Saved by Works...

CHRIST'S WORKS!

by

James Prest

TEACH Services, Inc.
www.TEACHServices.com

**PRINTED IN
THE UNITED STATES OF AMERICA**

World rights reserved. This book or any portion thereof may not be copied or reproduced in any form or manner whatever, except as provided by law, without the written permission of the publisher, except by a reviewer who may quote brief passages in a review.

The author assumes full responsibility for the accuracy of all facts and quotations as cited in this book.

Copyright © 2010 TEACH Services, Inc.
ISBN-13: 978-1-57258-644-4
Library of Congress Control Number: 2010941939

Published by
TEACH Services, Inc.
www.TEACHServices.com

Dedication

This book is dedicated to those who don't love Jesus, those who think they do, those who are not sure if they do, and those who really do love Him.

Unless otherwise noted, all scripture is quoted from the King James Version. In addition, all scripture that is italicized was added as emphasis by the author.

Acknowledgments

"O give thanks unto the LORD; for he is good: for his mercy endureth for ever.
"O give thanks unto the God of gods: for his mercy endureth for ever.
"O give thanks to the Lord of lords: for his mercy endureth for ever.
"To him who alone doeth great wonders: for his mercy endureth for ever.
"To him that by wisdom made the heavens: for his mercy endureth for ever.
"To him that stretched out the earth above the waters: for his mercy endureth for ever.
"To him that made great lights: for his mercy endureth for ever:
"The sun to rule by day: for his mercy endureth for ever:
"The moon and stars to rule by night: for his mercy endureth for ever.
"To him that smote Egypt in their firstborn: for his mercy endureth for ever:
"And brought out Israel from among them: for his mercy endureth for ever:
"With a strong hand, and with a stretched out arm: for his mercy endureth for ever.
"To him which divided the Red sea into parts: for his mercy endureth for ever:
"And made Israel to pass through the midst of it: for his

mercy endureth for ever:
"But overthrew Pharaoh and his host in the Red sea: for his mercy endureth for ever.
"To him which led his people through the wilderness: for his mercy endureth for ever.
"To him which smote great kings: for his mercy endureth for ever:
"And slew famous kings: for his mercy endureth for ever:
"Sihon king of the Amorites: for his mercy endureth for ever:
"And Og the king of Bashan: for his mercy endureth for ever:
"And gave their land for an heritage: for his mercy endureth for ever:
"Even an heritage unto Israel his servant: for his mercy endureth for ever.
"Who remembered us in our low estate: for his mercy endureth for ever:
"And hath redeemed us from our enemies: for his mercy endureth for ever.
"Who giveth food to all flesh: for his mercy endureth for ever.
"O give thanks unto the God of heaven: for his mercy endureth for ever" (Ps. 136).

I would also like to thank my mother, Evelyn Prest, for raising me the way she did, which has helped to make me who I am. I give thanks to Ace Hedger, a child of God by faith, in whose heart Christ lives and reigns. He has helped me to better understand that grandest of all themes that I have written about in this book. And thanks also to my faithful editor, Brian White.

Table of Contents

Acknowledgments v

Preface viii

Chapter 1 “If any man will” 1

Chapter 2 “Choose you this day” 19

Chapter 3 “And this is the victory . . .” 41

Chapter 4 “Ye shall be free indeed” 63

Chapter 5 “A way of escape” 172

Chapter 6 “This is life eternal” 190

Chapter 7 “Ye shall receive power” 197

Chapter 8 “There is a friend . . .” 211

Chapter 9 “Take no thought . . .” 231

Chapter 10 “All things . . .” 251

Chapter 11 “The truth shall make you free” 264

Source References 268

Preface

I was raised as a complete worldling for the first twelve years or so of my life. After that I began to learn about God through the influence of my father. Upon learning, I understood what was right and knew in part the way I should be living, but I rebelled against God in my heart while outwardly professing to be a Christian one day a week. Eventually I openly went back to the world and renounced my title of Christian. It was when I was sixteen years old and my life couldn't seem to get any worse than it was that my Dad offered me a book to read that revealed to my understanding, in sharp clarity, the two sides in the great controversy and the love of Jesus.

It was this love that turned my downward course to the heavenward way. In my rebellion, I had figured that I would just live how I wanted to at the present moment, and when all was said and done, I would just be consumed in flames and that would be the end of it. What didn't hit me at that time was that I would not merely perish with that being the only and final result. When I saw more clearly the love of Jesus for my very own soul, I realized that if I were lost all of what Christ did in utter love to save me would be in vain and others would be lost as the result of my influence. How could I abuse such love? How could I choose eternal death for another? Christ then put

Preface

within my heart a principle that has kept me from giving up. I could not, without a struggle, make the choice that would break my Lord's heart and throw others into perdition when they might have had everlasting life. Through many difficulties since, the Lord has kept me by His constraining love.

The origin of this book is traced back to when a young lady asked me if I would write articles for *The Youth Messenger* in our church. "Sure!" I replied, "I won't even consider it a sacrifice." I had recently been learning some most beautiful truths that had abundantly blessed me and had helped to transform my life for the better. I was desirous of sharing these precious truths with others and I thought that this would be a good opportunity to do so, so I began writing.

Upon finishing several articles, various circumstances prevented *The Youth Messenger* from accepting my writings. I wasn't thrilled at first. I insisted on sharing with others the blessings that I had received, and I quickly got the idea to turn the articles into book chapters, and so I just kept writing.

But even though the things about which I was writing were beautiful, God had different plans for my book—plans that were far more glorious than I could have imagined. While I had understood it in part years in the past, my knowledge of Christ our Righteousness had been slowly growing. Through the providence of God, I was placed in connection with a young man named Ace Hedger. Together we helped each other to better understand this most precious truth, though I will say that I learned more from him than he from me. He has, by the grace of God, made a major impact on the final product of this book. Chapter four, a vital chapter, would not exist were it not for his influence being used by the Lord Jesus.

You will notice that I often quote from other writings in this book. I see no point in saying again what has already been clearly presented by another. While many readers will have a tendency to acknowledge the writings quoted and will respect them far more than mine, I do not desire that they shall be quoted with an authoritative voice. The Word of God is to be taken as the only authority for the things brought to view in this book. I quote other writings for their ability to move and charm the reader and for the profoundness of the things they bring to view that will help the Christian in their everyday life.

This book is not written in support or defense of any Christian denomination, nor is its purpose to attack any particular church or religion. The intention of this book is not to bring a single person to accept the creed of anyone. Its whole aim is to be a savor of life to the reader. I cannot say that this is not a doctrinal book, for a doctrine is a teaching, and the Bible is the lesson book of the world. The sole focus of this book is to show what exactly it means to depend *entirely* upon God for absolutely *everything* and to impress upon the reader's mind the utter necessity of this vital principle. I have nothing to hide that I should feel any need to make my book to appear like it is what it is not: "For I am not ashamed of the gospel of Christ: for it is the power of God unto salvation to every one that believeth" (Rom 1:16).

I do not profess to know everything. There is One who "knoweth all things" (1 John 3:20). I am only a finite mortal. I do not desire my audience to merely read this book and accept everything that I say as pure truth, but rather I want them to study the Scriptures that it brings to view. I want them to be a faithful Berean and to search the Scriptures daily, to see whether or not the things I have presented are so (Act 17:11). "Thus saith the LORD; Cursed be the man that trusteth in man, and maketh flesh his arm" (Jer. 17:5). "There is a way which seemeth right unto a man, but the end thereof are the ways of death" (Prov. 14:12).

I have sought to arrange the chapters of this book in such a way as to enable the reader to have just the knowledge that he needs before he can understand and receive the highest benefit of following chapters. The only thing that I most strongly request for the sake of the reader is that you do not jump around from chapter to chapter in this book. If you do, there is a very good chance that you will wish you didn't. I don't want you to become confused as to what I am saying. Start with chapter one and read it through chronologically until you finish reading chapter seven. Then you are at liberty to jump around from chapter to chapter. I only say this because I know that some people (such as myself) like to jump around in a book, picking out and reading those chapters whose title grabs their attention the most. You will not want to do this with this book.

After having finished reading the whole book, I believe it would do the reader well to read chapters two through five again; at least. This book is very simple, but very deep, and I don't want the reader to miss one iota of the precious truths that have brought me such great joy in Christ.

To the reader of this book, I have many things to say, but I cannot say them all. However, if it mean anything to you, I will say this: I would, by the grace of God, cheerfully consent to give myself over to a lifetime of the screaming horrors of the Inquisition, if only the reader could but fully understand, as I do, the truth of Christ our Righteousness as presented in this book, and how it is to be practically applied in his own life. I have given it my best to put into words that which will enable the reader to fully grasp how Christ's righteousness applies to him, but it is God alone that "revealeth the deep and secret things" (Dan 2:22). I pray that His Spirit will attend this book. Not for my purposes, but for His. Amen.

"One interest will prevail, one subject will swallow up every other, — Christ our righteousness."

~ *Review and Herald*, December 23, 1890, par. 19

Chapter 1

"If any man will"
John 7:17

Jesus said, "My doctrine is not mine, but his that sent me. If any man will do his will, he shall know of the doctrine, whether it be of God, or whether I speak of myself" (John 7:16, 17). Full of significance are these words that come to us straight from the Son of God Himself. Here Christ unmistakably outlines what exactly man must do to come to a knowledge of true doctrine. *"If any man will do His will, he shall know of the doctrine."* But what is the doctrine? Jesus does not say. The only thing that He says is how to come to a knowledge of it. "If any man will do his will." This is the requirement. Should the truth of heaven be revealed to be something other than what you thought it was, would you do the will of God by accepting the light given and live your life accordingly? Or would you resist the light, insisting that it cannot be correct because it does not line up with your ideas of truth? If you are not willing to accept the truth that God may give, and be willing to live by it, then there is no hope in the words of Christ that you shall ever come to a knowledge of truth. Jesus gives no exceptions. Will you know of the doctrine? Jesus answers, "If any man will do his will, *he shall know of the doctrine.*"

God forces no man to believe truth anymore than He forces them to accept a lie. There is no reason to fear that upon studying a certain

Saved by Works... Christ's Works!

Bible topic you will be forced into believing error if you open yourself up to something that cuts across your established views of truth. Jesus says plainly that if a man is willing to do God's will, he shall know what true doctrine is. He said also that the Holy Spirit "will guide you into all truth" (John 16:13). We can therefore rest safe in these words of the One who died for us. We should never be afraid of searching the Scriptures for God has given them to us that we might not be afraid. "And ye shall seek me, and find me, when ye shall search for me with all your heart. And I will be found of you, saith the LORD" (Jer. 29:13, 14).

When studying the Scriptures, it is crucial to put all of our ideas of truth aside, to put them *all* on the shelf, and study the Scriptures in the light of the Scriptures, and not in the light of our established opinions. There is no internal or external force exhibited that would keep you from picking back up again those cherished views of truth and holding them close to your heart. You are free to believe whatever you will. But the requirement that Jesus gives us to come to a knowledge of true doctrine is that we be willing to accept the light that He may give.

"Do you ask, What shall I do to be saved? You must lay your preconceived opinions, your hereditary and cultivated ideas, at the door of investigation. If you search the Scriptures to vindicate your own opinions, you will never reach the truth. Search in order to learn what the Lord says. If conviction comes as you search, if you see that your cherished opinions are not in harmony with the truth, do not misinterpret the truth in order to suit your own belief, but accept the light given. Open mind and heart that you may behold wondrous things out of God's word."[1]

"How shall we search the Scriptures? Shall we drive our stakes of doctrine one after another, and then try to make all Scripture meet our established opinions, or shall we take our ideas and views to the

Chapter 1 — "If any man will"

Scriptures, and measure our theories on every side by the Scriptures of truth? Many who read and even teach the Bible, do not comprehend the precious truth they are teaching or studying. Men entertain errors, when the truth is clearly marked out, and if they would but bring their doctrines to the Word of God, and not read the Word of God in the light of their doctrines, to prove their ideas right, they would not walk in darkness and blindness, or cherish error. Many give the words of Scripture a meaning that suits their own opinions, and they mislead themselves and deceive others by their misinterpretations of God's Word. As we take up the study of God's Word, we should do so with humble hearts. All selfishness, all love of originality, should be laid aside. Long-cherished opinions must not be regarded as infallible. It was the unwillingness of the Jews to give up their long established traditions that proved their ruin. They were determined not to see any flaw in their own opinions or in their expositions of the Scriptures; but however long men may have entertained certain views, if they are not clearly sustained by the written word, they should be discarded. . . . Those who sincerely desire truth will not be reluctant to lay open their positions for investigation and criticism, and will not be annoyed if their opinions and ideas are crossed."[2]

"How shall we search the Scriptures in order to understand what they teach? We should come to the investigation of God's Word with a contrite heart, a teachable and prayerful spirit. We are not to think, as did the Jews, that our own ideas and opinions are infallible; nor with the papists, that certain individuals are the sole guardians of truth and knowledge, that men have no right to search the Scriptures for themselves, but must accept the explanations given by the fathers of the church. We should not study the Bible for the purpose of sustaining our preconceived opinions, but with the single object of learning what God has said.

Saved by Works... Christ's Works!

"Some have feared that if in even a single point they acknowledge themselves in error, other minds would be led to doubt the whole theory of truth. Therefore they have felt that investigation should not be permitted, that it would tend to dissension and disunion. But if such is to be the result of investigation, the sooner it comes the better. If there are those whose faith in God's Word will not stand the test of an investigation of the Scriptures, the sooner they are revealed the better; for then the way will be opened to show them their error. We cannot hold that a position once taken, an idea once advocated, is not, under any circumstances, to be relinquished. There is but One who is infallible—He who is the way, the truth, and the life.

"Those who allow prejudice to bar the mind against the reception of truth cannot receive the divine enlightenment. Yet, when a view of Scripture is presented, many do not ask, Is it true—in harmony with God's Word? but, By whom is it advocated? and unless it comes through the very channel that pleases them, they do not accept it. So thoroughly satisfied are they with their own ideas that they will not examine the Scripture evidence with a desire to learn, but refuse to be interested, merely because of their prejudices.

"The Lord often works where we least expect Him; He surprises us by revealing His power through instruments of His own choice, while He passes by the men to whom we have looked as those through whom light should come. God desires us to receive the truth upon its own merits—because it is truth.

"The Bible must not be interpreted to suit the ideas of men, however long they may have held these ideas to be true. We are not to accept the opinion of commentators as the voice of God; they were erring mortals like ourselves. God has given reasoning powers to us as well as to them. We should make the Bible its own expositor.

"All should be careful about presenting new views of Scripture

Chapter 1 — "If any man will"

before they have given these points thorough study, and are fully prepared to sustain them from the Bible. Introduce nothing that will cause dissension, without clear evidence that in it God is giving a special message for this time.

"But beware of rejecting that which is truth. The great danger with our people has been that of depending upon men and making flesh their arm. Those who have not been in the habit of searching the Bible for themselves, or weighing evidence, have confidence in the leading men, and accept the decisions they make; and thus many will reject the very messages God sends to His people, if these leading brethren do not accept them.

"No one should claim that he has all the light there is for God's people. The Lord will not tolerate this. He has said, 'I have set before thee an open door, and no man can shut it.' [Revelation 3:8]. Even if all our leading men should refuse light and truth, that door will still remain open. The Lord will raise up men who will give the people the message for this time.

"Truth is eternal, and conflict with error will only make manifest its strength. We should never refuse to examine the Scriptures with those who, we have reason to believe, desire to know what is truth. Suppose a brother held a view that differed from yours, and he should come to you, proposing that you sit down with him and make an investigation of that point in the Scriptures; should you rise up, filled with prejudice, and condemn his ideas, while refusing to give him a candid hearing? The only right way would be to sit down as Christians and investigate the position presented in the light of God's Word, which will reveal truth and unmask error. To ridicule his ideas would not weaken his position in the least if it were false, or strengthen your position if it were true. If the pillars of our faith will not stand the test of investigation, it is time that we knew it. There must be no spirit of Phariseeism

Saved by Works... Christ's Works!

cherished among us.

"We should come with reverence to the study of the Bible, feeling that we are in the presence of God. All lightness and trifling should be laid aside. While some portions of the Word are easily understood, the true meaning of other parts is not so readily discerned. There must be patient study and meditation and earnest prayer. Every student, as he opens the Scriptures, should ask for the enlightenment of the Holy Spirit; and the promise is sure that it will be given.

"The spirit in which you come to the investigation of the Scriptures will determine the character of the assistant at your side. Angels from the world of light will be with those who in humility of heart seek for divine guidance. But if the Bible is opened with irreverence, with a feeling of self-sufficiency, if the heart is filled with prejudice, Satan is beside you, and he will set the plain statements of God's Word in a perverted light.

"There are some who indulge in levity, sarcasm, and even mockery toward those who differ with them. Others present an array of objections to any new view; and when these objections are plainly answered by the words of Scripture, they do not acknowledge the evidence presented, nor allow themselves to be convinced. Their questioning is not for the purpose of arriving at truth, but was intended merely to confuse the minds of others.

"Some have thought it an evidence of intellectual keenness and superiority to perplex minds in regard to what is truth. They resort to subtlety of argument, to playing upon words; they take unjust advantage in asking questions. When their questions have been fairly answered, they will turn the subject, bring up another point to avoid acknowledging the truth. We should beware of indulging the spirit which controlled the Jews. They would not learn of Christ, because His explanation of the Scriptures did not agree with their ideas; there-

Chapter 1 — "If any man will"

fore they became spies upon His track, 'laying wait for Him, and seeking to catch something out of His mouth, that they might accuse Him.' [Luke 11:54]. Let us not bring upon ourselves the fearful denunciation of the Saviour's words, 'Woe unto you, lawyers! for ye have taken away the key of knowledge: ye entered not in yourselves, and them that were entering in ye hindered.' [Luke 11:52].

"It does not require much learning or ability to ask questions that are difficult to answer. A child may ask questions over which the wisest men may be puzzled. Let us not engage in a contest of this kind. The very same unbelief exists in our time as prevailed in the days of Christ. Now as then the desire for preferment and the praise of men leads people away from the simplicity of true godliness. There is no pride so dangerous as spiritual pride.

"Young men should search the Scriptures for themselves. They are not to feel that it is sufficient for those older in experience to find out the truth; that the younger ones can accept it from them as authority. The Jews perished as a nation because they were drawn from the truth of the Bible by their rulers, priests, and elders. Had they heeded the lessons of Jesus, and searched the Scriptures for themselves, they would not have perished.

"Young men in our ranks are watching to see in what spirit the ministers come to the investigation of the Scriptures; whether they have a teachable spirit, and are humble enough to accept evidence, and receive light from the messengers whom God chooses to send.

"We must study the truth for ourselves. No man should be relied upon to think for us. No matter who he is, or in what position he may be placed, we are not to look upon any man as a criterion for us. We are to counsel together, and to be subject one to another; but at the same time we are to exercise the ability God has given us, in order to learn what is truth. Each one of us must look to God for divine enlightenment. We must individually develop a character that will stand the test in the day of God. We must not become set in our ideas, and think that no one should interfere with our opinions.

"When a point of doctrine that you do not understand comes to your attention, go to God on your knees, that you may understand what is truth and not be found as were the Jews fighting against God. While warning men to beware of accepting anything unless it is truth, we should also warn them not to imperil their souls by rejecting messages of light, but to press out of the darkness by earnest study of the Word of God.

"When Nathanael came to Jesus, the Saviour exclaimed, 'Behold an Israelite indeed, in whom is no guile!' Nathanael said, 'Whence knowest thou me?' Jesus answered, 'When thou wast under the fig tree, I saw thee.' [John 1:47, 48]. And Jesus will see us also in the secret places of prayer, if we seek Him for light that we may know what is truth.

"If a brother is teaching error, those who are in responsible positions ought to know it; and if he is teaching truth, they ought to take their stand at his side. We should all know what is being taught among us; for if it is truth, we need to know it. . . . We are all under obligation to God to understand what He sends us. He has given directions by which we may test every doctrine,—'To the law and to the testimony: if they speak not according to this word, it is because there is no light in them.' [Isaiah 8:20]. But if it is according to this test, do not be so full of prejudice that you cannot acknowledge a point simply because it does not agree with your ideas."[3]

"There should be liberty given for a frank investigation of truth, that each may know for himself what is the truth. . . . Precious light is to shine forth from the Word of God, and let no one presume to dictate what shall or what shall not be brought before the people in

Chapter 1 — "If any man will"

the messages of enlightenment that He shall send, and so quench the Spirit of God. Whatever may be his position of authority, no one has a right to shut away the light from the people. When a message comes in the name of the Lord to His people, no one may excuse himself from an investigation of its claims. No one can afford to stand back in an attitude of indifference and self-confidence, and say: 'I know what is truth. I am satisfied with my position. I have set my stakes, and I will not be moved away from my position, whatever may come. I will not listen to the message of this messenger; for I know that it can not be truth.'. . .

". . . put away all egotism, all self-confidence, and pride of opinion; if a message comes that you do not understand, take pains that you may hear the reasons the messenger may give, comparing scripture with scripture, that you may know whether or not it is sustained by the Word of God. If you believe that the position taken have not the Word of God for their foundation, if the position you hold on the subject can not be controverted, then produce your strong reasons; for your position will not be shaken by coming in contact with error. There is no virtue or manliness in keeping up a continual warfare in the dark, closing your eyes lest you may see, closing your ears lest you may hear, hardening your heart in ignorance and unbelief lest you may have to humble yourselves and acknowledge that you have received light on some points of truth. To hold yourselves aloof from an investigation of truth is not the way to carry out the Saviour's injunction to 'search the Scriptures.' Is it digging for hidden treasures to call the results of some one's labor a mass of rubbish, and make no critical examination to see whether or not there are precious jewels of truth in the collection of thought which you condemn? Will those who have almost everything to learn keep themselves away from every meeting where there is an opportunity to investigate the messages that come to the people, simply because they imagine the views held by the teachers of the truth may be out of harmony with what they have conceived as truth? Thus it was that the Jews did in the days of Christ, and we are warned not to do as they did, and be led to choose darkness rather than light, because there was in them an evil heart of unbelief in departing from the living God. No one of those who imagine that they know it all is too old or too intelligent to learn from the humblest of the messengers of the living God."[4]

"The fact that there is no controversy or agitation among God's people should not be regarded as conclusive evidence that they are holding fast to sound doctrine. There is reason to fear that they may not be clearly discriminating between truth and error. When no new questions are started by investigation of the Scriptures, when no difference of opinion arises which will set men to searching the Bible for themselves to make sure that they have the truth, there will be many now, as in ancient times, who will hold to tradition and worship they know not what."[5]

"But God will have a people upon the earth to maintain the Bible, and the Bible only, as the standard of all doctrines and the basis of all reforms. The opinions of learned men, the deductions of science, the creeds or decisions of ecclesiastical councils, as numerous and discordant as are the churches which they represent, the voice of the majority—not one nor all of these should be regarded as evidence for or against any point of religious faith. Before accepting any doctrine or precept, we should demand a plain 'Thus saith the Lord' in its support.

"Satan is constantly endeavoring to attract attention to man in the place of God. He leads the people to look to bishops, to pastors, to professors of theology, as their guides, instead of searching the Scriptures to learn their duty for themselves. Then, by controlling the minds of these leaders, he can influence the multitudes according to his will.

Chapter 1 — "If any man will"

"When Christ came to speak the words of life, the common people heard Him gladly; and many, even of the priests and rulers, believed on Him. But the chief of the priesthood and the leading men of the nation were determined to condemn and repudiate His teachings. Though they were baffled in all their efforts to find accusations against Him, though they could not but feel the influence of the divine power and wisdom attending His words, yet they incased themselves in prejudice; they rejected the clearest evidence of His Messiahship, lest they should be forced to become His disciples. These opponents of Jesus were men whom the people had been taught from infancy to reverence, to whose authority they had been accustomed implicitly to bow. 'How is it,' they asked, 'that our rulers and learned scribes do not believe on Jesus? Would not these pious men receive Him if He were the Christ?' It was the influence of such teachers that led the Jewish nation to reject their Redeemer."[6]

"The will and voice of finite man are not to be interpreted as the voice of God."[7]

"The spirit which actuated those priests and rulers is still manifested by many who make a high profession of piety. They refuse to examine the testimony of the Scriptures concerning the special truths for this time. They point to their own numbers, wealth, and popularity, and look with contempt upon the advocates of truth as few, poor, and unpopular, having a faith that separates them from the world.

"Christ foresaw that the undue assumption of authority indulged by the scribes and Pharisees would not cease with the dispersion of the Jews. He had a prophetic view of the work of exalting human authority to rule the conscience, which has been so terrible a curse to the church in all ages. And His fearful denunciations of the scribes and Pharisees, and His warnings to the people not to follow these blind leaders, were placed on record as an admonition to future generations."[8]

Saved by Works. . . Christ's Works!

"It was the work of the Reformation to restore to men the word of God; but is it not too true that in the churches of our time men are taught to rest their faith upon their creed and the teachings of their church rather than on the Scriptures? Said Charles Beecher, speaking of the Protestant churches: 'They shrink from any rude word against creeds with the same sensitiveness with which those holy fathers would have shrunk from a rude word against the rising veneration of saints and martyrs which they were fostering. . . . The Protestant evangelical denominations have so tied up one another's hands, and their own, that, between them all, a man cannot become a preacher at all, anywhere, without accepting some book besides the Bible. . . . There is nothing imaginary in the statement that the creed power is now beginning to prohibit the Bible as really as Rome did, though in a subtler way.'"[9]

"The Bible, and the Bible alone, is to be our creed, the sole bond of union; all who bow to this holy word will be in harmony. Our own views and ideas must not control our efforts. Man is fallible, but God's word is infallible. Instead of wrangling with one another, let men exalt the Lord. Let us meet all opposition as did our Master, saying, 'It is written.' Let us lift up the banner on which is inscribed, The Bible our rule of faith and discipline."[10]

"Do not carry your creed to the Bible, and read the Scriptures in the light of that creed. If you find that your opinions are opposed to a plain 'Thus saith the Lord,' or to any command or prohibition He has given, give heed to the Word of God rather than to the sayings of men. Let every controversy or dispute be settled by 'It is written.'"[11]

"The question is, 'What is truth?' It is not how many years have I believed that makes it the truth. You must bring your creed to the Bible and let the light of the Bible define your creed and show where it comes short and where the difficulty is. The Bible is to be your standard, the living oracles of Jehovah are to be your guide. You are to dig for the truth as for hidden treasures. You are to find where the treasure is, and then you are to plow every inch of that field to get the jewels. You are to work the mines of truth for new gems, for new diamonds, and you will find them.

"You know how it is with the papal power. The people have no right to interpret the Scriptures for themselves. They must have someone else interpret the Scriptures for them. Have you no mind? Have you no reason? Has not God given judgment to the common people just as well as He has to the priests and rulers? When Christ, the Lord of life and glory, came to our world, if they had known Him, they never would have crucified Him. God had told them to search the Scriptures: 'In them ye think ye have eternal life: and they are they which testify of Me' (John 5:39).

"God help us to be Bible students. Until you can see the reason for it yourself and a 'thus saith the Lord' in the Scriptures, don't trust any living man to interpret the Bible for you. And when you can see this, you know it for yourself, and know it to be the truth of God. You will say, 'I have read it, I have seen it, and my own heart takes hold upon it, and it is the truth God has spoken to me from His Word.' Now this is what we are to be—individual Christians. We need to have an individual, personal experience. We need to be converted, as did the Jews. If you see a little light, you are not to stand back and say, 'I will wait until my brethren have seen it.' If you do, you will go on in darkness."[12]

"Notwithstanding the Bible is full of warnings against false teachers, many are ready thus to commit the keeping of their souls to the clergy. There are today thousands of professors of religion who can give no other reason for points of faith which they hold than that they were so instructed by their religious leaders. They pass by the Sav-

Saved by Works... Christ's Works!

iour's teachings almost unnoticed, and place implicit confidence in the words of the ministers. But are ministers infallible? How can we trust our souls to their guidance unless we know from God's Word that they are light bearers? A lack of moral courage to step aside from the beaten track of the world leads many to follow in the steps of learned men; and by their reluctance to investigate for themselves, they are becoming hopelessly fastened in the chains of error. They see that the truth for this time is plainly brought to view in the Bible; and they feel the power of the Holy Spirit attending its proclamation; yet they allow the opposition of the clergy to turn them from the light. Though reason and conscience are convinced, these deluded souls dare not think differently from the minister; and their individual judgment, their eternal interests, are sacrificed to the unbelief, the pride and prejudice, of another.

"Many are the ways by which Satan works through human influence to bind his captives. He secures multitudes to himself by attaching them by the silken cords of affection to those who are enemies of the cross of Christ. Whatever this attachment may be, parental, filial, conjugal, or social, the effect is the same; the opposers of truth exert their power to control the conscience, and the souls held under their sway have not sufficient courage or independence to obey their own convictions of duty.

"The truth and the glory of God are inseparable; it is impossible for us, with the Bible within our reach, to honor God by erroneous opinions. Many claim that it matters not what one believes, if his life is only right. But *the life is molded by the faith.* If light and truth is within our reach, and we neglect to improve the privilege of hearing and seeing it, we virtually reject it; we are choosing darkness rather than light.

"'There is a way that seemeth right unto a man, but the end thereof are the ways of death.' Proverbs 16:25. Ignorance is no excuse for er-

Chapter 1 — "If any man will"

ror or sin, when there is every opportunity to know the will of God. A man is traveling and comes to a place where there are several roads and a guideboard indicating where each one leads. If he disregards the guideboard, and takes whichever road seems to him to be right, he may be ever so sincere, but will in all probability find himself on the wrong road.

"God has given us His word that we may become acquainted with its teachings and know for ourselves what He requires of us. When the lawyer came to Jesus with the inquiry, 'What shall I do to inherit eternal life?' the Saviour referred him to the Scriptures, saying: 'What is written in the law? how readest thou?' Ignorance will not excuse young or old, nor release them from the punishment due for the transgression of God's law; because there is in their hands a faithful presentation of that law and of its principles and claims. It is not enough to have good intentions; it is not enough to do what a man thinks is right or what the minister tells him is right. His soul's salvation is at stake, and he should search the Scriptures for himself. However strong may be his convictions, however confident he may be that the minister knows what is truth, this is not his foundation. He has a chart pointing out every waymark on the heavenward journey, and he ought not to guess at anything.

"It is the first and highest duty of every rational being to learn from the Scriptures what is truth, and then to walk in the light and encourage others to follow his example. We should day by day study the Bible diligently, weighing every thought and comparing scripture with scripture. With divine help we are to form our opinions for ourselves as we are to answer for ourselves before God.

"The truths most plainly revealed in the Bible have been involved in doubt and darkness by learned men, who, with a pretense of great wisdom, teach that the Scriptures have a mystical, a secret, spiritual meaning not apparent in the language employed. These men are false teachers. It was to such a class that Jesus declared: 'Ye know not the Scriptures, neither the power of God.' Mark 12:24. The language of the Bible should be explained according to its obvious meaning, unless a symbol or figure is employed. Christ has given the promise: 'If any man will do His will, he shall know of the doctrine.' John 7:17. If men would but take the Bible as it reads, if there were no false teachers to mislead and confuse their minds, a work would be accomplished that would make angels glad and that would bring into the fold of Christ thousands upon thousands who are now wandering in error.

"We should exert all the powers of the mind in the study of the Scriptures and should task the understanding to comprehend, as far as mortals can, the deep things of God; yet we must not forget that the docility and submission of a child is the true spirit of the learner. Scriptural difficulties can never be mastered by the same methods that are employed in grappling with philosophical problems. We should not engage in the study of the Bible with that self-reliance with which so many enter the domains of science, but with a prayerful dependence upon God and a sincere desire to learn His will. We must come with a humble and teachable spirit to obtain knowledge from the great I AM. Otherwise, evil angels will so blind our minds and harden our hearts that we shall not be impressed by the truth.

"Many a portion of Scripture which learned men pronounce a mystery, or pass over as unimportant, is full of comfort and instruction to him who has been taught in the school of Christ. One reason why many theologians have no clearer understanding of God's Word is, they close their eyes to truths which they do not wish to practice. An understanding of Bible truth depends not so much on the power of intellect brought to the search as on the singleness of purpose, the earnest longing after righteousness.

Chapter 1 — "If any man will"

"The Bible should never be studied without prayer. The Holy Spirit alone can cause us to feel the importance of those things easy to be understood, or prevent us from wresting truths difficult of comprehension. It is the office of heavenly angels to prepare the heart so to comprehend God's word that we shall be charmed with its beauty, admonished by its warnings, or animated and strengthened by its promises. We should make the psalmist's petition our own: 'Open Thou mine eyes, that I may behold wondrous things out of Thy law.' Psalm 119:18. Temptations often appear irresistible because, through neglect of prayer and the study of the Bible, the tempted one cannot readily remember God's promises and meet Satan with the Scripture weapons. But angels are round about those who are willing to be taught in divine things; and in the time of great necessity they will bring to their remembrance the very truths which are needed. Thus 'when the enemy shall come in like a flood, the Spirit of the Lord shall lift up a standard against him.' Isaiah 59:19."[13]

How are we to know whether someone is teaching us the truth? "We are not bidden to prove them by their fair speeches and exalted professions. They are to be judged by the word of God. 'To the law and to the testimony: if they speak not according to this word it is because there is no light in them.' 'Cease, my son, to hear the instruction that causeth to err from the words of knowledge.' Isaiah 8:20; Proverbs 19:27. What message do these teachers bring? Does it lead you to reverence and fear God? Does it lead you to manifest your love for Him by loyalty to His commandments? If men do not feel the weight of the moral law; if they make light of God's precepts; if they break one of the least of His commandments, and teach men so, they shall be of no esteem in the sight of heaven. We may know that their claims are without foundation. They are doing the very work that originated with the prince of darkness, the enemy of God."[14]

Saved by Works. . . Christ's Works!

The True Witness says, "I know thy works, that thou art neither cold nor hot: I would thou wert cold or hot. So then because thou art lukewarm, and neither cold nor hot, I will spue thee out of my mouth. Because thou sayest, I am rich, and increased with goods, and have need of nothing; and knowest not that thou art wretched, and miserable, and poor, and blind, and naked: I counsel thee to buy of me gold tried in the fire, that thou mayest be rich; and white raiment, that thou mayest be clothed, and that the shame of thy nakedness do not appear; and anoint thine eyes with eyesalve, that thou mayest see" (Rev. 3:15-18).

"What greater deception can come upon human minds than a confidence that they are right when they are all wrong! The message of the True Witness finds the people of God in a sad deception, yet honest in that deception. They know not that their condition is deplorable in the sight of God. While those addressed are flattering themselves that they are in an exalted spiritual condition, the message of the True Witness breaks their security by the startling denunciation of their true condition of spiritual blindness, poverty, and wretchedness. The testimony, so cutting and severe, cannot be a mistake, for it is the True Witness who speaks, and His testimony must be correct."[15]

"As many as I love, I rebuke and chasten: be zealous therefore, and repent. Behold, I stand at the door, and knock: if any man hear my voice, and open the door, I will come in to him, and will sup with him, and he with me" (Rev. 3:19, 20).

"When the doctrine we accept kills sin in the heart, purifies the soul from defilement, bears fruit unto holiness, we may know that it is the truth of God. When benevolence, kindness, tenderheartedness, sympathy, are manifest in our lives; when the joy of right doing is in our hearts; when we exalt Christ, and not self, we may know that our faith is of the right order."[16]

Chapter 2

"Choose you this day"
Joshua 24:15

"The greatest want of the world is the want of men—men who will not be bought or sold, men who in their inmost souls are true and honest, men who do not fear to call sin by its right name, men whose conscience is as true to duty as the needle to the pole, men who will stand for the right though the heavens fall."[1]

Today, many of us look with great admiration at people like Job, Elijah, David, Daniel, Stephen, Paul, and many of those other faithful men. We are amazed to see such examples of faith, zeal, love, devotion, perseverance, boldness, and firm obedience to God even in the face of fearful and terrible death, or even life, and we say in awe, "Wow! I wish I could be like that! I wish I could be like those men were for God!" I would like to emphasize the requirement for all to stop *wishing* to be like these men and start *being* like them today.

In the book of Daniel, we read the great secret to his success—"Daniel purposed in his heart" (Dan. 1:8). In other words, Daniel decided in his mind that it was his purpose, his choice, to refuse to break the law of God in the least particular; he was determined to serve God with his *heart*. Sometimes people get the idea that Daniel and all of these other great men of God served their Creator with their emotions, their feelings, their moods, and their impulses, that these were always

Saved by Works... Christ's Works!

in harmony with God's law and that this is why they were able to obey. To this idea we must decidedly say "no." These men served God with their will; they served God with their choices. To believe that these holy men always felt like obeying God is a false idea.

Jesus said, "If any man will come after me, let him deny himself, and take up his cross daily, and follow me" (Luke 9:23). To deny yourself means to go against what you feel like doing. This is God's requirement for us today, and it was the requirement for them then, for God's law has never changed. If these men were required to deny themselves, then they didn't always feel like obeying. In all honesty, ask yourself the question, "Is it truly self-denial for me to do something that I really feel like doing?" If not, then you must also realize that the faithful men of old could not have always served God because they felt like it. The Bible says of Daniel that he "purposed in his heart;" it does not say that he "felt in his feelings."

In Ezekiel 36 we read of God's promise to change our hearts. He says, "A new heart also will I give you, and a new spirit will I put within you: and I will take away the stony heart out of your flesh, and I will give you an heart of flesh. And I will put my spirit within you, and cause you to walk in my statutes, and ye shall keep my judgments, and do them" (Eze. 36:26, 27). This promise of a change of heart does not mean that we will never have evil emotions and feelings rise up in us. Many people stumble and fall in the narrow path because they think God's promise to take away their evil hearts and give them good ones meant that they would never have evil feelings enter them again and that they would always feel like doing what is right. This is a dangerous error.

The reason that many people use their emotions and feelings to judge whether or not they really want to serve God is because they feel their emotions more than anything else, so they seem more real to

Chapter 2 — "Choose you this day"

them than anything else. Therefore, whatever their emotions tell them must be so. These people think that their emotions and feelings are their heart, their true self, and this is one reason why they are so often discouraged.

This problem comes in its force when our emotions make us feel that our heart is not right with God. In our mind we want and desire to serve God, but because we feel that our heart really wants to do evil—because our heart does not feel true, sincere, honest, holy, and converted—we assume that it wants to do evil and that that is because we are not fully surrendered to God. This then makes us feel like a hypocrite, a fake Christian.

The difference must be made clear. Those faithful men of the past did what was right regardless of the consequences. They ignored their feelings, denied their emotions, and chose to obey God whether they felt like it or not. They chose to give themselves wholly to God, and whether or not they felt like they were completely His, they lived as if they felt this way. They were wholly God's by choice, obedient to Him by choice, not by feelings, not by impulses, not because their emotions pushed them to do what was right but because they *chose* to be wholly God's and because they *chose* do right by their *choices*.

It is impossible for anyone to do something that he does not want to do unless he is perfectly forced and cannot resist doing it in the least particular. Anything and everything we do then is by choice. You may choose to do something that you do not *feel* like doing, but you cannot choose to do anything that you do not *want* to do. If you do something, it is because you wanted to do it. If you choose to do something, then regardless of the reasons that you don't *feel* like you want to do it, and maybe even the reasons that you really don't *want* to do it, you want it enough to choose it above everything else. If in the end you are lost and are deprived of eternal life, it is because you chose to die, you *wanted* to die, and God will only be giving you what you wanted. If you choose to serve God, if you choose to be saved, it is because you *want* to serve God and be saved regardless of how you feel and regardless of the consequences.

Often Christians get the idea that committing sin is a part of life, that violating God's law is a common and normal thing that has always been and always will be. "I sin every day," they say. It is true that they may sin every day, but that is because they choose to sin. Even though they will deny it with their words, some believe deep inside of themselves that living a completely sinless life is impossible. They cannot imagine living a single day without doing something evil; it is something they cannot fathom. Believing as they do, they make God a liar. The Lord said, "I am the Almighty God; walk before me, and be thou perfect" (Gen. 17:1). In the Sermon on the Mount, Christ merely reemphasized this command. In Matthew 5:48 He bids us, "Be ye therefore perfect," and "all His biddings are enablings."[2] Is it not written in the Scriptures, "Be ye holy; for I am holy" (1 Peter 1:16)?

Not only do men make God a liar by their beliefs but they put themselves in a position where their failure is guaranteed. Just because you always break God's law doesn't mean you must always do so. Just because you have never lived a sinless day in your life doesn't mean it has to be that way. Stop insisting that because it has always been, it always *has to be*. If you will be truly converted, if you will be fully surrendered to God, if you will choose to obey the Lord even in the face of death, you will overcome in God's strength.

"Many are inquiring, '*How* am I to make the surrender of myself to God?' You desire to give yourself to Him, but you are weak in moral power, in slavery to doubt, and controlled by the habits of your life of sin. . . . What you need to understand is the true force of the will. This is the governing power in the nature of man, the power of deci-

Chapter 2 — "Choose you this day"

sion, or of choice. Everything depends on the right action of the will. The power of choice God has given to men; it is theirs to exercise. You cannot change your heart, you cannot of yourself give to God its affections; but you can *choose* to serve Him. You can give Him your will; He will then work in you to will and to do according to His good pleasure."[3] "It is through the will that sin retains its hold upon us."[4]

"God has given us the power of choice; it is ours to exercise. We cannot change our hearts, we cannot control our thoughts, our impulses, our affections. We cannot make ourselves pure, fit for God's service. But we can *choose* to serve God, we can give Him our will; then He will work in us to will and to do according to His good pleasure."[5] "Every human being possessed of reason has power to choose the right. In every experience of life, God's word to us is, 'Choose you this day whom ye will serve.' Joshua 24:15. Everyone may place his will on the side of the will of God, may choose to obey Him, and by thus linking himself with divine agencies, he may stand where nothing can force him to do evil."[6] Christ's followers "are to have power to resist evil, power that neither earth, nor death, nor hell can master, power that will enable them to overcome as Christ overcame."[7]

"You must remember that your will is the spring of all your actions. This will, that forms so important a factor in the character of man, was at the Fall given into the control of Satan; and he has ever since been working in man to will and to do of his own pleasure."[8] "Satan knows that he cannot overcome man unless he can control his will."[9]

"Desires for goodness and holiness are right as far as they go; but if you stop here, they will avail nothing. Many will be lost while hoping and desiring to be Christians. They do not come to the point of yielding the will to God. They do not now *choose* to be Christians."[10] They say with Agrippa, "Almost thou persuadest me to be a Christian"

Saved by Works. . . Christ's Works!

(Acts 26:28). "Almost Christians, yet not fully Christians, they seem near the kingdom of heaven, but they cannot enter there. Almost but not wholly saved, means to be not almost but wholly lost."[11]

Jesus said, "No man can serve two masters" (Matt. 6:24). "Christ does not say that man will not or shall not serve two masters, but that he *cannot*. . . . No one can occupy a neutral position; there is no middle class, who neither love God nor serve the enemy of righteousness. . . . He who does not give himself wholly to God is under the control of another power, listening to another voice, whose suggestions are of an entirely different character. Half-and-half service places the human agent on the side of the enemy as a successful ally of the hosts of darkness."[12] "Unless we do yield ourselves to the control of Christ, we shall be dominated by the wicked one. We must inevitably be under the control of the one or the other of the two great powers that are contending for the supremacy of the world. It is not necessary for us deliberately to choose the service of the kingdom of darkness in order to come under its dominion. We have only to neglect to ally ourselves with the kingdom of light. If we do not co-operate with the heavenly agencies, Satan will take possession of the heart, and will make it his abiding place."[13]

"Halfhearted Christians are worse than infidels; for their deceptive words and noncommittal position lead many astray. The infidel shows his colors. The lukewarm Christian deceives both parties. He is neither a good worldling nor a good Christian. Satan uses him to do a work that no one else can do."[14] To the worldling he appears as a detestable hypocrite and strengthens the unbeliever in his unbelief, and to the Christian he is a hidden enemy who makes it appear that the whole heart need not be involved in the warfare against sin and Satan.

There are people in this world, even those who earnestly desire to be wholehearted Christians, who long to do what is right and fol-

Chapter 2 — "Choose you this day"

low God all the way. Because of their desire, they will ask people to teach them lessons on how to be strong, how to be pleasant, how to be kind and loving, how to not be faultfinding, how to be positive, and how to have faith—lessons which will inspire them to do right. They research the matter and try to find a book, preacher, or friend which will show them the way. They search the Bible for the way to overcome their sins. They are looking, searching, and desiring to find the path to perfect peace and victory. This is the answer that God gives to them, "Choose you this day" (Joshua 24:15). If anyone desires to truly serve the Lord in everything he does, then simply choose Him. If you choose the path of obedience, if you choose to believe what God has said, and having made your choice to act upon it, God will do for you what you cannot do for yourself. God will act upon your right choice for you; in place of you; instead of you. Making an entire surrender to God is so simple it is hard to explain. Simply choose Him, His way, and choose to believe, whether you feel like believing or not.

"The Christian life is a battle and a march. But the victory to be gained is not won by human power. The field of conflict is the domain of the heart. The battle which we have to fight—the greatest battle that was ever fought by man—is the surrender of self to the will of God, the yielding of the heart to the sovereignty of love."[15] Though the battle against self is the greatest battle ever fought, victory is sure if you will simply choose it *and stick to that choice.*

Jesus said, "Without me ye can do nothing" (John 15:5). When Jesus said nothing, He really meant *nothing*. "God could not for a moment stay His hand, or man would faint and die."[16] Every moment of time, our very existence, is in Christ's hands, and thus everything we do has its source in Him. Of ourselves we have no power to overcome sin, but we can choose Christ as our master. God has given us the ability to choose, but if Satan could, he would not allow us this choice.

Saved by Works... Christ's Works!

The only thing you can do in this great controversy between Christ and Satan is to choose whom you will serve. If you choose Christ, He will fight the battle *for* you; He will fight the battle in your place; He will fight in your stead. "Ye shall not need to fight in this battle" (2 Chron. 20:17), "for the battle is not yours, but God's" (verse 15). Yes, you must stand on the battlefield, and yes, you will have to run in full force toward the enemy, but only by your choice—Christ does the fighting part for you, and He will win.

"When Christ took human nature upon Him, He bound humanity to Himself by a tie of love that can never be broken by any power save the choice of man himself. Satan will constantly present allurements to induce us to break this tie—to choose to separate ourselves from Christ. Here is where we need to watch, to strive, to pray, that nothing may entice us to *choose* another master; for we are always free to do this. But let us keep our eyes fixed upon Christ, and He will preserve us. Looking unto Jesus, we are safe. Nothing can pluck us out of His hand."[17] "The soul that has given himself to Christ is more precious in His sight than the whole world. The Saviour would have passed through the agony of Calvary that one might be saved in His kingdom. He will never abandon one for whom He has died. Unless His followers *choose* to leave Him, He will hold them fast."[18]

All are called upon now to make a stand, to make a decision for eternity and choose Christ. Eternal salvation for yourself and for others depends upon the choice you now make. "How long halt ye between two opinions?" (1 Kings 18:21). This question is not "Whom will you serve?" but "How long are you going to stand around without making a decision?" As for Joshua's question, he did not merely say, "Choose you whom ye will serve." He said, "Choose you *this day* whom ye will serve," meaning "Make your decision *now* whom you are going to obey." If you do not choose now, then your choice is al-

Chapter 2 — "Choose you this day"

ready made. By your indecision you have already decided. You have made a choice that will ruin souls for eternity. Jesus said, "He that is not with me is against me; and he that gathereth not with me scattereth abroad" (Matt. 12:30). You are and will be wholly the devil's until you give yourself, by choice, wholly to Christ.

Do not say to yourself, "I cannot serve Jesus. I cannot overcome." If you cannot, it is because you *will* not serve Him; you *will* not overcome. If you choose a master other than Christ, you choose failure. "Let no one say, I cannot remedy my defects of character. If you come to this decision, you will certainly fail of obtaining everlasting life. The impossibility lies in your own will. If you will not, then you can not overcome."[19]

Do not say to yourself, "I will try to serve Jesus and overcome!" There is no such thing as trying to serve Jesus. Remember, Jesus said, "He that is not with me is against me; and he that gathereth not with me scattereth abroad" (Matt. 12:30). You either serve Jesus wholly or you don't serve Jesus at all. There is no trying in the matter. You either serve Him or you do not. You cannot shine as the light of the world while you are a child of darkness. It is impossible! Just what light is it that you think you are going to shine when you are nothing but darkness? Until you are a child of light, the possibility of shining doesn't exist.

Everything comes down to your choices, your decisions. Choose to be as kind, loving, pleasant, self-denying, and self-sacrificing as your Savior. Choose to be as obedient as Job. Choose to be as firm as Daniel. Choose to be as bold as Elijah. Choose to be as strong as Stephen. Choose to be as persevering as Paul. Choose to be as fearless as David. Choose to overcome a perverted appetite. Choose to overcome the fashions and pleasures of the world. Choose to overcome cherished sins. Choose to make your own personal, whole-hearted, self-denying sacrifices to save souls, lest their blood be required at your hands (Eze. 3:18; 33:8). Choose to honor God in eating, drinking, dressing, and conversation. In "whatsoever ye do," choose to do it "all to the glory of God" (1 Cor. 10:31).

Make the choice to use every talent for Christ. Choose to use all of your time, your money, your health, your strength, your energy, your fullest and most thorough and persevering efforts, your thoughts, your influence, your everything for Him. He requires it all. Invest it all then, and spare nothing! "Whatsoever ye do in word or deed," choose to "do all in the name of the Lord Jesus" (Col. 3:17). And if whatever you are about to do cannot be rightly done in Christ's name, then choose to not do it.

Choose to spend time daily with Jesus in prayer while you go about your duties and in reading His Word. Choose to study deeply under God's direction and know the truth for yourself, to know what is right versus what is wrong, to distinguish the truth from error, lest you be deceived to your own eternal death. Choose to surrender your cherished theories, ideas, and opinions to the authority of God's Word. Choose to believe God's promises—belief is a choice! Choose to be as trusting in God as the child who believes his loving parents. Choose to be like those great men of the past who lived, suffered, and died for Christ, and make this choice even if you must travel the path alone, for as you travel, it may seem that you will have to go alone.

Choose to fill "the greatest want of the world." Choose Jesus as your Master. Choose salvation. *Choose! Choose! Choose!* This is what you must do. And you must make your choice *now*, whether you feel like it or not! The time to choose has expired, and yet God still gives you one more chance! What will you do with this one more gift of God's patient love? What will you do with this one more second given you to choose Christ before it is forever too late and the great clock of

Chapter 2 — "Choose you this day"

time ticks its last tock before it explodes at probation's midnight end? Oh that all would heed the counsel, "Seek ye the LORD while He may be found" (Isa. 55:6).

But do not deceive yourself! "Know ye not, that to whom ye yield yourselves servants to obey, his servants ye are to whom ye obey; whether of sin unto death, or of obedience unto righteousness?" (Rom. 6:16). If you think that you are a wholehearted servant of Jesus Christ and yet still commit sin, then your master is not Christ, but Satan. Your deeds will determine who your master is. If you continue to choose sin over obedience to the Word of God, then "Ye are of your father the devil, and the lusts of your father ye will do" (John 8:44). To insist that you are a true follower of Jesus while you are living in sin is a terrible thing. "Woe unto them that call evil good, and good evil; that put darkness for light, and light for darkness; that put bitter for sweet, and sweet for bitter!" (Isa. 5:20).

"If you choose to follow Jesus, you must obey the word, 'If any man will come after me, let him deny himself, and take up his cross, and follow me' (Matthew 16:24)."[20] "Christ demands all. . . . This is a self-denying way. And when you think that the way is too strait, that there is too much self-denial in this narrow path; when you say, How hard to give up all, ask yourselves the question, What did Christ give up for me? This question puts anything that we may call self-denial in the shade. Behold Him in the garden, sweating great drops of blood. A solitary angel is sent from heaven to strengthen the Son of God. Follow Him on His way to the judgment hall, while He is derided, mocked, and insulted by that infuriated mob. Behold Him clothed in that old purple kingly robe. Hear the coarse jest and cruel mocking. See them place upon that noble brow the crown of thorns, and then smite Him with a reed, causing the thorns to penetrate His temples, and the blood to flow from that holy brow. Hear that murderous throng eagerly crying for the blood of the Son of God. He is delivered into their hands, and they lead the noble sufferer away, pale, weak, and fainting, to His crucifixion. He is stretched upon the wooden cross, and the nails are driven through His tender hands and feet. Behold Him hanging upon the cross those dreadful hours of agony until the angels veil their faces from the horrid scene, and the sun hides its light, refusing to behold. Think of these things, and then ask, Is the way too strait? No, no."[21]

"But what do we give up, when we give all? A sin-polluted heart, for Jesus to purify, to cleanse by His own blood, and to save by His matchless love. And yet men think it hard to give up all! I am ashamed to hear it spoken of, ashamed to write it."[22]

We are taught in the parable of the lost sheep that "if there had been but one lost soul, Christ would have died for that one."[23] That means that if you were the only person that was ever lost, Jesus would still have made the same great sacrifice to save just *you*. We understand that "the Saviour would have passed through the agony of Calvary that one might be saved in His kingdom."[24] Yes! Even if that one was only you!

Dear friends, "Jesus did not count heaven a place to be desired while we were lost."[25] What was heaven to the King of heaven if you weren't there to enjoy it with Him? What was heaven to Love Himself if you weren't there for Him to love? Were there not millions upon millions of angels with whom He could enjoy heaven? Were there not all of these angels that He could love, along with all the rest of the created universe? But I suppose that since He left heaven just for you, you must be very dear to His heart. Because of this, because He loves you so much that the paradise of God was not paradise to Him without you there, He chose to leave heaven, come down here to earth, and make a great effort to save you and bring you home.

In this great effort to save you, Christ had "to meet life's peril in

Chapter 2 — "Choose you this day"

common with every human soul, to fight the battle as every child of humanity must fight it, at the risk of failure and eternal loss."[26] "Christ risked all. For our redemption, heaven itself was imperiled."[27] "Satan saw that he must either conquer or be conquered. The issues of the conflict involved too much to be entrusted to his confederate angels. He must personally conduct the warfare. All the energies of apostasy were rallied against the Son of God. Christ was made the mark of every weapon of hell."[28] Do you realize what Christ risked for your very own soul? If Christ, the infinite God of the universe, committed a single sin, I ask you, where would have been the Savior to redeem Him from the eternal penalty of the law? "The wages of sin is death" (Rom. 6:23).

"Never can the cost of our redemption be realized until the redeemed shall stand with the Redeemer before the throne of God. Then as the glories of the eternal home burst upon our enraptured senses we shall remember that Jesus left all this for us, that He not only became an exile from the heavenly courts, but for us took the risk of failure and eternal loss. Then we shall cast our crowns at His feet, and raise the song, 'Worthy is the Lamb that was slain to receive power, and riches, and wisdom, and strength, and honor, and glory, and blessing.' Revelation 5:12."[29]

Jesus Christ came down from heaven to earth and lived a life of toil for thirty-three and a half years while every weapon of hell was aimed at Him. Then, for your sake, He died a most miserable death, suffering beyond what you can ever imagine, and He did all of this with the hope that you would accept His great sacrifice, choose His salvation, and finally be with Him in paradise. What a sacrifice for the King of heaven to make! And that, knowing that it all might be in vain if you chose another master. Oh how much He has risked in the hope that you might choose Him! Oh how much hope He has placed

Saved by Works... Christ's Works!

on your one, solitary decision for or against Him! What are you going to do about it? What are you going to decide? Whom are you going to choose?

"Jesus longs to save you, to give you peace and rest and assurance while you live, and to bestow upon you eternal life in His kingdom; but no one will be compelled to be saved. Jesus says, 'Choose ye this day whom ye will serve.'"[30] "In the work of redemption there is no compulsion. No external force is employed. Under the influence of the Spirit of God, man is left free to choose whom he will serve. In the change that takes place when the soul surrenders to Christ, there is the highest sense of freedom. The expulsion of sin is the act of the soul itself."[31]

"In the day of final judgment, every lost soul will understand the nature of his own rejection of truth. The cross will be presented, and its real bearing will be seen by every mind that has been blinded by transgression. Before the vision of Calvary with its mysterious Victim, sinners will stand condemned. Every lying excuse will be swept away. Human apostasy will appear in its heinous character. Men will see what their choice has been."[32]

"If the love of Jesus does not subdue the heart, there are no means by which we can be reached."[33] There is no greater appeal that can be given to the sinner to choose to give his whole heart and life to God than a knowledge of Christ's love for him. This love is the greatest power in the universe, and it is the only thing that can melt the sinner's hard heart of cold stone.

Picture Him there, bowed low at the gates of paradise, face downward in inexpressible sorrow. His chest heaving up and down from the choking sobs of a broken heart. Trembling, He longingly reaches out His pierced hand toward the sinner who is on the opposite side of the gates as He slowly separates Himself from the treasured object of His

Chapter 2 — "Choose you this day"

fathomless love. From His soft, tender, forgiving eyes, rapidly fall as from a bottle, the holy tears of unselfish love as He mourns in deepest sorrow for the sinner's lot. The fountain of His tears is broken up as he lifts His head to behold the horribly terrified face of the sinner. In painful tones of heart-wrenching agony, He cries between His surging sobs, "How shall I give thee up . . . ? how shall I deliver thee . . . ?" (Hosea 11:8). The shadow of a great, untold woe has come upon Him. He loathes to give the sinner up to desolate destruction. In groans of keen, insuppressible pangs of sharpest agony, He sorrowfully declares to the sinner from hesitant, quivering, and unwilling lips, "Depart from me" (Matt. 7:23). This is the separation struggle.

No longer does Jesus cry to God to spare the sinner a little longer. Most gladly He would if there were the faintest hope that the sinner would receive Him, but for too long the merciful pleadings of divine love have been to the sinner only an aggravation, a disturber of his false peace. Christ's yearning heart, in love that would not be repressed nor let the sinner go, had pleaded for years, but no longer will enduring love and patient mercy plead. They have not been desired, cherished, or appreciated, but hatefully ignored, scorned, and abused. "A long-suffering Saviour held out every inducement for the sinner to receive Him, to repent, and to be cleansed from the defilement of sin,"[34] but the sinner would not. Christ had done all that infinite wisdom, power, and love could do. Because Jesus did not count heaven a place to be desired while we were lost, He drained the dregs of death for every man and bore their woeful guilt that they might live with Him in paradise. But for the sinner His sufferings have been in vain. In mercy to them, He gives them up to suffer the wages of their sins—death. He will not have them suffer eternally where the false pleasures of sin and selfishness will never again be enjoyed. They have loved and cherished their sins—they have clung to them—and He allows

Saved by Works. . . Christ's Works!

them their choice.

With the separation struggle in no wise abated, His burning wrath against sin is stirred. This is the guilty one who has brought misery and death to His child. This is the culprit who has now eternally separated His child from Him. Those selfless tears that infinite love has shed for the sinner now become hot from His wrath. His enraged flaming fury is now executed in the eternal destruction of sin. Sin will be utterly, miserably, and eternally eradicated in the most intense fires of the hottest hell for what it has done to His precious child. This is the wrath of the Lamb.

"To sin, wherever found, 'our God is a consuming fire.' Hebrews 12:29. In all who submit to His power the Spirit of God will consume sin. But if men cling to sin, they become identified with it. Then the glory of God, which destroys sin, must destroy them."[35]

Because sin has been harbored and cherished in his heart, the sinner will feel the heated wrath of God against sin. The enduring love of Christ that for so long has cried in tearful agony to spare, spare the sinner a little longer, now, in mercy, cries for the sinner's death. He will not have His children continue to live a life of selfish sin in this world only to suffer its woeful results. Into His compassionate and sympathetic ears have poured the painful strains of crying, rejected humanity throughout all the ages of this world, and He will allow them to suffer no longer. In pity and sympathy to the sinner, Love Himself must end the sinful life.

Oh how difficult it would be for an earthly father or mother to end the life of their beloved children, and yet we think it an easy and even enjoyable thing for Him whose heart of divine love passeth knowledge! I declare unto you, *there is nothing intensely harder, more extremely difficult, or most nearly impossible for the heart of infinite love to do!* "As I live, saith the Lord GOD, I have no pleasure in the

Chapter 2 — "Choose you this day"

death of the wicked" (Eze. 33:11). In the destruction of the sinner, God's scorching wrath and His limitless love are stirred to their deepest depths. Again, this is the separation struggle; behold, this is the wrath of the Lamb.

"The forbearance that God has exercised toward the wicked, emboldens men in transgression; but their punishment will be none the less certain and terrible for being long delayed. 'The Lord shall rise up as in Mount Perazim, He shall be wroth as in the valley of Gibeon, that he may do his work, his strange work; and bring to pass his act, his strange act.' Isaiah 28:21. To our merciful God the act of punishment is a strange act. 'As I live, saith the Lord God, I have no pleasure in the death of the wicked; but that the wicked turn from his way and live.' Ezekiel 33:11. The Lord is 'merciful and gracious, long-suffering, and abundant in goodness and truth, . . . forgiving iniquity and transgression and sin.' Yet He will 'by no means clear the guilty.' Exodus 34:6, 7. While he does not delight in vengeance, he will execute judgment upon the transgressors of his law. He is forced to do this, to preserve the inhabitants of the earth from utter depravity and ruin. In order to save some he must cut off those who have become hardened in sin. 'The Lord is slow to anger, and great in power, and will not at all acquit the wicked.' Nahum 1:3. By terrible things in righteousness he will vindicate the authority of his downtrodden law. And the very fact of his reluctance to execute justice testifies to the enormity of the sins that call forth His judgments and to the severity of the retribution awaiting the transgressor."[36]

There is only one thing in all the universe that shall never receive even a single atom from the smallest of drops of God's mercy, and that is sin. The Scriptures declare of Jesus that God "hath made him to be sin for us, who knew no sin; that we might be made the righteousness of God" (2 Cor. 5:21). Oh awe-striking thought! Christ, the all-

Saved by Works... Christ's Works!

powerful God, became sin that you might be saved. The wrath of God that Jesus suffered for the longest of hours was a wrath in which there was no mercy. God's wrath against sin scorched the heart of Christ and wrung it through and through. The weight of all the sins of all men, with all of their tremblingly weighty guilt, crushed out Christ's life while He was on the cross. But "it is because He would not save Himself that the sinner has hope of pardon and favor with God."[37]

Behold Him. "The spotless Son of God hung upon the cross, His flesh lacerated with stripes; those hands so often reached out in blessing, nailed to the wooden bars; those feet so tireless on ministries of love, spiked to the tree; that royal head pierced by the crown of thorns; those quivering lips shaped to the cry of woe. And all that He endured—the blood drops that flowed from His head, His hands, His feet, the agony that racked His frame, and the unutterable anguish that filled His soul at the hiding of His Father's face—speaks to each child of humanity, declaring, It is for thee that the Son of God consents to bear this burden of guilt; for thee He spoils the domain of death, and opens the gates of Paradise. He who stilled the angry waves and walked the foam-capped billows, who made devils tremble and disease flee, who opened blind eyes and called forth the dead to life,—offers Himself upon the cross as a sacrifice, and this from love to thee. He, the Sin Bearer, endures the wrath of divine justice, and for thy sake becomes sin itself."[38] And as you view with amazement the terrible scene, your angel points saying, "Behold the Lamb of God, which taketh away the sin of the world" (John 1:29).

"The True Witness says, 'Behold, I stand at the door, and knock.' Revelation 3:20. Every warning, reproof, and entreaty in the word of God or through His messengers is a knock at the door of the heart. It is the voice of Jesus asking for entrance. With every knock unheeded, the disposition to open becomes weaker. The impressions of the Holy

Chapter 2 — "Choose you this day"

Spirit if disregarded today, will not be as strong tomorrow. The heart becomes less impressible, and lapses into a perilous unconsciousness of the shortness of life, and of the great eternity beyond."[39]

"Every time you fail to open the door of your heart to Christ, you become more and more unwilling to listen to the voice of Him that speaketh. You diminish your chance of responding to the last appeal of mercy. Let it not be written of you, as of ancient Israel, 'Ephraim is joined to idols; let him alone.' Hosea 4:17."[40] "Mercy may plead for years and be slighted and rejected; but there comes a time when mercy makes her last plea. The heart becomes so hardened that it ceases to respond to the Spirit of God. Then the sweet, winning voice entreats the sinner no longer, and reproofs and warnings cease."[41]

"Mercy's sweet call is now sounding; but it will soon die away. Probation's hour will soon be ended. The seven last plagues will fall, and then those who have chosen the pleasures of the world and rebelled against God, will cry for mercy when there will be none to answer their prayers. But a voice will be heard,—'Thou art weighed in the balance and found wanting.' And as they realize that they have no shelter from the dreadful storm of God's wrath, they will plead for one little hour of probation that they may again hear the sweet voice, inviting, 'every one that thirsteth, come ye to the waters.' It will then fall upon the ear, in that dreadful hour, 'Too late! too late!'"[42]

"That voice which penetrates the ear of the dead, they know. How often have its plaintive, tender tones called them to repentance. How often has it been heard in the touching entreaties of a friend, a brother, a Redeemer. To the rejecters of His grace no other could be so full of condemnation, so burdened with denunciation, as that voice which has so long pleaded: 'Turn ye, turn ye from your evil ways; for why will ye die?' Ezekiel 33:11. Oh, that it were to them the voice of a stranger! Says Jesus: 'I have called, and ye refused; I have stretched out My hand, and no man regarded; but ye have set at nought all My counsel, and would none of My reproof.' Proverbs 1:24, 25. That voice awakens memories which they would fain blot out—warnings despised, invitations refused, privileges slighted."[43]

"Scorner of His love, He addresses you today. It is 'thou, even thou,' who shouldest know the things that belong to thy peace. Christ is shedding bitter tears for you, who have no tears to shed for yourself. Already that fatal hardness of heart which destroyed the Pharisees is manifest in you. And every evidence of the grace of God, every ray of divine light, is either melting and subduing the soul, or confirming it in hopeless impenitence."[44]

"If the invitations given now are refused, if we persist in disobedience, we shall have no second probation. 'Choose you this day whom ye will serve,'— God or Mammon. Now, while it is called today, if ye will hear his voice, harden not your hearts, lest it be the last invitation of mercy."[45]

"I call heaven and earth to record this day against you, that I have set before you life and death, blessing and cursing: therefore *choose* life, that both thou and thy seed may live" (Deut. 30:19). "Behold, *now* is the accepted time; behold, *now* is the day of salvation" (2 Cor. 6:2, italics added).

Chapter 2 — "Choose you this day"

TICK, TOCK. . .

There is a gentle loving whisper,
A tiny little "tick,"
That tells us, "Time's about to end,
And judgment will come quick!"

There is a tender pleading sound,
A tiny little "tock,"
That tells us, "Come and join My sheep,
Quickly come and join My flock."

There is a sweet familiar noise,
A tiny little "tick,"
That tells us, "Stop building here on earth.
It soon will burn, yes, every brick!"

There is a soft and quiet voice,
A tiny little "tock,"
That tells us, "Hurry up and choose!
Soon will die probation's clock!"

There is a dying, fading speech,
A silent "tick"-like sound,
That tells us, "Quickly die the death!
Salvation comes once around."

Saved by Works... Christ's Works!

> There is a fainting, hard to hear,
> Tiny little "tock,"
> That tells us, "Christ is at the door,
> And it may be His last knock?"
>
> There is a silent, "No wait! Come back!
> The tiny 'tick' is lost!"
> "Too long hast thou refused Me now;
> And great will be the cost!"
>
> Will you dear child ignore this voice?
> This tiny "tock" and "tick"?
> Will you abuse the Saviour's love?
> Oh decide, and make it quick!

Chapter 3

"And this is the victory . . ."
1 John 5:4

David's Battle

All of us admire the little shepherd boy David for his heroic act in slaying Goliath. We wonder at his faith, his trust in God, and how he could be so perfectly confident of victory as he walked toward that heavily armed and protected giant with only a few small stones, a leather strap, and not a trace of fear in his heart. To all appearances, David was outmatched! A ruddy little shepherd boy versus a nearly ten-foot-tall man of war! How is it that David knew for a fact that he would have victory over this mammoth-sized Philistine? The answer: he believed God's promises.

The Bible is full of these promises. In this book God has promised that He will provide for all the needs of His children, that He will help them in every time of difficulty, that He will keep them from harm, and that He will forgive their sins and give them power to be perfect overcomers in everything, along with countless other things. But the only way that we can have these promises fulfilled to us is if we believe that God will do what He has promised. "According to your faith," says Jesus, "be it unto you" (Matt. 9:29).

Here is how many people determine whether or not they have faith. First, they get this feeling that tells them God's promise is ful-

Saved by Works... Christ's Works!

filled. Then, because they feel that God's Word is fulfilled, it must be true and factual. And because of the feeling which brings the fact, they then decide that they have faith. But this feeling-fact-faith process is all wrong, and it is unbiblical. In reality, first comes our faith, then God's promise is fulfilled, and then it is up to Him whether or not He will give you feeling. Therefore the process works like this: faith, fact, feeling.

There was nothing magical about David's faith that delivered Goliath into his hands. It was God's promise fulfilled that made this youth a conqueror. The important thing was that David believed *in God*. The Philistines believed in false gods, and these gods didn't save them. David believed in the true God, and that is what was important. In both cases, the faith of the Philistines and the faith of David were the same. The thing that made the mighty difference was what they believed in.

If you want to have faith like David to overcome the giants in your life, you cannot be wandering all over the battlefield with the question of whether or not you have faith, because if you do, Goliath will surely take your head off in the meantime.

We often think that faith in God is something hard to understand. It is something we want, yes; but we don't fully understand or know how to get it. But the truth is that faith is so incredibly simple. In fact, you already have it. Here are a few questions to confirm this. How do you know that Columbus sailed to America? Did you see him when he arrived on the American shores of the Atlantic? Did you talk with him? Did he tell you the whole story of his trip? If not, then how do you know that Columbus sailed to America? It is very simple, because you believe it. Here is another question. Chances are you have never been to Antarctica. How, then, do you know that Antarctica exists?

"Oh," but you say, "it is different believing in something that will happen *in the future*. It is different believing that God will do some-

Chapter 3 — "And this is the victory . . ."

thing for me in the time ahead, just like David did as he was marching toward Goliath." How is it different? In both cases, you have not seen, smelled, tasted, or touched the object of your faith. The only other sense of the five you have that could possibly make anything outside of you more real is the sense of hearing. You have heard about Antarctica and its existence, but you have also heard about how God will always work for us in the future, that we have no need to fear, and that it is impossible for Him to lie (Heb. 6:18). Therefore, if you believe that Antarctica exists, having no other way of knowing that it is there than because others have said so, so you should believe in God's promises because others, and He Himself, have said that they will be fulfilled. The Bible teaches that "faith cometh by hearing" (Rom. 10:17). You have already heard that God will fulfill His promises, so now just choose to accept the testimony given.

"If we receive the witness of men, the witness of God is greater: for this is the witness of God which he hath testified of his Son. He that believeth on the Son of God hath the witness in himself: *he that believeth not God hath made him a liar; because he believeth not the record that God gave* of his Son" (1 John 5:9, 10).

If you are not going to trust in God because you don't know Him well enough, then you must apply the same principle to all aspects of life or else you are a hypocrite. How sad it is that you can trust sinful, fallen, corrupted humanity, but you cannot trust your holy, righteous, and loving Father in heaven. You can trust evil men's words, wicked men's hands, but not those lips that came to speak peace to your soul, not those hands that were pierced to save you from pain, suffering, and eternal death. Oh how wicked of us to doubt such love! No wonder that "whatsoever is not of faith is sin" (Rom. 14:23). Faith can lack experience with its object and still be faith.

Now back to the battlefield. David comes before King Saul

and says that he accepts the challenge of Goliath. Everyone present laughs. The monarch says to David, "Thou art not able to go against this Philistine to fight with him: for thou art but a youth, and he a man of war from his youth" (1 Sam. 17:33). King Saul tried hard to turn David from his purpose of fighting with the giant, but David would not budge. Saul finally gave up and said, "Go, and the LORD be with thee" (1 Sam. 17:37).

David makes his way to the battlefield. He chooses five smooth stones out of the brook and then heads straight for the giant. Goliath comes forward, thinking to meet the greatest warrior of the Israelite army. When he sees David, he is very angry to be thus mocked by being given a child to fight with. The armies of Israel tremble as they watch David head for the haughty warrior. "What!" they cry, "A sheep-herding child is going to decide our fate?" The armies of the Philistines roll with laughter. Only a few men dare to question who will win the battle.

Stopping here, let us consider a few things. David is surrounded by two huge armies that believe he is going to lose the battle. He sees this heavily-protected and well-armed giant towering above him in comparison with his shepherd clothing and bag of rocks. Even if David did defeat the giant, he would be the first person to run smack into the entire Philistine army, and he would do it alone, because all of Israel's army would be too far back to help him. Yet despite all this, with a ring of fearlessness in his voice and a look of victory upon his face, David says boldly in reply to the angry, cursing threats of Goliath, "Thou comest to me with a sword, and with a spear, and with a shield: but I come to thee in the name of the LORD of hosts, the God of the armies of Israel, whom thou hast defied. This day will the LORD deliver thee into mine hand" (1 Sam. 17:45, 46).

Put yourself for a minute in David's place on the actual battle-

Chapter 3 — "And this is the victory..."

field. How would you feel? You would probably feel like a cornered little puppy about to uncontrollably wet itself. You would feel sure of defeat, sure that you would be dead in the next few seconds—unless of course, you could run fast enough back toward the armies of Israel before Goliath, with his oversized legs, trampled you underfoot. But, why, we question, did David not feel like this? The real question is, how do you know that he didn't?

"Feeling is not faith; emotion is not faith,"[1] but for some reason we do not understand this. The Scriptures remain silent in support of the idea that one does not really believe unless he feels like it. "Feeling is not faith. Faith is simply to take God at His word."[2] We have absolutely no place to say that David didn't feel like he would lose, that he didn't feel outmatched, for chances are, he did. Just consider Satan, our great enemy, for evidence. He had been successfully mocking God's people and God Himself for thirty-nine days. For the devil to be silenced and shamed by a little shepherd boy is not something he can afford. Therefore, with all his hellish weapons aimed at David, he may have nearly forced David to doubt his God by making him feel like God would not protect him. But David, fighting with all his willpower against the clamors of these false emotions inside of him, looks outside of himself to his all-powerful God, and refuses to consent to even consider the suggested thought of doubting God's promise of victory.

We need to understand far more clearly than we do that "feeling is not faith; the two are distinct. Faith is ours to exercise, but joyful feeling and the blessing are God's to give. The grace of God comes to the soul through the channel of living faith, and that faith it is in our power to exercise."[3] And the best time to exercise this faith is when our overwhelming emotions urge us to doubt. Faith is not exercised very much when everything feels like it will be okay. Exercising faith is marching into battle alone when every weapon of earth and hell is aimed at you and the feeling of perfect failure seeks to crowd out every speck of trust in God from the soul.

"Confound not faith and feeling together. They are distinct. Faith is ours to exercise. This faith we must keep in exercise. Believe, believe. Let your faith take hold of the blessing, and it is yours. Your feelings have *nothing* to do with this faith. When faith brings the blessing to your heart, and you rejoice in the blessing, it is no more faith, but feeling."[4]

"Faith is not sight; faith is not feeling; faith is not reality. 'Faith is the substance of things hoped for, the evidence of things not seen.' To abide in faith is to put aside feeling and selfish desires, to walk humbly with the Lord, to appropriate His promises, and apply them to *all* occasions, believing that God will work out his own plans and purposes in your heart and life by the sanctification of your character; it is to rely entirely, to trust implicitly, upon the faithfulness of God. If this course is followed, others will see the special fruits of the Spirit manifested in the life and character."[5]

"What you need to understand is the true force of the will. This is the governing power in the nature of man, the power of decision, or of choice. *Everything* depends on the right action of the will. The power of choice God has given to men; it is theirs to exercise."[6] It is your choice to believe and to exercise faith.

"If you fight the fight of faith with all your *will power*, you will conquer. Your feelings, your impressions, your emotions, are not to be trusted, for they are not reliable . . . You must be determined to believe, although nothing seems true and real to you. . . . You cannot control your impulses, your emotions, as you may desire; but you can control the will, and you can make an entire change in your life. By yielding up your will to Christ, your life will be hid with Christ in God and allied to the power which is above all principalities and powers. You

Chapter 3 — "And this is the victory . . ."

will have strength from God that will hold you fast to His strength; and a new life, even the life of living faith, will be possible to you. But your will must co-operate with God's will."[7]

Faith is one of the simplest concepts, but it is made to appear very complicated by confused people. Faith is a choice. The devil cannot force you to sin, and therefore he cannot force you to doubt, "for whatsoever is not of faith is sin" (Rom. 14:23). And if Satan cannot force you to doubt, then you must have a choice in the matter. The only thing that you can do is choose to believe, and *that choice is your faith!* That choice is exercising your faith. "Faith, *in itself,* is an act of the mind."[8] If there is anything more to exercising faith than simply choosing it, you will not have this, whatever it is, until you first choose to have faith—until you first choose to believe. You can either choose to believe what God has said or you can choose to doubt what He has said; either way, it is your choice. No one can force you to doubt.

Here are a few questions for you. Do you *believe* that God created the heavens and the earth, or do you *know* that God created the heavens and the earth? Do you *believe* that Jesus died to save sinners, or do you *know* that Jesus died to save sinners? Do you *believe* that Jesus loves you, or do you *know* that Jesus loves you? Do you *believe* that Jesus will fulfill His promises, or do you *know* that Jesus *does* fulfill His promises? Do you trace this line of thought? When it comes to dealing with God's Word and promises, true faith is choosing to acknowledge existing facts. But how do you know that the facts exist? Let us turn that question around. How do you know that they don't exist? Think about it! Is God true, or is He a liar? Do you *really* believe that He is not faithful to perform that which He has promised? Believing is knowing.

Faith is acknowledging that "God is true" (2 Cor. 1:18). And since God is true, then all of His unchangeable promises must be true also,

Saved by Works... Christ's Works!

or else God is not true but a liar. But we know that God is not a liar (Heb. 6:18) and that God is true. When it comes to receiving blessings from God, acknowledging that God is true is all that faith is, and this is all that faith will ever be. God is true. We believe that God is true, and we know that God is true; therefore, we do believe, and the promise that we claim *is* fulfilled to us.

But let us go to the highest of all authority, above all reasoning, theological deductions, and opinions of men. What does Jesus say that faith is? "And when Jesus was entered into Capernaum, there came unto him a centurion, beseeching him, and saying, Lord, my servant lieth at home sick of the palsy, grievously tormented. And Jesus saith unto him, I will come and heal him. The centurion answered and said, Lord, I am not worthy that thou shouldest come under my roof: but speak the word only, and my servant shall be healed. For I am a man under authority, having soldiers under me: and I say to this man, Go, and he goeth; and to another, Come, and he cometh; and to my servant, Do this, and he doeth it" (Matt. 8:5-9). "As I represent the power of Rome, and my soldiers recognize my authority as supreme, so dost Thou represent the power of the Infinite God, and all created things obey Thy word. Thou canst command the disease to depart, and it shall obey Thee. Thou canst summon Thy heavenly messengers, and they shall impart healing virtue. Speak but the word, and my servant shall be healed."[9] "When Jesus heard it, he marvelled, and said to them that followed, Verily I say unto you, I have not found so great faith, no, not in Israel. . . . And Jesus said unto the centurion, Go thy way; and as thou hast believed, so be it done unto thee. And his servant was healed in the selfsame hour" (Matt. 8:10, 13).

Jesus said that this centurion had "great faith." The centurion said, "*Speak the word only,* and my servant shall be healed." The centurion acknowledged that Christ's word had authority and power over sick-

Chapter 3 — "And this is the victory . . ."

ness and that all Christ had to do was speak and the sickness would obey His authority. So then, faith is acknowledging the authority and power that God's Word has, expecting it to do the thing that it says, depending upon that word to do it, and *knowing* that it does do it. This is all that the centurion did, and Jesus called it "great faith."

"Now the just shall live by faith" (Heb. 10:38). And what is faith? Faith is depending upon God's Word to do what it says. Therefore, "Man shall not live by bread alone, but by every word that proceedeth out of the mouth of God" (Matt. 4:4). How shall a just man live? By faith—by depending upon every word of God to do the thing that it says.

Paul says that "God hath dealt to every man the measure of faith" (Rom. 12:3). That is to say, God has dealt to every man, both good and evil, the ability to acknowledge the ultimate authority and power of His spoken word and to depend upon that word to do what it says. The word "hath" signifies past tense, meaning you already *have* faith. "Faith in Christ is not the work of nature, but the work of God on human minds, wrought in the very soul by the Holy Spirit."[10] This faith that every man already has is called "the gift of God" (Eph. 2:8). "Faith that enables us to receive God's gifts is itself a gift, of which some measure is imparted to every human being. It grows as exercised in appropriating the word of God. In order to strengthen faith, we must often bring it in contact with the word."[11]

Even though all men already have faith, they often perceive that they do not. We read the story of the father who cried out to Jesus saying, "Lord, have mercy on my son" (Matt. 17:15), "for he is mine only child. And, lo, a spirit taketh him" (Luke 9:38, 39). "And wheresoever he taketh him, he teareth him: and he foameth, and gnasheth with his teeth, and pineth away" (Mark 9:18). "Ofttimes he falleth into the fire, and oft into the water" (Matt. 17:15). "And I spake to thy disciples that

Saved by Works. . . Christ's Works!

they should cast him out; and they could not" (Mark 9:18).

"He answereth him, and saith, O faithless generation, how long shall I be with you? how long shall I suffer you? bring him unto me. And they brought him unto him: and when he saw him, straightway the spirit tare him; and he fell on the ground, and wallowed foaming. And he asked his father, How long is it ago since this came unto him? And he said, Of a child" (Mark 9:19-21). "The father told the story of long years of suffering, and then, as if he could endure no more, exclaimed, 'If Thou canst do anything, have compassion on us, and help us.' [Mark 9:22] 'If Thou canst!' Even now the father questioned the power of Christ.

"Jesus answers, 'If thou canst believe, all things are possible to him that believeth.' [Mark 9:23] There is no lack of power on the part of Christ; the healing of the son depends upon the father's faith. With a burst of tears, realizing his own weakness, the father casts himself upon Christ's mercy, with the cry, 'Lord, I believe; help Thou mine unbelief.' [Mark 9:24]

"Jesus turns to the suffering one, and says, 'Thou dumb and deaf spirit, I charge thee, come out of him, and enter no more into him.' [Mark 9:25] There is a cry, an agonized struggle. The demon, in passing, seems about to rend the life from his victim. Then the boy lies motionless, and apparently lifeless. The multitude whisper, 'He is dead.' [Mark 9:26] But Jesus takes him by the hand, and lifting him up, presents him, in perfect soundness of mind and body, to his father. Father and son praise the name of their Deliverer. The multitude are 'amazed at the mighty power of God,' [Luke 9:43] while the scribes, defeated and crestfallen, turn sullenly away.

"'If Thou canst do anything, have compassion on us, and help us.' How many a sin-burdened soul has echoed that prayer. And to all, the pitying Saviour's answer is, 'If thou canst believe, all things are pos-

Chapter 3 — "And this is the victory..."

sible to him that believeth.' It is faith that connects us with heaven, and brings us strength for coping with the powers of darkness. In Christ, God has provided means for subduing every sinful trait, and resisting every temptation, however strong. But many *feel* that they lack faith, and therefore they remain away from Christ. Let these souls, in their helpless unworthiness, cast themselves upon the mercy of their compassionate Saviour. Look not to self, but to Christ. He who healed the sick and cast out demons when He walked among men is the same mighty Redeemer today. Faith comes by the word of God. Then grasp His promise, 'Him that cometh to Me I will in no wise cast out.' John 6:37. Cast yourself at His feet with the cry, 'Lord, I believe; help Thou mine unbelief.' You can never perish while you do this—never."[12]

The father had questioned and doubted Christ's power, saying, "If thou canst." By thus doubting, he imperiled his child, for the healing of the son depended upon the father's faith. When Jesus answered the father's question saying, "If thou canst believe, all things are possible to him that believeth," the father, in realizing his own weakness, had to concede to another's strength—*Christ's strength*. He acknowledged the power that Christ had, but because he didn't *feel* like he believed, he replied, "Lord, I believe; help Thou mine unbelief."

Now, if the healing of the son depended upon the father's faith and the son was in fact healed by Christ, then the father must have had faith. The father's pleading cry revealed contradictory sentiments. "I believe," he says, "but I don't believe, so help my unbelief." This man had faith or else his son would not have been healed. That which called forth his contradicting cry was his feelings, but feelings are not faith. "Satan will, if he is unsuspected, give feelings and impressions. These are not safe guides."[13]

When the father cried out saying, "Lord I believe; help Thou mine unbelief," Jesus saw that he had faith in His power. Christ knew that the man's feelings were giving him so much difficulty, and He, totally disregarding the father's feelings, looked over them as of no account and set the captive child free. And this same Jesus of old, that set the child free from the power of Satan, will do the same for us today. He will overlook feelings and acknowledge the simple faith that man has in His power.

This is the reason that you can never perish while you cry out to Christ, as did this poor father. If you cry out to Jesus in the same way that this man did, your faith lays hold on Christ's strength. From this most precious story we learn that faith is merely realizing your own weakness and simply acknowledging the power of God in your behalf. "My strength," Christ says, "is made perfect in weakness" (2 Cor. 12:9).

"Faith is simply to take God at His word."[14] "Faith, in itself, is an act of the mind."[15] Faith is a choice. Faith is realizing your own weakness and choosing to acknowledge the power and authority of God's Word, choosing to acknowledge, not God's theories, but God's facts, and *knowing* that they are facts. And this choice, this knowing, this act of the mind, this taking God at His word is the assurance (according to the original Greek) of the things you are hoping for. It is the evidence you have of the things you cannot see (Heb. 11:1). While it is true that faith is not reality, it is faith that allows God's Word to make His promise a reality. When it comes to the Word of God, faith is not theorizing that something is true; faith is *knowing* that it is true. "The word is nigh thee, even in thy mouth, and in thy heart: that is, the word of faith" (Rom. 10:8).

As for Abraham, "being not weak in faith, he considered not his own body now dead, when he was about an hundred years old, neither yet the deadness of Sarah's womb: He staggered not at the promise of God through unbelief; but was strong in faith, giving glory to God"

Chapter 3 — "And this is the victory . . ."

(Rom 4:19, 20). Jesus spoke of men who had "little faith" (Matt. 6:30; 8:26; 14:31; 16:8; Luke 12:28). And He spoke of men who had "great faith" (Matt. 15:28). In order to increase from having "little faith" to "great faith," to go from being "weak in faith" to "strong in faith," faith needs to be exercised. But exercising faith through acknowledging the power of God's Word requires no great effort. It is just a mere acknowledgment.

The understanding that we most need is "understanding how to exercise faith. This is the science of the gospel. The Scripture declares, 'Without faith it is impossible to please God.' The knowledge of what the Scripture means when urging upon us the necessity of cultivating faith, is more essential than any other knowledge that can be acquired. We suffer much trouble and grief because of our unbelief, and our ignorance of how to exercise faith. We must break through the clouds of unbelief. We can not have a healthy Christian experience, we can not obey the gospel unto salvation, until the science of faith is better understood, and until more faith is exercised."[16]

It is the strong faith of Jesus that will allow God to do for us everything that He has promised. Our daily food and water, our clothing, our difficulties and trials, our education, our lifework, our spouses, our children, our daily victory over sin, and our salvation will all be taken care of and provided for if we will but believe our loving Father in heaven in the same way as we believe wicked men on earth. We have faith and trust in sinful human beings without thinking that this faith is anything special, and yet we wonder in astonishment after a faith and trust that believes in Him who cannot lie. What!? Has Satan so successfully lied to us about faith that we wholeheartedly trust lying and misinformed mortals but do not dare to trust a righteous and immortal God who knows everything? We trust God with the management of the universe, that He will watch over everything and make sure it runs

Saved by Works... Christ's Works!

in perfect order from the greatest galaxy down to the smallest atom in unlimited space, but we don't think that He is capable of successfully managing our small little lives? Oh what nonsense!

You are now challenged to set your will on the believing side. March straight toward the full armies of hell with the all-powerful shield of a living faith, and do it alone if no one will go with you. Charge in full force toward the dragon and all his hosts with the earth-shaking and trumpet-like war cry of a holy faith ringing from your lips. Remember, it is not your belief that will give you the sure victory but what you believe in, which is God's power. David ran toward this smaller-than-actual-size giant with the full assurance that "the captain of the LORD's host" (Joshua 5:15) was at his right hand, and that he would therefore not be moved (Ps. 16:8).

David claimed God's promises, and this is why he won the battle. We can also claim both the promise and the victory. We have been assured that "a thousand shall fall at thy side, and ten thousand at thy right hand; but it shall not come nigh thee" (Ps. 91:7). "When thou passest through the waters, I will be with thee; and through the rivers, they shall not overflow thee: when thou walkest through the fire, thou shalt not be burned; neither shall the flame kindle upon thee" (Isa. 43:2). "No weapon that is formed against thee shall prosper" (Isa. 54:17). "Thou shalt tread upon the lion and adder: the young lion and the dragon shalt thou trample under feet" (Ps. 91:13). "Behold, I give unto you power to tread on serpents and scorpions, and over all the power of the enemy: and nothing shall by any means hurt you" (Luke 10:19).

Remember that "ye shall not need to fight in this battle" (2 Chron. 20:17), "for the battle is not yours, but God's" (verse 15). Therefore "set yourselves," and your will, on the believing side; "stand ye still, and see the salvation of the LORD with you . . . fear not, nor be dis-

Chapter 3 — "And this is the victory . . ."

mayed . . . go out against them: for the LORD will be with you" (verse 17).

Our Battle

The demands of the law of God are high, for Jesus says, "Be ye therefore perfect" (Matt. 5:48). This word perfect, in the original Greek, means complete in mental and moral character. "God will accept only those who are determined to aim high. He places every human agent under obligation to do his best. Moral perfection is required of all. Never should we lower the standard of righteousness in order to accommodate inherited or cultivated tendencies to wrong-doing. We need to understand that imperfection of character is sin. All righteous attributes of character dwell in God as a perfect, harmonious whole, and every one who receives Christ as a personal Saviour is privileged to possess these attributes."[17]

"God's ideal for His children is higher than the highest human thought can reach. 'Be ye therefore perfect, even as your Father which is in heaven is perfect.' This command is a promise. The plan of redemption contemplates our complete recovery from the power of Satan. Christ always separates the contrite soul from sin. He came to destroy the works of the devil, and He has made provision that the Holy Spirit shall be imparted to every repentant soul, to keep him from sinning."[18]

To many of us perfection of character is something we know is required, but we put off its obtainment into the future, thinking that though we can be perfect it is something that we cannot have right now. It is something that we might be able to possess in the far distant future, but now?—impossible! What could be more false than this? And what could be more dangerous? "He who has not sufficient faith in Christ to believe that he can keep him from sinning, has not the faith

Saved by Works... Christ's Works!

that will give him an entrance into the kingdom of God."[19]

One reason we think in this erroneous way is that though we might believe that Christ has indeed forgiven our past sins and set us free from the wages of our sins, which is death, we do not believe that Christ has set us free from *the power of sin* itself. We still reckon that sin has power over us to conform us to its will, and because we consider this, it is true in our lives.

Jesus said, "Whosoever committeth sin is the servant of sin" (John 8:34). If a man is a servant of sin, the implication is that the master of this man is sin itself. Every master has a law that is to be obeyed. Paul expressed the fact that sin has a law when speaking concerning himself: "For I delight in the law of God after the inward man: But I see another law in my members, warring against the law of my mind, and bringing me into captivity to the *law of sin* which is in my members" (Rom. 7:22, 23). Having this law of sin within himself, Paul cried out, "O wretched man that I am! who shall deliver me from the body of this death?" (verse 24).

Many Christians take their character improvement and end it just about here. Though Paul said that he had this law of sin inside of himself, and then gave his mournful cry, he goes on in the next chapter to say, "The law of the Spirit of life in Christ Jesus hath made me free from the law of sin and death" (Rom. 8:2). This is where many Christians fail. They do not reckon themselves as being made free from the law of sin but suppose themselves to be somewhat bound by this law even still. They reckon that this law of sin still has a power over them, and as a result, it brings them in captivity to itself. These people do not fully believe that "if the Son . . . shall make you free, ye shall be free indeed" (John 8:36). They do not depend upon the Word of God to do the thing that it says. The freedom that Christ gives is a perfect freedom—a freedom in which there is no trace of bondage.

Chapter 3 — "And this is the victory . . ."

But because we do not believe this, because we lack faith to claim this freedom, we are *not* made free.

From the moment that Jesus died victorious on the cross, "Christ's followers were to look upon Satan as a conquered foe. Upon the cross, Jesus was to gain the victory *for* them; that victory He desired them to accept as their own. 'Behold,' He said, 'I give unto you power to tread on serpents and scorpions, and over all the power of the enemy: and nothing shall by any means hurt you.'"[20] "When Christ bowed his head and died, he bore the pillars of Satan's kingdom with him to the earth."[21] From the moment Christ cried out on the cross, "It is finished" (John 19:30), it was sure that man would be made perfectly free from the power of sin and Satan if he would but choose and believe it to be so.

In the reality of it all, Satan is a defeated foe. He was conquered by the Lord Jesus at Calvary, but so many Christians look at Satan as someone who still needs to be conquered. But what is the purpose of trying to overcome Satan? He has already lost the war! He has only just as much power as the believer ascribes to him through unbelief in the Word of God, unbelief in the good news. God's Word declares us to be set free from the power of Satan the moment we accept this truth as a fact, but if we, as Christians, do not believe this, we will not avail ourselves of the freedom that is so freely ours.

The command came to God's people long ago saying, "Ye shall not need to fight in this battle: set yourselves, stand ye still, and see the salvation of the LORD with you, O Judah and Jerusalem: fear not, nor be dismayed; to morrow go out against them: for the LORD will be *with you*" (2 Chron. 20:17). What was the reason that they did not need to fight in the battle? It was because the Lord was going to be *with them*. So here the lesson is made unmistakably clear that when God is with us we need not do anything but let Him fight for us: "for

Saved by Works... Christ's Works!

the battle is not yours, but God's" (verse 15). And Christ has promised us saying, "Lo, I am *with you* always, even unto the end of the world" (Matt. 28:20). Therefore, when Satan comes to fight for your soul, understand that Christ is with you and that Satan therefore stands, *already conquered.*

"The life is molded by the faith."[22] If a small child came to you and told you that if you did not give him $100 he would beat you up, you would probably grin a little bit and then say to him, "That is just not how it works, sonny. You see . . ." But why would you do that? It is simple, because you do not believe that he has the authority to demand your money from you or that he is even able to beat you up. But suppose you *really believed* what the child said; would you not end up quickly handing him $100 to avoid being pulverized? "The life *is* molded by the faith." If you believe that Satan has power over you, then you will do what he says. But if you believe that God has taken that power away from him and that he has no power over you whatsoever because God's Word has declared you free, then you will live your life accordingly. "The life *is* molded by the faith."

The Lord Jesus has promised that all who accept, choose, and believe in His promises shall be set free from the power of sin and from the power of Satan. The problem is that when people leave the service of Satan to enter the service of Christ they often carry their old master along with them, listen to and believe his lies, tremble at his threats, and as a result, find themselves serving him once again. This way of dealing with our old master is very foolish and extremely dangerous.

Let us say that you worked for a company under the direct control of the owner, and then, after years of service, you leave this company and begin working for an opposing company with a different owner who offered far better benefits. Would you still consider yourself under the authority of your first employer? Would he have any place to

Chapter 3 — "And this is the victory . . ."

tell you what to do? Would you not raise an eyebrow, in question of who he thinks he is, if he should start ordering you around? Would you not remind him that he is no longer your boss and that you are now working for a different company under a new owner? If he, seeming unconscious of the fact that you no longer work for him, threatened to make your life more difficult or to take away your retirement plan, would you not inform him that he has no power to make your life harder and that you now have a new and far better retirement plan than he ever had or ever could offer? Need the application be made?

The Bible makes it clear just how we are to respond to our old master. Paul asks, "How shall we, that are dead to sin, live any longer therein?" (Rom. 6:2). Just as a dead man would respond to his master, so we are to respond to sin. "He that is dead is freed from sin. . . . For in that he died, he died unto sin once: but in that he liveth, he liveth unto God. Likewise reckon ye also yourselves to be dead indeed unto sin, but alive unto God through Jesus Christ our Lord" (verses 7-11). "For when ye were the servants of sin, ye were free from righteousness" (verse 20). "Being then made free from sin, ye became the servants of righteousness" (verse 18).

When the apostle Paul said "reckon ye also yourselves to be dead indeed unto sin," he was not saying that we should reckon something that is really not true and that we should find some sneaky way into tricking ourselves into believing a lie to the end that somehow we might be better able to overcome sin. Paul was aware of the fact that if someone does reckon himself as dead to sin, then he *is* dead to sin because he is believing that God's Word has set him free from sin. If man does not reckon himself as free from sin, then he is *not* free from sin, because "according to your faith be it unto you" (Matt. 9:29). And when man reckons himself as free from sin, he is to remember the glorious fact that "he that is dead is *freed* from sin." And, "being then

Saved by Works. . . Christ's Works!

made free from sin, ye become the servants of righteousness."

"*Through faith*, the believer passes from the position of a rebel, a child of sin and Satan, to the position of a loyal subject of Christ Jesus."[23] "The dominion of evil is broken, and through faith the soul is kept from sin."[24] When you choose to leave the armies of the dragon host and put on the "whole armour of God" (Eph. 6:11) and join yourself to the armies of Christ, the devil has no more authority to dictate to you his commands. You are under the authority of God, and if Satan has a problem with that, he will have to go and talk to God about it. When the devil comes to you with his commands, rebuke him! Being thus resisted, "he will flee from you" (James 4:7). As long as you continue to choose Christ as your Captain and understand that sin and Satan no longer have any power over you whatsoever, you will be safe from the power of sin. But the moment you believe that sin and Satan still have a power over you, beware!

"Abundant grace has been provided that the believing soul may be kept free from sin; for all heaven, with its limitless resources, has been placed at our command."[25] "Trials and temptations may come; but the child of God, whether minister or layman, knows that Jesus is his helper. Although we may be weak and helpless in ourselves, all the forces of heaven are at the command of the believing child of God, and the hosts of hell cannot make him depart from the right course if he will cling to God by living faith."[26] "Through the grace given us we may achieve victories that because of our own erroneous and preconceived opinions, our defects of character, our smallness of faith, have seemed impossible."[27]

Chapter 3 — "And this is the victory..."

Christ My Righteousness

I was a poor wretch,
The chiefest of sinners.
There was no doom more sure,
Nor future more grimmer.

But looking toward You,
A ray of hope glistened.
You promised me life,
So I continued to listen.

I saw Your great love,
And what sin had done.
A new living principle
Had within me begun.

You'd forgiven my sins
And removed a great burden.
By faith I received
Against my name: Pardoned.

Then I tried to be righteous,
I gave it my best,
But freedom from sin?
I could find no rest.

Saved by Works... Christ's Works!

> I tried wielding God's power,
> But it didn't work.
> Then finally I realized
> That *He does the works*.
>
> So I examined my heart
> And saw it was vile.
> By faith Christ came inside me,
> Once cleansed from all guile.
>
> So by grace, all alone:
> Through faith justified,
> A sinless life *He* lives,
> By faith sanctified.
>
> And I've loved Him e'er since
> The works *He* has done;
> He paid the *full* price,
> By His love I've been won.

Chapter 4

"Ye shall be free indeed"
John 8:36

The Problem

When by faith we accept the freedom Christ has freely offered to us and cease to serve our old master called sin, there is, however, the danger that we will then start serving God as our master. While we are to reckon ourselves as free from the law of sin and free from Satan's service, we are not to reckon ourselves as servants of God, nor are we to reckon Him as our Master. The reason that we are not to do this is because, "When the fulness of the time was come, God sent forth his Son, made of a woman, made under the law, To redeem them that were under the law, that we might receive the adoption of sons. And because ye are sons, God hath sent forth the Spirit of his Son into your hearts, crying, Abba, Father. *Wherefore thou art no more a servant, but a son*; and if a son, then an heir of God through Christ" (Gal. 4:4-7).

The difference between a servant and a son is this. The servant works for wages, but the son works out of love for his father and receives an inheritance at no cost. There are far too many Christians who serve God as their Master, but not as their Father; they accept Christ as their Lord, but not as their Brother (Matt. 12:50). When they do this, they most assuredly become legalists, as generally revealed by their lives, and they think that they, by doing the works of the law, shall

63

obtain righteousness and eternal life. "Christ is become of no effect unto you, whosoever of you are justified by the law; ye are fallen from grace. For we through the Spirit wait for the hope of righteousness by faith" (Gal. 5:4, 5). "I do not frustrate the grace of God: for if righteousness come by the law, then Christ is dead in vain" (Gal. 2:21).

God does not care what we *do*, but rather He places all the importance upon who we *are*, because He knows that if we *are* His children, whatever we *do* will be according to His will, for children obey their fathers from a heart that is filled with love. Therefore, God wants us to *be* His children and not merely *do* His will. When we merely try to do God's will, we make our salvation—our inheritance—a matter of works. When we do this, we "frustrate the grace of God" and are found "fallen from grace."

Of Christ we read, "But as many as received him, to them gave he power to become the sons of God, even to them that believe on his name: Which were born, not of blood, nor of the will of the flesh, nor of the will of man, but of God" (John 1:12, 13). To those who fully receive the Lord Jesus, it is theirs to be the sons of God. "For as many as are led by the Spirit of God, they are the sons of God" (Rom. 8:14). "Not those whose hearts are touched by the Spirit, not those who now and then yield to its power, but they that are led by the Spirit, are the sons of God."[1] If someone is led by another it is because one of them is following the other. All those who choose to completely follow the leading of the Holy Spirit are the sons of God. And "if ye be led of the Spirit, ye are not under the law" (Gal. 5:18).

To not be under the law means to not be under a master, but under a father. Paul expresses this in his letter to the Galatians: "Wherefore the law was our schoolmaster to bring us unto Christ, that we might be justified by faith. But after that faith is come, we are no longer under a schoolmaster" (Gal. 3:24, 25). Why does Paul say we are no longer

Chapter 4 — "Ye shall be free indeed"

under the law? The next verse answers: *"For ye are all the children of God by faith in Christ Jesus"* (verse 26).

Paul, addressing the Galatians who desired to be under the law, that is, under the service of works, said, "Tell me, ye that desire to be under the law, do ye not hear the law? For it is written, that Abraham had two sons, the one by a bondmaid, the other by a freewoman. But he who was of the bondwoman was born after the flesh; but he of the freewoman was by promise" (Gal. 4:21-23). Note the words *bondwoman*, signifying bondage, and *freewoman*, signifying freedom. Paul continues saying, "Now we, brethren, as Isaac was, are the children of promise. But as then he that was born after the flesh persecuted him that was born after the Spirit, even so it is now. Nevertheless what saith the scripture? Cast out the bondwoman and her son: for the son of the bondwoman shall not be heir with the son of the freewoman. So then, brethren, we are not children of the bondwoman, but of the free" (verses 28-31).

Those who choose to be children of the bondwoman will, like her child, serve the father because they are servants, as the result of their being born of a servant. But those who choose to be children of the freewoman, the wife of the father, will serve the father out of love because he is their father. Because the Galatians were called to a higher position than that of a mere servant, they were told, "Brethren, we are not children of the bondwoman, but of the free." And it is for this same reason that in the very next verse Paul exhorts us saying, "Stand fast therefore in the liberty wherewith Christ hath made us free, and be not entangled again with the yoke of bondage" (Gal. 5:1). This yoke of bondage he is referring to is legalism. We are to live under the grace of God, which offers to us salvation at no cost, by allowing Him to adopt us as His children. But we are not to resort to going back to being under the law—to working for our inheritance.

Saved by Works... Christ's Works!

God wants us to serve Him, yes, but He wants us to serve Him with an attitude of love—a love that delights so much to please its object that the word service never even crosses the mind of the server.

We should never say, "I *need* to obey God," but rather, "I *like* to obey God." We should never say, "I *should* obey God," but rather, "I *desire* to obey God." We should never say, "I *have to* obey God," but rather, "I *enjoy* obeying God." We should never say, "I have *no choice* and will therefore obey God," but rather, "I choose to obey God because I *love* Him." The attitudes of *like, desire, enjoy,* and *love* are of a far different spirit than those of *must, should, have to,* and *no choice.* Jesus said, "He that hath my commandments, and keepeth them, he it is that loveth me" (John 14:21). "If a man love me, he will keep my words . . . He that loveth me not keepeth not my sayings" (verses 23, 24). Of Christ, "we love him, because he first loved us" (1 John 4:19). If this is the case, then our service to Him will be a service of utter love and greatest pleasure, not of duty, not of requirement, and not of fear, but of a love that delights to serve and please its object. The false types of service just mentioned, that seek, consciously or unconsciously, to purchase God's gifts, are of a very disgusting spirit.

"Oh!" men may say, "but we don't serve God with any of these false types of service!" A question for them then is what type of service do you serve Him with? If man cannot fully, completely, and wholeheartedly say with Christ from the very deepest depths of his heart, "I delight to do thy will, O my God" (Ps. 40:8), then his service to Christ only brings pain to the Lord's heart of love.

"Our God is a tender, merciful Father. His service should not be looked upon as a heart-saddening, distressing exercise. It should be a pleasure to worship the Lord and to take part in His work. God would not have His children, for whom so great salvation has been provided, act as if He were a hard, exacting taskmaster. He is their best friend;

Chapter 4 — "Ye shall be free indeed"

and when they worship Him, He expects to be with them, to bless and comfort them, filling their hearts with joy and love. The Lord desires His children to take comfort in His service and to find more pleasure than hardship in His work. He desires that those who come to worship Him shall carry away with them precious thoughts of His care and love, that they may be cheered in all the employments of daily life, that they may have grace to deal honestly and faithfully in all things."[2]

When the heart is overflowing with love for Christ, it will be our overflowing delight of love to perfectly fulfill His every command and suggestion, and this is the type of service Christ wants. The commandment says, "Thou shalt love the Lord thy God with *all* thy heart, and with *all* thy soul, and with *all* thy mind" (Matt. 22:37). "You must be devoted, yes, consecrated to God. He wants the whole heart. He is a jealous God, and he requires the whole heart, and the warmest affections."[3] "He wants the whole heart and interest, or He will have none."[4]

"In both the Old and the New Testament the marriage relation is employed to represent the tender and sacred union that exists between Christ and His people, the redeemed ones whom He has purchased at the cost of Calvary. 'Fear not,' He says; 'thy Maker is thine husband; the Lord of hosts is His name; and thy Redeemer, the Holy One of Israel.' 'Turn, O backsliding children, saith the Lord; for I am married unto you.' Isaiah 54:4, 5; Jeremiah 3:14. In the 'Song of Songs' we hear the bride's voice saying, 'My Beloved is mine, and I am His.' And He who is to her 'the chiefest among ten thousand' speaks to His chosen one, 'Thou art all fair, My love; there is no spot in thee.' Song of Solomon 2:16; 5:10; 4:7."[5] Dear child, Jesus does not just love you; Jesus is *in love* with you.

The marriage relationship is the tie that binds closest together those two people who love each other. Far deeper than any other human relation, the love and attention between husband and wife is unmatched. The slightest reserve on the part of either becomes a means of separating the two lovers from each other. Each heart must give to the other its all and nothing short of this. Nothing can be held back without imperiling the life of this closest union of love.

Many who are just entering manhood and womanhood long, with such an intensity of longing, to enter into this lifelong relationship with the object of their supreme affection. They consider it absolutely no sacrifice whatsoever to give all they have and are to their beloved one. For them to hold back the slightest amount of their heart from lavishing itself upon the other in the tenderest love that lies in all the deepest depths of their being would be to them far worse than death. If you have ever longed for such a union as this with any, then wait no longer. Christ, the "KING OF KINGS, AND LORD OF LORDS" (Rev. 19:16), the One who is "altogether lovely" (S. of Sol. 5:16) offers Himself to you to be the object of this deepest affection. Evidence heaped upon toppling evidence has been brought forth as a witness that He loves you far more than the entire world. There is no greater lover than Him. There is no one who can make you happier. He is love Himself, and only one who is deceived by Satan would not most eagerly accept His offer without thinking twice. And the instant you accept His offer, then just as surely "as the bridegroom rejoiceth over the bride, so shall thy God rejoice over thee" (Isa. 62:5).

Christ is represented in the book of Revelation as pleading at the door of the heart for admittance. But Christ is not merely waiting to be let in so that He can come in and rule your life. The Lord Jesus is standing at your heart's door, eagerly waiting for you to open to Him. At His feet is a box containing a wedding dress, whiter than snow. In His pocket, a golden ring of proposal, set with stones most precious. From the window you may only see the bouquet of roses He is holding

Chapter 4 — "Ye shall be free indeed"

behind His back, but do you realize that it is with these very roses that He comes to ask for your hand and make you His bride? Even now Christ is on His knees presenting before you the wedding ring. The One who is "altogether lovely" is offering to you His companionship, His mansions, and above all, His love. Will you turn Him down? Will you not throw yourself into His arms with tears of utter joy and accept His loving offer as too good to be true? Or will you coldly reply to His excited inquiry, "I'm sorry but I cannot give You my love. I have other interests, and I love these all too much. It is just too great a sacrifice to love You who first loved me." Too great a sacrifice!? Who would not be shocked at such a reply? Oh tell me poor deceived one. Tell me, just what sacrifice is involved in being the bride of God!? Will you call His offer a galling yoke, a burden hard to be borne? Will you call it a sacrifice? "Jesus does not require of man any real sacrifice; for whatever we are asked to surrender is only that which we are better off without. We are only letting go the lesser, the more worthless, for the greater, the more valuable."[6]

Jesus says, "Behold, I stand at the door, and knock" (Rev. 3:20). Wake up, sleepy Christians, and open to Christ quickly before He leaves! Be not as the woman in the Song of Solomon! "I sleep," she says, "but my heart waketh: it is the voice of my beloved that knocketh." Her beloved says to her, "Open to me, my sister, my love, my dove, my undefiled: for my head is filled with dew, and my locks with the drops of the night" (S. of Sol. 5:2). But instead of moving quickly to open to him whom she professes to love more than herself, she responds, "I have put off my coat; how shall I put it on? I have washed my feet; how shall I defile them? My beloved put in his hand by the hole of the door, and my bowels were moved for him. I rose up to open to my beloved; and my hands dropped with myrrh, and my fingers with sweet smelling myrrh, upon the handles of the lock. I opened to my beloved; but my beloved had withdrawn himself, and was gone: my soul failed when he spake: I sought him, but I could not find him; I called him, but he gave me no answer. The watchmen that went about the city found me, they smote me, they wounded me; the keepers of the walls took away my veil from me" (verses 3-8).

Christ's promise is, "I will betroth thee unto me for ever; yea, I will betroth thee unto me in righteousness, and in judgment, and in lovingkindness, and in mercies. I will even betroth thee unto me in faithfulness: and thou shalt know the LORD" (Hosea 2:19, 20). Jesus says to you, "Rise up, my love, my fair one, and come away. For, lo, the winter is past, the rain is over and gone; The flowers appear on the earth; the time of the singing of birds is come, and the voice of the turtle is heard in our land; The fig tree putteth forth her green figs, and the vines with the tender grape give a good smell. Arise, my love, my fair one, and come away" (S. of Sol. 2:10-13).

"Behold," your Beloved says, "I come quickly: hold that fast which thou hast, that no man take thy crown" (Rev. 3:11). Did you notice that Jesus calls the "crown of life" (James 1:12) "thy crown"? But just like it was with Christ, so it must be with us. "Before the crown must come the cross."[7]

"Whosoever he be of you that forsaketh not all that he hath, he cannot be my disciple" (Luke 14:33). "And whosoever doth not bear his cross, and come after me, cannot be my disciple" (verse 27). Such texts as these seem to make the married life with Christ appear as a torturous struggle, but in reality, it is not so. Christ has already made His proposal to you, and now the day of the wedding has come.

As you make your way to the place of crucifixion bearing your cross, don't think about how hard men say it is, but understand that you are walking up the aisle where you and your Beloved will be pronounced Husband and wife. That purple robe that others use as a

Chapter 4 — "Ye shall be free indeed"

means of mocking you is evidence that you are the royal bride, and that the Groom's desire is toward you. As that crown of thorns is mercilessly beaten into your head, focus not on the cruel stinging spikes, but realize that this crown of stinging roses adorns you and is the one worn only by the King's wife. When you reach the altar of sacrifice and are willingly bound to the cross by those cruel nails, remember that those nails are the blessed vows that bind you to your beloved Husband. That old cruel and rugged cross that you are called upon by your Beloved to bear is laced with glowing lilies. The blood that you and your Beloved have both shed upon the cross is the sweetest wine you could ever taste when, as precious Husband and wife, you drink it together on your wedding day.

And while you are hanging upon the cross and are asked by shocked onlookers, "What is thy beloved more than another beloved, O thou fairest among women?" (S. of Sol. 5:9), you are to answer them saying, "My beloved is mine, and I am his" (S. of Sol. 2:16). "I am my beloved's, and his desire is toward me" (S. of Sol. 7:10). "My beloved is . . . the chiefest among ten thousand" (S. of Sol. 5:10). "He is altogether lovely. This is my beloved, and this is my friend, O daughters of Jerusalem" (verse 16).

Everyone who bears the name of Christian needs to forever dismiss the ideas of toils and struggles, obedience, and mere service to Christ, for though these things are necessary, they so often give the wrong impression upon the mind. The Lord said through Hosea, "I desired *mercy*, and *not sacrifice*; and the knowledge of God more than burnt offerings" (Hosea 6:6). David speaks to the Lord saying, "Thou desirest not sacrifice; else would I give it: thou delightest not in burnt offering" (Ps. 51:16). And the Lord Jesus Himself says, "I will have mercy, and not sacrifice" (Matt. 9:13).

"God does not require sacrifice, but mercy."[8] Instead of these no-

Saved by Works... Christ's Works!

tions of torture and pain, obedience and sacrifice, drown yourselves in the deep warming oceans of Christ's love. He has caused wave after wave of His love to swell and to surge and then to so abundantly fall upon you. Let this love envelope you and shut you in to where you can neither see nor feel anything else. Accept, every waking moment of your life, His proposal to make you His bride. Live every second in that moment of exciting romance. Love Him as your bridegroom. Don't serve Him! Forget about serving Him! Just love Him. And better yet, forget about loving Him. Just focus on His love for you. The only way that we can possibly love Christ is "because he first loved us" (1 John 4:19).

But men say, "Whosoever he be of you that forsaketh not all that he hath, he cannot be my disciple" (Luke 14:33). Does not Paul say to "present your bodies a living sacrifice, holy, acceptable unto God, which is your reasonable service"? (Rom. 12:1). Be careful not to forget the burden that the Lord has enjoined upon us. Burden? What burden?

Thus saith the Lord, "When this people, or the prophet, or a priest, shall ask thee, saying, What is the burden of the LORD? thou shalt then say unto them, What burden? I will even forsake you, saith the LORD. And as for the prophet, and the priest, and the people, that shall say, The burden of the LORD, I will even punish that man and his house. Thus shall ye say every one to his neighbour, and every one to his brother, What hath the LORD answered? and, What hath the LORD spoken? And the burden of the LORD shall ye mention no more: for every man's word shall be his burden; *for ye have perverted the words of the living God*, of the LORD of hosts our God. Thus shalt thou say to the prophet, What hath the LORD answered thee? and, What hath the LORD spoken? But since ye say, The burden of the LORD; therefore thus saith the LORD; Because ye say this word,

Chapter 4 — "Ye shall be free indeed"

The burden of the LORD, and I have sent unto you, saying, Ye shall not say, The burden of the LORD; Therefore, behold, I, even I, will utterly forget you, and I will forsake you, and the city that I gave you and your fathers, and cast you out of my presence: And I will bring an everlasting reproach upon you, and a perpetual shame, which shall not be forgotten" (Jer. 23:33-40). "When the requirements of God are accounted a burden because they cut across human inclination, we may know that the life is not a Christian life."[9]

The terms "sacrifice" and "self-denial," when they are spoken of in the context of doing something for Jesus, are merely just terms to the true follower of Christ. They are cutting words that rebuke the hypocritical Christian and reveal the condition of eternal life to the worldling. But to the one who really *loves* Christ, they are just terms. To the real Christian, sacrifice and self-denial are merely words of technicality, not an experiential reality.

"Do you talk about self-denial? What did Christ give for us? When you think it hard that Christ requires all, go to Calvary, and weep there over such a thought. Behold the hands and feet of your Deliverer torn by the cruel nails that you may be washed from sin by His own blood!"[10] "When, as erring, sinful beings, we come to Christ and become partakers of His pardoning grace, love springs up in the heart. Every burden is light, for the yoke that Christ imposes is easy. Duty becomes a delight, and sacrifice a pleasure. The path that before seemed shrouded in darkness, becomes bright with beams from the Sun of Righteousness."[11]

Christ died in such a way that we might live, but we live in such a way that He might die. Christ counted it no sacrifice to do *everything* for us, but we count it an all-consuming sacrifice to do *anything* for Him. The law that demands the death of the transgressor still declares, "Thou shalt love the Lord thy God with *all* thy heart, and with *all* thy soul, and with *all* thy mind" (Matt. 22:37). We have every reason in the world to love Christ with everything that we have and are, to love Him to the point that it would be most devastating to us to fail to fulfill the smallest of His wishes. But we have a problem.

The Solution

Startlingly, strangely, and sadly, you will find it difficult to love Christ as your all in all: "Because the carnal mind is enmity against God: for it is not subject to the law of God, neither indeed can be" (Rom. 8:7). What you need to do then is to give your heart to God, but "you are not able, of yourself, to bring your purposes and desires and inclinations into submission to the will of God; but if you are 'willing to be made willing,' God will accomplish the work for you."[12] What you need is a new heart that is emptied of self so it can be filled with Christ. "But no man can empty himself of self. We can only consent for Christ to accomplish the work. Then the language of the soul will be, Lord, take my heart; for I cannot give it. It is Thy property. Keep it pure, for I cannot keep it for Thee. Save me in spite of myself, my weak, unchristlike self. Mold me, fashion me, raise me into a pure and holy atmosphere, where the rich current of Thy love can flow through my soul."[13] You cannot empty your heart of self, but God says, "I will take away the stony heart out of your flesh" (Eze. 36:26). This is a precious promise, and we are to receive the fulfillment of this promise in the same way that we receive all of God's promises, *by faith*.

You cannot make your "desperately wicked" (Jer. 17:9) heart to love Christ; "man cannot transform himself by the exercise of his will. He possesses no power by which this change can be effected."[14] "You cannot change your heart, you cannot of yourself give to God its affections; but you can choose to serve Him. You can give Him your will; He will then work in you to will and to do according to His good plea-

Chapter 4 — "Ye shall be free indeed"

sure [Phil. 2:13]."[15] The promise is then fulfilled: "A new heart also will I give you, and a new spirit will I put within you" (Eze. 36:26). The instant you make that choice to believe that He has caused you to love Him it becomes a living, breathing fact. "You cannot atone for your past sins; you cannot change your heart and make yourself holy. But God promises to do all this for you through Christ. You believe that promise. You confess your sins and give yourself to God. You will to serve Him. Just as surely as you do this, God will fulfill His word to you. If you believe the promise,—believe that you are forgiven and cleansed,—*God supplies the fact*; you are made whole . . . It is so if you believe it."[16] Just surrender the fact that you can't do these things for yourself, and let Christ do them for you.

"I will put my spirit within you" (Eze. 36:27). "When the Spirit of God takes possession of the heart, it transforms the life. Sinful thoughts are put away, evil deeds are renounced; love, humility, and peace take the place of anger, envy, and strife. Joy takes the place of sadness, and the countenance reflects the light of heaven. No one sees the hand that lifts the burden, or beholds the light descend from the courts above. The blessing comes when *by faith* the soul surrenders itself to God. Then that power which no human eye can see creates a new being in the image of God."[17]

"When the soul surrenders itself to Christ, a new power takes possession of the new heart. A change is wrought which man can never accomplish for himself. It is a supernatural work, bringing a supernatural element into human nature. The soul that is yielded to Christ becomes His own fortress, which He holds in a revolted world, and He intends that no authority shall be known in it but His own. A soul thus kept in possession by the heavenly agencies is impregnable to the assaults of Satan."[18]

Jesus has given the new covenant promise, "I will dwell in them"

Saved by Works. . . Christ's Works!

(2 Cor. 6:16). Paul tells us just how Jesus is to dwell in our hearts when he wrote to the saints which were in Ephesus. He says, "I bow my knees unto the Father of our Lord Jesus Christ . . . That he would grant you, according to the riches of his glory, to be strengthened with might by his Spirit in the inner man; That Christ may dwell in your hearts *by faith*" (Eph. 3:14-17). By your simply believing the promise, Christ Jesus dwells in your heart. "Through this simple act of *believing* God, the Holy Spirit *has* begotten a new life in your heart. You are as a child born into the family of God, and He loves you as He loves His Son."[19]

"Whereby are given unto us exceeding great and precious promises: that by these ye might be partakers of the divine nature, having escaped the corruption that is in the world through lust" (2 Peter 1:4). The promise that Christ will dwell in our hearts by faith enables us to be partakers of His divine nature, because by faith, He and His nature are now in the heart.

When Christ *is* in the heart, it is impossible for man *to* sin. "Whosoever is born of God doth not commit sin; for his seed remaineth in him: and he cannot sin, because he is born of God" (1 John 3:9). God's seed in this verse is referring to God's child or Son. Genesis 4:25 clarifies this, "And Adam knew his wife again; and she bare a son, and called his name Seth: For God, said she, hath appointed me another seed instead of Abel, whom Cain slew." (See also Galatians 3:16.) In 1 John 3:9, the word "cannot" in the original Greek is broken down into two parts, a negative part such as *not*, *never*, or *no*, and the other part meaning *able* or *possible*. Combining the two parts, we have *not possible*, or shall we say, *impossible*. When "Jesus Christ, the Son of God" (Mark 1:1) is in the heart, to commit sin is an impossibility. When Christ lived upon the earth, He "did no sin" (1 Peter 2:22). Though He "was in all points tempted like as we are," He was found

Chapter 4 — "Ye shall be free indeed"

"without sin" (Heb. 4:15). Jesus Christ is "the same yesterday, and to day, and for ever" (Heb. 13:8), and when He is in the heart, only good can come forth from it.

That is not to say that if a man "believes" that Christ is in his heart and he is knowingly breaking God's commandments that it is not sin. God has made very clear what sin is: "sin is the transgression of the law" (1 John 3:4). Who's law? "There is one lawgiver, who is able to save and to destroy" (James 4:12). "The LORD is our lawgiver" (Isa. 33:22). If man believes that since Christ is "in his heart" he can violate God's law without sinning, such a man is calling God a liar. God says, "Sin is the transgression of the law," while this man says, "Sin is not the transgression of the law, because I transgress it without sinning." Whom do you believe? Such a faith, one that leads men to transgress God's law, is not faith but presumption.

"Woe unto them that call evil good, and good evil; that put darkness for light, and light for darkness; that put bitter for sweet, and sweet for bitter!" (Isa. 5:20). "To the law and to the testimony: if they speak not according to this word, it is because there is no light in them" (Isa. 8:20). "A mere profession of discipleship is of no value. The faith in Christ which saves the soul is not what it is represented to be by many. 'Believe, believe,' they say, 'and you need not keep the law.' But a belief that does not lead to obedience is presumption. The apostle John says, 'He that saith, I know Him, and keepeth not His commandments, is a liar, and the truth is not in him.' 1 John 2:4. Let none cherish the idea that special providences or miraculous manifestations are to be the proof of the genuineness of their work or of the ideas they advocate. When persons will speak lightly of the word of God, and set their impressions, feelings, and exercises above the divine standard, we may know that they have no light in them."[20] "Impressions and feelings are no sure evidence that a person is led by the

Saved by Works... Christ's Works!

Lord. Satan will, if he is unsuspected, give feelings and impressions. These are not safe guides."[21] "This then is the message which we have heard of him, and declare unto you, that God is light, and in him is no darkness at all. If we say that we have fellowship with him, and walk in darkness, we lie, and do not the truth" (1 John 1:5, 6).

When Christ *is* in the heart, it is impossible for man *to* sin, but when Christ is *not* in the heart, it is impossible for man *not* to sin. The human heart "is deceitful above all things, and desperately wicked" (Jer. 17:9). "The carnal mind is enmity against God: for it is not subject to the law of God, neither indeed can be" (Rom. 8:7). "We are all as an unclean thing" (Isa. 64:6), and "who can bring a clean thing out of an unclean? not one" (Job 14:4). "A good tree cannot bring forth evil fruit, neither can a corrupt tree bring forth good fruit" (Matt. 7:18). "Either make the tree good, and his fruit good; or else make the tree corrupt, and his fruit corrupt: for the tree is known by his fruit. O generation of vipers, how can ye, being evil, speak good things? for out of the abundance of the heart the mouth speaketh" (Matt. 12:33, 34). "A good man out of the good treasure of his heart bringeth forth that which is good; and an evil man out of the evil treasure of his heart bringeth forth that which is evil" (Luke 6:45). "Can the Ethiopian change his skin, or the leopard his spots? then may ye also do good, that are accustomed to do evil" (Jer. 13:23). "Doth a fountain send forth at the same place sweet water and bitter? Can the fig tree, my brethren, bear olive berries? either a vine, figs? so can no fountain both yield salt water and fresh" (James 3:11, 12). Cleanse only the fountain and the streams will be pure.

"By nature the heart is evil, and 'who can bring a clean thing out of an unclean? not one.' Job 14:4. No human invention can find a remedy for the sinning soul. 'The carnal mind is enmity against God: for it is not subject to the law of God, neither indeed can be.' 'Out of the heart proceed evil thoughts, murders, adulteries, fornications, thefts, false witness, blasphemies.' Romans 8:7; Matthew 15:19. The fountain of the heart must be purified before the streams can become pure. He who is trying to reach heaven by his own works in keeping the law is attempting an impossibility. There is no safety for one who has merely a legal religion, a form of godliness. The Christian's life is not a modification or improvement of the old, but a transformation of nature. There is a death to self and sin, and a new life altogether."[22]

Just as one cannot possibly bring a clean substance out of perfect filth, so can no man do righteous works when he is unrighteous. Just as a corrupt tree cannot possibly bring forth good fruit, so can no man do good works when his heart is evil. Just as a fountain cannot possibly bring forth salt water and fresh water at the same place, so can no good heart bring forth both good and evil works. It can only bring forth one, and which one it brings forth depends upon the type of fountain it is. If it is a saltwater fountain, it will bring forth *only* saltwater. If it is a freshwater fountain, it will bring forth *only* freshwater. If the heart is good, it will bring forth good and only good without the faintest trace of evil. But if the heart is evil, it will bring forth evil and only evil without the faintest trace of good. If you sin, it is because your heart is evil. If you do righteousness, it is because your heart is good. The actions of man do not determine the condition of his heart; the condition of his heart determines his actions. The actions are merely the outward sign as to the condition of the inward thing. "Little children, let no man deceive you: he that doeth righteousness is righteous, even as he is righteous. He that committeth sin is of the devil" (1 John 3:7, 8).

If it seems that we are doing both good and evil in our lives, we must conclude that our hearts are evil, or else we would be saying that the evil that we are doing is not really evil, but good. Now it may seem like doing this would also be dangerous, because then we would be saying that the good we do is not really good, but evil, and "woe unto them that call evil good, and good evil" (Isa. 5:20). However, when we understand that "the heart is *deceitful above all things*, and desperately wicked" (Jer. 17:9), we will soon believe that the "good" works it *seems* like we do are laced with evil, and that we just do not readily see it, before we would ever dare to say that evil is not really evil, but rather that it is good. If we truly have good hearts, then good works and only good works can be manifested in the life.

"Often the question arises, Why, then, are there so many, claiming to believe God's word, in whom there is not seen a reformation in words, in spirit, and in character? Why are there so many who cannot bear opposition to their purposes and plans, who manifest an unholy temper, and whose words are harsh, overbearing, and passionate? There is seen in their lives the same love of self, the same selfish indulgence, the same temper and hasty speech, that is seen in the life of the worldling. There is the same sensitive pride, the same yielding to natural inclination, the same perversity of character, as if the truth were wholly unknown to them. The reason is that they are not converted."[23]

"The change of heart by which we become children of God is in the Bible spoken of as birth. Again, it is compared to the germination of the good seed sown by the husbandman. In like manner those who are just converted to Christ are, 'as new-born babes,' to 'grow up' to the stature of men and women in Christ Jesus. 1 Peter 2:2; Ephesians 4:15."[24]

True conversion takes place when man chooses to believe that God's love and power saves his and transforms his heart to love his Creator, and as a result of this choice, it becomes a fact because of God's immutable promise. Jesus says, "Verily, verily, I say unto thee, Except a man be born again, he cannot see the kingdom of God" (John

Chapter 4 — "Ye shall be free indeed"

3:3). "Except ye be converted . . . ye shall not enter into the kingdom of heaven" (Matt. 18:3). This conversion is a state of being that can be entered and exited at will. As long as we choose to claim the promise of the word by faith, it is true. The moment we doubt the promise of the Word, our heart becomes evil, and therefore, evil is the only fruit that can then be brought forth. But should we choose to reverse our course and wholeheartedly believe the promises of God's Word, the heart is made good through faith and the good fruits of righteousness will shine forth from the life.

"Above all, taking the shield of faith, wherewith ye shall be able to quench all the fiery darts of the wicked" (Eph. 6:16). "The *only* safeguard against evil is the indwelling of Christ in the heart through faith in His righteousness. It is because selfishness exists in our hearts that temptation has power over us. But when we behold the great love of God, selfishness appears to us in its hideous and repulsive character, and we desire to have it expelled from the soul. As the Holy Spirit glorifies Christ, our hearts are softened and subdued, the temptation loses its power, and the grace of Christ *transforms* the character."[25] Thus Paul says, "the goodness of God leadeth thee to repentance" (Rom. 2:4). When someone is truly converted, his character is changed. But it is not changed by any effort of his own. His character is not changed because he prays, because he studies his Bible, because he hangs around the right crowds, or because of his strong efforts to resist temptation and do good; his character is *transformed* by the converting power of the love of Jesus Christ.

"The LORD hath appeared of old unto me, saying, Yea, *I have loved thee* with an everlasting love: therefore *with lovingkindness have I drawn thee*" (Jer. 31:3). Jesus said, "And I, if I be lifted up from the earth, will draw all men unto me" (John 12:32). Christ must be revealed to the sinner as the Savior dying for the sins of the world, and

Saved by Works... Christ's Works!

as we behold the Lamb of God upon the cross of Calvary, the mystery of redemption begins to unfold to our minds and the goodness of God leads us to repentance. In dying for sinners, Christ manifested a love that is incomprehensible, and as the sinner beholds this love, it softens the heart, impresses the mind, and inspires contrition in the soul.

"It is true that men sometimes become ashamed of their sinful ways, and give up some of their evil habits, before they are conscious that they are being drawn to Christ. But whenever they make an effort to reform, from a sincere desire to do right, it is the power of Christ that is drawing them. An influence of which they are unconscious works upon the soul, and the conscience is quickened, and the outward life is amended. And as Christ draws them to look upon His cross, to behold Him whom their sins have pierced, the commandment comes home to the conscience. The wickedness of their life, the deep-seated sin of the soul, is revealed to them. They begin to comprehend something of the righteousness of Christ, and exclaim, 'What is sin, that it should require such a sacrifice for the redemption of its victim? Was all this love, all this suffering, all this humiliation, demanded, that we might not perish, but have everlasting life?'

"The sinner may resist this love, may refuse to be drawn to Christ; but if he does not resist he *will* be drawn to Jesus; a knowledge of the plan of salvation will lead him to the foot of the cross in repentance for his sins, which have caused the sufferings of God's dear Son."[26]

"Then the Spirit of God through faith produces a new life in the soul. The thoughts and desires are brought into obedience to the will of Christ. The heart, the mind, are created anew in the image of Him who works in us to subdue all things to Himself. Then the law of God is written in the mind and heart, and we can say with Christ, 'I delight to do Thy will, O my God.' Psalm 40:8."[27]

After claiming the promise that God has changed your heart and

Chapter 4 — "Ye shall be free indeed"

has caused you to love Him, do not be discouraged if you do not feel like you love God. True love is not a feeling. Love is a living, acting, working principle. Feelings may follow love, but love does not always follow feelings. "Do not wait to feel that you are made whole, but say, 'I believe it; it is so, not because I feel it, but because God has promised.'"[28] "The feelings, whether encouraging or discouraging, should not be made the test of the spiritual condition. By *God's Word* we are to determine our true standing before Him."[29]

But wherein lies the strength of God's promise? How can we be sure that if we believe it, it is so? The power behind all the promises lies in the almighty word of God. "By the word of the LORD were the heavens made; and all the host of them by the breath of his mouth. . . . Let all the earth fear the LORD: let all the inhabitants of the world stand in awe of him. For he spake, and it was done; he commanded, and it stood fast" (Ps. 33:6-9). God's Word has creative power. If He says that something is so, that something instantly becomes so. This is why it is "impossible for God to lie" (Heb. 6:18; see also Titus 1:2). Should God speak saying, "There are two suns in the sky," the instant He finished speaking it, immediately another sun would pop into existence. Though it would be a lie for us to say that there are two suns in the sky, it would not be a lie if God said it, because whatever He says becomes a fact.

Paul teaches that God is one who "calleth those things which be not as though they were" (Rom 4:17). Now if a man talks about something that is not as though it was, he is being deceitful; in short, he is lying. Paul says that God does this very thing, and the reason that God can do this without lying is because "He 'calleth those things which be not as though they were' (Psalm 33:9; Romans 4:17); *for when He calls them, they are.*"[30]

This brings an entirely new outlook to all of the promises of God's

Saved by Works. . . Christ's Works!

Word. It assures the soul with unmistakable evidence that the things God has said *are so* because, since He said them, they became so—that is, if they weren't already. The only thing God requires in order for His promises to be fulfilled to you is that you believe them to be true. Understanding why God cannot possibly lie, *even if He wanted to,* is one of the most faith-inspiring facts in existence. When one understands why it is impossible for God to lie, can he doubt God's promises? "Whatever gift He promises, is in the promise itself. 'The seed is the word of God.' Luke 8:11. As surely as the oak is in the acorn, so surely is the gift of God in His promise. If we receive the promise, we have the gift."[31] How is this so? It's simple. The promise itself creates the gift. And the reason that the promise itself creates the gift that it promised is because the promise itself is the creative word of God.

In Genesis chapter 1, we have many illustrations of the power of God's word. "And God said, Let there be light: *and there was light. . . . And God said . . . and it was so*" (Gen. 1:3-7). "Through faith we understand that the worlds were framed *by the word of God*, so that things which are seen were not made of things which do appear" (Heb. 11:3).

But not only are all things created by His word, but He also sustains His creation by His word. "God, who at sundry times and in divers manners spake in time past unto the fathers by the prophets, Hath in these last days spoken unto us by his Son, whom he hath appointed heir of all things, by whom also he made the worlds; Who being the brightness of his glory, and the express image of his person, *and upholding all things by the word of his power*, when he had by himself purged our sins, sat down on the right hand of the Majesty on high" (Heb. 1:1-3).

And the words that God speaks will accomplish His purposes. "For as the rain cometh down, and the snow from heaven, and retur-

Chapter 4 — "Ye shall be free indeed"

neth not thither, but watereth the earth, and maketh it bring forth and bud, that it may give seed to the sower, and bread to the eater: *So shall my word be that goeth forth out of my mouth: it shall not return unto me void, but it shall accomplish that which I please, and it shall prosper in the thing whereto I sent it*" (Isa. 55:10, 11).

Do you remember the definition of "great faith" that Jesus gave when dealing with the centurion? *Do not ever forget this definition!* Faith is acknowledging the authority and power that God's Word has, expecting it to do the thing that it says, depending upon that word to do it, and *knowing* that it does it because it cannot possibly lie. And since faith is knowing that the Word does what it says because it cannot possibly do anything else, saving faith is only acknowledging every word of God as true *in behalf of your own soul*.

Whatever God says instantly becomes a fact. God has spoken to us through His Word: "I will take away the stony heart out of your flesh" (Eze. 36:26). This is what it means to surrender to God, to submit to Him. You cannot submit yourself to Him, for that would be doing a good thing, and it is impossible for us to do any good thing. "A new heart also will I give you" (Ibid.). "I will put my law in their inward parts, and write it in their hearts" (Jer. 31:33). "I will dwell in them" (2 Cor. 6:16). The fulfillment of these promises is based on the condition that we allow God, *by faith*, to do all of these things for us. It is based on the condition that we take these promises of the Word, depending upon them to do the things that they said, and acknowledging that they are done in our own behalf. As soon as we do this all of the combined forces of the universe, in their vast entirety, cannot stand before the *all*-powerful word of God to hinder the promise from being fulfilled. At the very instant the soul believes, Christ abides in his heart, and as long as that soul continues to believe this promise and acknowledge the power and authority that His word has in his own behalf, it is perfectly impossible for sin to be manifested in his life.

"The creative energy that called the worlds into existence is in the word of God. This word imparts power; it begets life. *Every command is a promise*; accepted by the will, received into the soul, it brings with it the life of the Infinite One. It transforms the nature and re-creates the soul in the image of God.

"The life thus imparted is in like manner sustained. *'By every word that proceedeth out of the mouth of God'* (Matthew 4:4) shall man live."[32]

But many people entertain this creation-evolution theory that while God made all things, all things evolved by themselves, sustained themselves, and rose to a higher plain of existence by themselves. But the Bible teaches that *God* upholds "all things *by the word* of His power" (Heb. 1:3). So it is with the creation of the new heart. God speaks it into existence, and *He* upholds and sustains it in its pure condition by His word. As long as we don't step between God's word and our new heart by trying to keep it pure ourselves, He will sustain it in a pure condition by His word *only*. Just believe that He does it for you and *it is done*.

If you believe that you can keep your heart pure by some effort of your own, then you must also reason that you don't need God's word to do it for you. When *you* attempt to keep your heart pure, you are taking upon yourself God's responsibility and are thus really putting yourself in His place. "Just do it yourself," the serpent says, "and ye shall be as gods" (Gen. 3:5). Do you covet God's position? Do you know that this is why Satan fell from heaven? "I will be like the most High," he said, and yet God said to him, "Thou shalt be brought down to hell, to the sides of the pit" (Isa. 14:14, 15). Will you be brought down to hell with him? The prophecy is yet to be fulfilled: "The devil that deceived them was cast into the lake of fire and brimstone . . . and

Chapter 4 — "Ye shall be free indeed"

whosoever was not found written in the book of life was cast into the lake of fire" (Rev 20:10, 15).

Man's part in the work of his own soul's salvation is to believe that God gives him a pure heart and maintains it in its pure condition by His word. Only believe that word, acknowledge its power in your behalf, depend wholly upon that power, and don't set yourself up as God and exalt yourself "above all that is called God, or that is worshipped" (2 Thess. 2:4). And thus believing this, there is no power in earth or hell that can corrupt your pure heart, for when God says it, it is.

And not only when God speaks is it, but it is *instantly*. Not in five trillion years, not in five years, not in five days or five hours, but instantly. If you don't believe that God's creation is instant, then it matters not whether you believe that it takes five billion eons or five milliseconds between the time God speaks before it is—if you give *any* space of time between the spoken word of God and the existence of the thing He spoke, then you are an evolutionist. "*The moment* we surrender ourselves to God, believing in him, we have his righteousness."[33] "All may *now* obtain holy hearts."[34]

"Abide in me, and I in you" (John 15:4). "To abide in Christ means that you shall be a partaker of the divine nature."[35] "Therefore if any man be in Christ, he is a new creature: old things are passed away; behold, all things are become new" (2 Cor. 5:17). This new creation of God, this new heart upon which is inscribed His law, which is created by the power of His word, He will also sustain and uphold by the word of His power. And that word which He speaks *will* accomplish that which He pleases.

The all-powerful word of God declares, "As many as received him, to them gave he power to become the sons of God, even to them that *believe* on his name: Which were born . . . of God" (John 1:12,

13). So then, those who are born of God are God's children, and they are "born again, not of corruptible seed, but of incorruptible, *by the word of God*, which liveth and abideth for ever" (1 Peter 1:23). "Whosoever is born of God doth not commit sin; for his seed remaineth in him: and he *cannot* sin, because he is born of God" (1 John 3:9). The words of Scripture are God's spoken words, just in written form. Therefore, we conclude that the reason you cannot sin if you are born of God is not because you have control of God's power, *but because it is God's power that has control of you*, "for ye are all the children of God *by faith* in Christ Jesus" (Gal. 3:26).

If it is true that when Christ is in man's heart by faith it is impossible for sin to be manifested in that man's life, we have three possibilities. First, God was ignorant and didn't know what He was talking about. Second, God was lying. Third, God was right. The first two options can be discarded because it is "impossible for God to lie" (Heb. 6:18) and He "knoweth all things" (1 John 3:20). And even if we could say that God was incorrect about the impossibility for man to sin when Christ is in the heart, the moment He said that it was so, *it was so*. Again, we therefore conclude that the reason you cannot sin if you are born of God is not because you have control of God's power, but *because it is God's power that has control of you.*

Paul says, "*I am carnal*, sold under sin. For that which I do I allow not: for what I would, that do I not; but what I hate, that do I. . . . For to will is present with me; but how to perform that which is good I find not. For the good that I would I do not: but the evil which I would not, that I do. . . . O wretched man that I am! who shall deliver me from the body of this death?" (Rom. 7:14-24). This is the experience of those whose minds are carnal, and "the carnal mind is enmity against God: for it is not subject to the law of God, neither indeed can be" (Rom. 8:7). "To be carnally minded is death" (verse 6). Paul wanted to do

Chapter 4 — "Ye shall be free indeed"

good and resist evil, but he could not do this because it was impossible for him to do good and resist evil. Only if God ruled in his heart could Paul overcome. Paul needed a new mind, a new heart, and then he would be able to keep the law. Paul needed the new covenant promise fulfilled to him.

"This is the covenant that I will make with them after those days, saith the Lord, I will put my laws into their *hearts*, and in their *minds* will I write them" (Heb. 10:16; see also Jer. 31:31-33). When this promise is fulfilled, then the experience that Paul was speaking about will vanish. And for Paul, it did vanish. He says, "The law of the Spirit of life in Christ Jesus hath made me free from the law of sin and death" (Rom. 8:2). The master called sin has two laws: 1) You will sin again, and 2) you will die. Paul was set free from both of these laws because the new covenant promise was fulfilled to him. "Be not conformed to this world," says Paul, "but be ye transformed by the renewing of your mind" (Rom. 12:2).

"I can do all things through Christ which strengtheneth me" (Phil. 4:13). Many people make the big mistake of thinking that *they* are going to *use* God's power to resist evil and to do good, but this is an impossibility. An evil heart cannot possibly do any good thing, even if it does use God's power. "It is true that there may be an outward correctness of deportment without the renewing power of Christ. The love of influence and the desire for the esteem of others may produce a well-ordered life. Self-respect may lead us to avoid the appearance of evil. A selfish heart may perform generous actions."[36] An evil man can do "good deeds" from a selfish motive, and while the deed he does may result in good, the deed itself is still wicked. A selfish heart may offer bread to the hungry so that men would never look at him as so covetous as to steal from another, but the heart is still corrupt, the motive is impure, and the deed is therefore evil, though it may result

Saved by Works... Christ's Works!

in some good.

"No mere external change is sufficient to bring us into harmony with God. There are many who try to reform by correcting this or that bad habit, and they hope in this way to become Christians, but they are beginning in the wrong place. Our first work is with the heart."[37] "The plan of beginning outside and trying to work inward has always failed, and always will fail. God's plan with you is to begin at the very seat of all difficulties, the heart, and then from out of the heart will issue the principles of righteousness; the reformation will be outward as well as inward."[38]

"All *true* obedience comes from the heart. It was heart work with Christ. And if we consent, He will so identify Himself with our thoughts and aims, so blend our hearts and minds into conformity to His will, that when obeying Him we shall be but carrying out our own impulses. The will, refined and sanctified, will find its highest delight in doing His service. When we know God as it is our privilege to know Him, our life *will be* a life of continual obedience. Through an appreciation of the character of Christ, through communion with God, sin will become hateful to us."[39]

"The man who attempts to keep the commandments of God from a sense of obligation merely—because he is required to do so—will never enter into the joy of obedience. *He does not obey.* When the requirements of God are accounted a burden because they cut across human inclination, we may know that the life is not a Christian life. True obedience is the outworking of a principle within. It springs from the love of righteousness, the love of the law of God. The essence of all righteousness is loyalty to our Redeemer. This will lead us to do right because it is right—because right doing is pleasing to God."[40]

Those who seek to resist evil and do good by using God's power will miserably fail. God will never give His power over to an evil heart

Chapter 4 — "Ye shall be free indeed"

so that it can go about to establish its own righteousness. Men may think that they are using God's power, but in reality they are either using Satan's power or their own. Those who attempt to use God's power this way may "have a zeal of God, but not according to knowledge. For they being ignorant of God's righteousness, and going about to establish their own righteousness, have not submitted themselves unto the righteousness of God. For Christ is the end of the law for righteousness to every one that believeth" (Rom. 10:2-4). It is not that the law is done away with or that the law is no longer to be kept, for it will be, but that "to every one that believeth" (Ibid.) that Jesus Christ is in him, *he* will not be keeping the law, because *Christ will be keeping it in, for, and through him,* "for *it is God which worketh* in you . . . to do of his good pleasure" (Phil. 2:13). Therefore it is true that "with the heart man believeth unto righteousness" (Rom 10:10).

"All our righteousnesses are as filthy rags" (Isa. 64:6). But what exactly is self-righteousness? Paul says, "I count all things but loss for the excellency of the knowledge of Christ Jesus my Lord: for whom I have suffered the loss of all things, and do count them but dung, that I may win Christ, And be found in him, *not having mine own righteousness, which is of the law, but that which is through the faith of Christ, the righteousness which is of God by faith*" (Phil. 3:8, 9).

Here it is made plain that we obtain the righteousness of God *by faith.* And faith is dependence upon the Word of God to do what it says. We are to obtain true righteousness by depending upon God's creative word to make us righteous. Now, *"whatsoever* is not of faith [dependence upon the Word] is sin" (Rom. 14:23). Therefore, if we depend upon anything other than the Word of God to make us righteous, and we depend upon it in any measure whatsoever, whether great or small, it is sin. Whatever "righteousness" is produced by depending upon something other than the Word of God is not true righteousness.

Saved by Works... Christ's Works!

A righteousness that is dependent upon self, even in the smallest iota, is self-righteousness. The righteousness of God is not obtained through dependence upon self to do what it says. It is obtained by dependence upon the Word, by dependence upon the Author of that Word, that His Word will do what it says. Utter dependence upon the Word of God *is utter dependence upon the Word of God.* It requires no effort on your part to depend completely upon the Word to do everything for you in your perfectly helpless condition. Those who strive to obtain righteousness by exerting every energy of their being, by their straining of every muscle, and their working of every nerve, are not depending upon the Word to do what it says, but are depending upon self and what self can do. And this "is sin."

Paul wanted to be found, he says, "*not having mine own righteousness*, which is of the law, *but that which is through the faith of Christ*, the righteousness which is of God by faith." This is simply to say that Paul did not want to depend upon his ability to keep the law to obtain righteousness, for this he says is his "own righteousness," which he himself defines as "sin." Rather, he wanted that "righteousness which is of God" which comes by depending wholly upon God's Word to do what it says.

"God is righteous" (Dan. 9:14), and "God is love" (1 John 4:8). Therefore, "righteousness is love,"[41] and love is a living, working, active principle. "Love is the *fulfilling* of the law" (Rom. 13:10). If love is not active in doing good for others, then it ceases to be love and becomes selfishness. Therefore, "righteousness is right doing."[42] Since righteousness is right doing, then self-righteousness would be the result of self's right-doing. So any effort of self to do right is a self-righteous effort. "All our righteousnesses are as filthy rags" (Isa. 64:6). The verse does not say, "all our righteousness *is* as filthy rags," but "all our righteousnesses *are* as filthy rags." Righteousnesses is plural, not

Chapter 4 — "Ye shall be free indeed"

singular. So all of our righteousnesses—right-doing's—are sin.

"Whatsoever is not of faith [dependence upon the Word] is sin" (Rom. 14:23). If we depend upon anything other than the Word for our righteousness, for our right-doings, it is sin. Righteousness is *active. Righteousness is right doing.* Therefore when good works need to be done, if we depend upon anything other than the Word to create that righteous action, it "is sin."

The Lord in heaven declares, "When I shall say to the righteous, that he shall surely live; *if he trust to his own righteousness*, and commit iniquity, all his *righteousnesses* shall not be remembered; but for his iniquity that he hath committed, he shall die for it" (Eze. 33:13). To put this simply, if man trusts to his own right-doing, "he shall die for it," and "all his righteousnesses," right-doings, "shall not be remembered."

Self-righteousnesses are sin. *Do not forget this!* The line is so fine between the righteousness of God by dependence upon the Word, and the righteousness of self by dependence upon self. This is where Satan has thousands upon thousands of honest souls blinded. They do not see their true condition as miserable self-righteous sinners, and therefore, they do not seek for that righteousness which will give them an entrance into the kingdom of God—"the righteousness which is of God *by faith.*"

But many will quote the following: "Work out *your own salvation* with fear and trembling" (Phil. 2:12); "Strive to enter in at the strait gate" (Luke 13:24); "Fight the good fight . . . lay hold on eternal life" (1 Tim. 6:12); "Resist the devil" (James 4:7); "The kingdom of heaven suffereth violence, and the violent take it by force" (Matt. 11:12); "As thy days, so shall thy strength be" (Deut. 33:25); and "The secret of success is the union of divine power *with human effort.*"[43] This is all perfectly true. But the question is, where are our efforts to be directed?

Saved by Works. . . Christ's Works!

Are our efforts to be made in working, or believing?

The people in Christ's time asked Him saying, "What shall we do, that we might work the works of God?" (John 6:28). They wanted to know where their efforts were to be directed so that they might work God's works. "Their question meant, What shall we do that we may deserve heaven? What is the price we are required to pay in order to obtain the life to come?"[44] Must they place their efforts toward obeying the rabbinical requirements, toward keeping the Ten Commandments, toward doing good deeds or toward loving each other? Or perhaps it was their duty to be baptized as John, who had called them to repentance, had directed. Jesus plainly answers their question and points out where their efforts are to be focused. "This is the work of God," He says, *"that ye believe* on Him whom He hath sent." This is where man's efforts are to be directed, in believing. "The price of heaven is Jesus. The way to heaven is *through faith* in 'the Lamb of God, which taketh away the sin of the world.' John 1:29."[45]

"When the question was asked Christ, 'What shall we do, that we might work the works of God?' He answered, 'This is the work of God, that ye believe on Him whom He hath sent.' John 6:28, 29. Repentance is turning from self to Christ; and when we receive Christ so that *through faith He can live His life in us*, good works will be manifest."[46] Jesus did not say that faith in Him is the preliminary work necessary to be saved, nor did He say that it is part of the work. He said, "This *is* the work." Nothing more than simple, saving faith in Christ is required of man for his salvation. Jesus paid it *all*. It is through Christ's works alone that we are brought into the favor of God.

The effort that we are to make is clearly the effort of choosing to believe the promise that Christ will dwell in our hearts and live through us. It is the effort to accept Him into the heart by believing in His promises. These are the only objects to which God requires us to

Chapter 4 — "Ye shall be free indeed"

direct our efforts. Never are your efforts to be placed in working, for you are not the one qualified to do the good works, nor could you do them if you wanted to. The works will be done, oh yes! But God will be doing them, not you. It is Christ living out His life within you and doing His works through you. We are only to say with Paul "I live; yet not I, *but Christ* liveth in me: and the life which I now live in the flesh I live by the faith of the Son of God" (Gal. 2:20).

Like the Jews of old, many Christians insist that they must do something other than believe in order to obtain their salvation. But Jesus clearly says, "Here it is! Just take it! It's yours! I've paid the price in full!" Why do we insist upon doing more than the Lord directs? Is it because we want some recognition from men for living a blameless life? Is it because upon arriving in heaven we want to be able to say, "*I* did it!"? "Shall the axe boast itself against him that heweth therewith? or shall the saw magnify itself against him that shaketh it?" (Isa. 10:15). "Behold," saith the Lord, "as the clay is in the potter's hand, so are ye in mine hand" (Jer. 18:6). "By grace are ye saved through faith; and that not of yourselves: it is the gift of God: Not of works, lest any man should boast" (Eph. 2:8, 9). "We cannot earn salvation, but we are to seek for it with as much interest and perseverance as though we would abandon everything in the world for it."[47]

There are far too many Christians who "have a zeal of God, but not according to knowledge. For they being ignorant of God's righteousness, and going about to establish *their own righteousness*, have *not submitted themselves unto the righteousness of God*" (Rom. 10:2, 3).

"Woe unto you, scribes and Pharisees, hypocrites! for ye are like unto whited sepulchres, which indeed appear beautiful outward, but are within full of dead men's bones, and of all uncleanness. Even so ye also outwardly appear righteous unto men, but within ye are full of

Saved by Works. . . Christ's Works!

hypocrisy and iniquity" (Matt. 23:27, 28). "Now do ye Pharisees make clean the outside of the cup and the platter; but your inward part is full of ravening and wickedness" (Luke 11:39). "Except your righteousness shall exceed the righteousness of the scribes and Pharisees, ye shall in no case enter into the kingdom of heaven" (Matt. 5:20).

"While the law is holy, the Jews could not attain righteousness by their own efforts to keep the law. The disciples of Christ must obtain righteousness of a different character from that of the Pharisees, if they would enter the kingdom of heaven. God offered them, in His Son, the perfect righteousness of the law. If they would open their hearts fully to receive Christ, then the very life of God, His love, would dwell in them, transforming them into His own likeness; and thus through God's free gift they would possess the righteousness which the law requires. But the Pharisees rejected Christ; 'being ignorant of God's righteousness, and going about to establish their own righteousness' (Romans 10:3), they would not submit themselves unto the righteousness of God."[48] "The righteousness of Christ, as a pure, white pearl, has no defect, no stain. No work of man can improve the great and precious gift of God. It is without a flaw."[49]

But alas! The Scripture says, "For not the hearers of the law are just before God, but the doers of the law shall be justified" (Rom. 2:13). Shall we then say that we must work for our salvation, for forgiveness and pardon, and for peace with God? Shall we throw out all hope of the joy that has just been set before us? No! If we had to do good works to be justified, we would be utterly doomed, for we cannot possibly do anything good. Why are the doers of the law justified then? Question: Can they possibly be justified if their hearts have not been cleansed? No, for this is one and the same thing. Now, if the heart is cleansed, is not the heart now good? And if the heart is good, can any evil work come from it? No, but only good can come forth from

Chapter 4 — "Ye shall be free indeed"

it because it is good. Thus, "the doers of the law shall be justified," but they are not justified because they worked for it, but as a result of being justified, they have been enabled to keep the good law, for it is now written on their hearts. "The doers of the law shall be justified." Do men argue that by works we are saved? Okay that's fine. Saved by works—*Christ's works!*

Justification is when the unclean soul is cleansed from the defilement of sin so that a clean thing may be brought out of it (Isa. 64:6; Job 14:4). To be justified by faith is to have the fountain of the heart purified from bitterness so that it may bring forth sweet water (James 3:11, 12). When one is justified, the tree is made good so the fruit may be good also. Justification is a change of heart, from evil to good, so that good works and *only* good works may be manifested in the life (Matt. 7:18; 12:33; Luke 6:45). It is all in the same promise. "Then will I sprinkle clean water upon you, and ye shall be clean: from all your filthiness, and from all your idols, will I cleanse you. A new heart also will I give you, and a new spirit will I put within you: and I will take away the stony heart out of your flesh, and I will give you an heart of flesh. And I will put my spirit within you, and cause you to walk in my statutes, and ye shall keep my judgments, and do them" (Eze. 36:25-27).

This is why justification by faith is the single most important truth ever taught. It shows that it is not merely just a forgiveness of sins in the past but that it is a transformation of heart so that the law may be kept at present and the fruits of righteousness may shine forth in the life. "God's forgiveness is not merely a judicial act by which He sets us free from condemnation. It is not only forgiveness for sin, but reclaiming from sin. It is the outflow of redeeming love that *transforms the heart*."[50]

"Christ is become of no effect unto you, whosoever of you are justified by the law; ye are fallen from grace" (Gal. 5:4). "Was not Abraham our father *justified by works*, when he had offered Isaac his son upon the altar? Seest thou how faith wrought with his works, and by works was faith made perfect? And the scripture was fulfilled which saith, *Abraham believed God, and it was imputed unto him for righteousness*: and he was called the Friend of God. Ye see then how that by works a man is justified, and not by faith only" (James 2:21-24). Because Abraham believed, he was justified, and Christ worked out His own law in Abraham's heart.

"Therefore *by the deeds of the law there shall no flesh be justified* in his sight: for by the law is the knowledge of sin. *But now the righteousness of God without the law is manifested*, being witnessed by the law and the prophets; Even the righteousness of God *which is by faith of Jesus Christ unto all and upon all them that believe*: for there is no difference: For all have sinned, and come short of the glory of God" (Rom. 3:20-23).

"What is justification by faith?—It is the work of God in laying the glory of man in the dust, and doing for man that which *it is not in his power to do for himself.* When men see their own nothingness, they are prepared to be clothed with the righteousness of Christ. When they begin to praise and exalt God all the day long, then by beholding they are becoming changed into the same image."[51]

You will never bring Christ into your heart by doing works that are acceptable to Him, because unless He is in the heart, you cannot do works that are acceptable to Him. You must choose to believe God's promise, "I [will] sprinkle clean water upon you, and ye shall be clean: from all your filthiness, and from all your idols, will I cleanse you. A new heart also will I give you, and a new spirit will I put within you: and I will take away the stony heart out of your flesh, and I will give you an heart of flesh. And I will put my spirit within you, and cause

Chapter 4 — "Ye shall be free indeed"

you to walk in my statutes, and ye shall keep my judgments, and do them" (Eze. 36:25-27). "I will dwell in them" (2 Cor. 6:16). Receive this promise by faith. This is *all* that you can ever do to be saved. This is the *only* requirement. A cleansing from sin, a removal of our evil hearts, and a new heart with Christ in it—it is *all* yours by faith. God promises to do all of these things for you. He says, "I will take away the stony heart out of your flesh." You cannot take out your stony heart; God takes it out by the power of His word with your mere consent. Receive the promise by faith. "A new heart also will I give you." There is nothing you can do to obtain this new heart from God. He creates it by the power of His word. He gives it to you; it is perfectly free. "I will dwell in you." All you must do is receive these most precious promises by faith and faith only. Then the self-fulfilling word of promise will itself create the fulfillment of the promise. "As surely as the oak is in the acorn, so surely is the gift of God in His promise. If we receive the promise, we have the gift."[52]

"Some who come to God by repentance and confession, and even believe that their sins are forgiven, still fail of claiming, as they should, the promises of God. They do not see that Jesus is an ever-present Saviour; and they are not ready to commit the keeping of their souls to him, relying upon him to perfect the work of grace begun in their hearts. While they think they are committing themselves to God, there is a great deal of self-dependence. There are conscientious souls that trust partly to God, and *partly to themselves*. They do not look to God, to be kept by His power, but depend upon watchfulness against temptation and the performance of certain duties for acceptance with him. *There are no victories in this kind of faith.* Such persons toil to no purpose; their souls are in continual bondage, and they find no rest until their burdens are laid at the feet of Jesus. There is need of constant watchfulness, and of earnest, loving devotion; but *these will*

Saved by Works... Christ's Works!

come naturally when the soul is kept by the power of God through faith."[53] "Clothed with the righteousness of Christ and not your own righteousness, you will not depend upon what you can do or what you will do."[54]

"By grace are ye saved through faith; and that not of yourselves: it is the gift of God" (Eph. 2:8). "Therefore being justified by faith, we have peace with God through our Lord Jesus Christ" (Rom. 5:1). "This is the will of God, even your sanctification" (1 Thess. 4:3). When we speak of justification, we speak of God's forgiveness for our past sins. When we speak of sanctification, we speak of the expelling of sin from the life at present, which includes the doing of good works, for "to him that knoweth to do good, and doeth it not, to him it is sin" (James 4:17). If "the only defense against evil is the indwelling of Christ in the heart through faith in His righteousness,"[55] then are we not sanctified the same way we are justified, by faith? Yes we are! Jesus made it very clear when speaking to Paul that men are "sanctified by faith" that is exercised in Him (Acts 26:18). And not just by faith, but by faith *only*! Jesus Christ "is made unto us wisdom, and righteousness, and sanctification, and redemption" (1 Cor. 1:30). If we then accept Christ into our hearts by faith, He is our sanctification.

"The followers of Christ are to become like Him—by the grace of God to form characters in harmony with the principles of His holy law. This is Bible sanctification. This work can be accomplished *only through faith in Christ*, by the power of the indwelling Spirit of God."[56]

Many Christians will say that men are to be active in the work of sanctification, while others say that it is a completely passive thing. But the fact of the matter is that it is both active and passive. We are to be active in choosing to believe that God submits our wills unto Himself, that He pardons us, and that Christ dwells in us. But we are to be passive in resisting sin and in doing good because Christ, and only

Chapter 4 — "Ye shall be free indeed"

Christ, does the works. "Behold, says the Lord, "as the clay is in the potter's hand, so are ye in mine hand" (Jer. 18:6).

All we must do is choose to believe. While in a technical sense it can be said that we do the works, in reality it is God that does the works, "for it is God which worketh in you . . . to do of his good pleasure" (Phil. 2:13). It is "not by works of righteousness which we have done, but according to his mercy he saved us" (Titus 3:5). "For he hath made him to be sin for us, who knew no sin; that we might be *made the righteousness of God in him*" (2 Cor. 5:21). So then we are sanctified, not because we have control of God's power but because God's power has control of us.

If man is the one who uses God's power in the process of sanctification, it would be man who would get the glory instead of God. Let us say that a man has a welding project. The man uses the power of the welder, a power which he himself can never possess, and through this power he completes his project with beauty and precision. But who would get the glory for the completion of the project? Would it not be the man? Was it not the man with the talented hand that used the lifeless welder to bring about the finished project? Would we give the glory to the inanimate machine that is perfectly useless of itself and must be controlled by the wisdom, skill, and power of the man? But shall the man be glorified more than God?

There is a class of people who say, "We are to have a faith that works," and they understand this to mean that because *they* "really believe," *they* work. They will quote, "For in Jesus Christ neither circumcision availeth any thing, nor uncircumcision; but faith which worketh by love" (Gal. 5:6). But true faith, in itself, cannot work. Faith meets the condition of God's promise so that He can work. It seems far more reasonable to say that faith works, or, faith is enabled, because of love. Or, stating the same thing backwards, love works faith in us, or love

Saved by Works... Christ's Works!

brings about faith in us. When we behold the love of Christ for us, it inspires us with faith, it inspires us to make a choice for Him. Faith works, or shall we say, faith is exercised in Jesus because we see His love for us. The love of Christ is the motive, the thing that is active or working is the faith, and it is faith that is exercised in Jesus because of His love for us. This is that "faith which worketh by love."

"Many have an idea that they must do some part of the work alone. They have trusted in Christ for the forgiveness of sin, but now they seek by their own efforts to live aright. But every such effort must fail. Jesus says, 'Without Me ye can do nothing.' Our growth in grace, our joy, our usefulness,—all depend upon our union with Christ. It is by communion with Him, daily, hourly,—by abiding in Him,—that we are to grow in grace. He is not only the Author, but the Finisher of our faith. It is Christ first and last and always. He is to be with us, not only at the beginning and the end of our course, but at every step of the way. David says, 'I have set the Lord always before me: because He is at my right hand, I shall not be moved.' Psalm 16:8." [57]

While it is not true that faith *does* works, it is true that faith *works*. Faith works in the sense that faith is *successful* in accepting God's works. But faith doesn't *do* the works. We are not to say, "I choose to believe, and therefore I will do good works." We are to say, "I choose to believe that God will do the works for me."

Do men ask, "What shall we do, that we might work the works of God?" (John 6:28). Let them hear carefully the Lord's answer: "This is the work of God, *that ye believe* on him whom he hath sent" (verse 29). Do you ask, "What must I do to be saved?" (Acts 16:30). Hear carefully the apostle's answer, "*Believe* on the Lord Jesus Christ, and thou shalt be saved" (verse 31). Do you ask, "What shall I do to inherit eternal life?" (Luke 10:25). Jesus, pointing to the law, says, "This do, and thou shalt live" (verse 28). But it is impossible for you to keep

Chapter 4 — "Ye shall be free indeed"

the law with a corrupt heart. Therefore Christ seeks to show you your need of a pure heart by pointing you to the law you cannot possibly keep, so you might pray, "Create in me a clean heart, O God; and renew a right spirit within me" (Ps. 51:10). Not fashion, not put together as man does, but create, by the power of Thy creative word, a new heart within me. "Wherefore the law was our schoolmaster to bring us unto Christ, that we might be justified by faith" (Gal. 3:24).

But Jesus is not completely finished answering the question, "What shall I do to inherit eternal life?" He continues with the parable of the good Samaritan.

"This Samaritan represents Christ."[58] "For there is none other name under heaven given among men, whereby we must be saved" (Acts 4:12). The thief represents the devil, for he came not "but for to steal, and to kill, and to destroy" (John 10:10)—"he was a murderer from the beginning" (John 8:44). The wounds we have received are the wounds of sin (Isa. 53:5), and "the wages of sin is death" (Rom. 6:23). "The oil is a symbol of the Holy Spirit,"[59] which God puts within us, enabling us to be partakers of the "sanctification of the Spirit" (2 Thess. 2:13; see also Zech. 4:1-6; Eze. 36:27; 1 Cor. 6:11). The wine represents the blood of Christ by which we are justified and washed from our sins (Matt. 26:28, 29; Rom. 5:9; Rev. 5:1). The raiment that was stolen from us was "the righteousness of saints" (Rev. 19:8), but through faith we can say with Isaiah, "I will greatly rejoice in the LORD, my soul shall be joyful in my God; for he hath clothed me with the garments of salvation, he hath covered me with the robe of righteousness, as a bridegroom decketh himself with ornaments, and as a bride adorneth herself with her jewels" (Isa. 61:10). The wounded man left as "half dead" represents us. And what did that man do to be saved? Did he work? Or did he submit to another's works? Did he put forth effort to be saved, or did he trust in the one who could save him?

Saved by Works... Christ's Works!

Was it by works he had done or was it according to the Samaritan's mercy that he was saved?

"It is impossible for us, of ourselves, to escape from the pit of sin in which we are sunken. Our hearts are evil, and we cannot change them. 'Who can bring a clean thing out of an unclean? not one.' 'The carnal mind is enmity against God: for it is not subject to the law of God, neither indeed can be.' Job 14:4; Romans 8:7. Education, culture, *the exercise of the will, human effort*, all have their proper sphere, *but here they are powerless*. They may produce an outward correctness of behavior, but they cannot change the heart; they cannot purify the springs of life. There must be a power *working from within*, a new life from above, before men can be changed from sin to holiness. *That power is Christ.* His grace alone can quicken the lifeless faculties of the soul, and attract it to God, to holiness."[60] "So then it is not of him that willeth, nor of him that runneth, but of God that sheweth mercy" (Rom. 9:16). Man is not to work; man is to *believe that Christ works!*

"The just shall live by faith" (Heb. 10:38). But who are the just? Simply, it must be those whom God makes just because they believe His promise of justification and depend upon that word of promise to justify them. And how are they to continue living as just? Very simply, "the just shall live *by faith*." Not by efforts of works but by efforts of faith is he to continue to live in a just condition. "This is the victory that overcometh the world, [not works, not efforts of righteousness, but] even our faith" (1 John 5:4).

"We do not earn salvation by our obedience; for salvation is the free gift of God, to be received *by faith*. But obedience is the fruit of faith. 'Ye know that He was manifested to take away our sins; and in Him is no sin. Whosoever abideth in Him sinneth not: whosoever sinneth hath not seen Him, neither known Him.' 1 John 3:5, 6. Here is the true test. If we abide in Christ, if the love of God dwells in us, our

Chapter 4 — "Ye shall be free indeed"

feelings, our thoughts, our purposes, our actions, will be in harmony with the will of God as expressed in the precepts of His holy law. 'Little children, let no man deceive you: he that doeth righteousness is righteous, even as He is righteous.' 1 John 3:7."[61]

"The proud heart strives to earn salvation; but both our title to heaven and our fitness for it are found in the righteousness of Christ."[62] "The righteousness by which we are justified is imputed; the righteousness by which we are sanctified is imparted. The first is our *title* to heaven, the second is our *fitness* for heaven."[63]

For God to impute righteousness to us is for Him to say, "I forgive you. Thou art righteous." And because He says it *and we believe it* (Rom. 5:1), it becomes a fact, and we are therefore justified, or made just before God. At the very moment we believe, Jesus says to us, "Now ye are clean *through the word which I have spoken unto you*" (John 15:3).

For God to impart righteousness to us is for Him to say, "My Son is living in your heart. The righteous works that He does through you are yours." And because He says it *and we believe it* (1 John 3:9; Eph. 3:17), it becomes a fact. In short, both justification and sanctification are given to us by our believing God when He says, "You are righteous, and My Son's righteousness is yours."

If a man is given a title to a car, it instantly becomes his car; he owns it. But if the man isn't fit to drive the car because he hasn't yet proved himself worthy of a driver's license, the car does him absolutely no good and he can't use it. So it is with heaven and eternal life. When we believe that God forgives our sins, we are justified, made righteous, and our title to heaven is sure. Jesus says that those who are righteous go "into life eternal" (Matt. 25:46). But while God has given to us our title to heaven by justifying us, before He allows us an entrance there, He first desires to see if we will be able to rightly use

Saved by Works... Christ's Works!

His gracious gift—He wants to see if we are fit for heaven.

If man will not live a justified life on earth for a few mere years, how could God expect him to live a sinless life in heaven throughout eternity? If we were allowed to enter into eternal life without having shown that we will keep God's law, through exercising faith and utter trust in the truthfulness of His Word, we would destroy heaven's peace just as a man who doesn't know how to drive a car would soon wreck, not only the car, but whatever got in his way as well. Upon entering paradise, because we never learned to exercise faith and trust in God wholly and implicitly while upon the earth, we would question the truthfulness of God while in heaven, and rebellion would arise once again. But the Word declares that "affliction *shall not* rise up the second time" (Nahum 1:9). Many people accept their title to heaven, but they never receive their driver's license; they are not fit for heaven. The heavenly driver's license, no less than the title to the car, is perfectly free if men will but take it through faith.

"The first thing to be learned by all who would become workers together with God is the lesson of self-distrust; then they are prepared to have *imparted* to them the character of Christ."[64] When you live as God would have you, you will understand that it is impossible for you to do good and that whatever good comes "from" you is not really coming from you, "for it is *God which worketh* in you both to will and to do of his good pleasure" (Phil. 2:13). It is not you that works with God's power to do good and resist evil; it is God which works with His own power while He dwells in your heart. He is the One who does the works; you merely consent for Him to do it. Christ does the works for us; He does the works in place of us; He does the works instead of us; and He does the works in and through us. Could this not be why Paul says, "If, when we were enemies, we were reconciled to God by the death of His Son, much more, being reconciled, we shall be saved by

Chapter 4 — "Ye shall be free indeed"

his life" (Rom. 5:10)?

"Only by overcoming as Christ overcame shall we win the crown of life."[65] But how did Jesus overcome? He said Himself, "I can of mine own self do nothing" (John 5:30). "The Father that dwelleth in me, he doeth the works" (John 14:10). Where then was Christ's works? Did Christ boast of Himself in what He had done? No! Jesus said, "I honour my Father . . . And I seek not mine own glory" (John 8:49, 50). "He that speaketh of himself seeketh his own glory: but he that seeketh his glory that sent him, the same is true, and no unrighteousness is in him" (John 7:18).

"It was possible for Adam, before the fall, to form a righteous character by obedience to God's law. But he failed to do this, and because of his sin our natures are fallen and we cannot make ourselves righteous. Since we are sinful, unholy, we cannot perfectly obey the holy law. We have no righteousness of our own with which to meet the claims of the law of God. But Christ has made a way of escape for us."[66] By believing in God's "exceeding great and precious promises," we become "partakers of the divine nature" (2 Peter 1:4). "He lived on earth amid trials and temptations such as we have to meet. He lived a sinless life. He died for us, and now He offers to take our sins and *give* us His righteousness. If you give yourself to Him, and accept Him as your Saviour, then, sinful as your life may have been, for His sake you are accounted righteous. Christ's character stands in place of your character, and you are accepted before God just as if you had not sinned.

"More than this, Christ changes the heart. He abides in your heart *by faith*. You are to maintain this connection with Christ *by faith* and the continual surrender of your will to Him; and so long as you do this, *He will work* in you to will and to do according to His good pleasure. So you may say, 'The life which I now live in the flesh I live by the

Saved by Works... Christ's Works!

faith of the Son of God, who loved me, and gave Himself for me.' Galatians 2:20. So Jesus said to His disciples, 'It is not ye that speak, but the Spirit of your Father which speaketh in you.' Matthew 10:20. Then with *Christ working* in you, you will manifest the same spirit and do the same good works—works of righteousness, obedience.

"So we have nothing in ourselves of which to boast. We have no ground for self-exaltation. Our only ground of hope is in the righteousness of Christ *imputed* to us, and in that wrought by *His Spirit working in and through* us."[67]

"Where is boasting then? It is excluded. By what law? of works? Nay: but by the law of faith" (Rom. 3:27). If men reach the standard of righteousness by faith and faith only, then God gets all the glory for the good works. Not more, not most, not nearly all, but He gets *all* the glory. Why would Christians have a problem with this? Is it because they want some of the glory for themselves? The example of Jesus condemns such. "I honour my Father," He says, "And I seek not mine own glory" (John 8:49, 50). Lucifer fell from heaven through seeking his own glory (Isa. 14:13, 14), and God knew from the beginning that men "could be saved through Christ only as *by faith* they should make His life their own."[68]

"Abide in me, and I in you. As the branch cannot bear fruit of itself, except it abide in the vine; no more can ye, except ye abide in me. I am the vine, ye are the branches: He that abideth in me, and I in him, the same bringeth forth much fruit: for without me ye can do nothing" (John 15:4, 5).

"The *only* defense against evil is the indwelling of Christ in the heart through faith in His righteousness. Unless we become *vitally* connected with God, we can never resist the unhallowed effects of self-love, self-indulgence, and temptation to sin. We may leave off many bad habits, for the time we may part company with Satan; but

Chapter 4 — "Ye shall be free indeed"

without a *vital* connection with God, through the surrender of ourselves to Him moment by moment, we shall be overcome. Without a personal acquaintance with Christ, and a continual communion, we are at the mercy of the enemy, and shall do his bidding in the end."[69]

Paul gives the counsel, "Examine yourselves, whether ye be in the faith; prove your own selves. Know ye not your own selves, how that Jesus Christ is in you, except ye be reprobates?" (2 Cor. 13:5). According to the original Greek definition, to be a reprobate means to be an unapproved, rejected castaway. To be rejected by God is a terrible thought! "Do not forget to examine yourselves whether you are in the faith. Prove your own selves, for unless Christ is in you, you are reprobates."[70]

"Do you ask, 'How am I to abide in Christ?' In the same way as you received Him at first. 'As ye have therefore received Christ Jesus the Lord, so walk ye in Him.' 'The just shall live by faith.' Colossians 2:6; Hebrews 10:38. You gave yourself to God, to be His wholly, to serve and obey Him, and you took Christ as your Saviour. You could not yourself atone for your sins or change your heart; but having given yourself to God, you believe that He for Christ's sake did all this for you. By *faith* you became Christ's, and by faith you are to grow up in Him—by giving and taking. You are to *give* all,—your heart, your will, your service,—give yourself to Him to obey all His requirements; and you must *take* all,—Christ, the fullness of all blessing, to abide in your heart, to be your strength, your righteousness, your everlasting helper,—to give you power to obey."[71]

The doing of good works will save no one. Why not? Because works are the fruit, not the root, of man's salvation. Good works are the outward evidence that one is saved, not the fact that helps to save him. The penitent thief on the cross next to Jesus did not really have much of a chance to do works toward his salvation, for he was dying,

Saved by Works... Christ's Works!

and yet Jesus said to him, "Today shalt thou be with me in paradise" (Luke 23:43). If there is any man who claims salvation and does not the works of those who are saved, then he is either deceived as to what constitutes the law or he is a liar, for "ye shall know them by their fruits" (Matt. 7:16). "For every tree is known by his own fruit. For of thorns men do not gather figs, nor of a bramble bush gather they grapes" (Luke 6:44). "Every good tree bringeth forth good fruit; but a corrupt tree bringeth forth evil fruit" (Matt. 7:17).

Many people will oppose this message of righteousness by faith and only faith. They ask the question, "What doth it profit, my brethren, though a man say he hath faith, and have not works? can faith save him?" (James 2:14). No! Faith cannot save anyone, but faith enables God to save all who will believe, because then, "being justified by faith" (Rom. 5:1), they will have Christ working in them to do His good pleasure, and they will then be sanctified by faith. But, they cry, "faith, if it hath not works, is dead, being alone" (James 2:17). But it has never here been proposed that we have faith without works. But it has been proposed that we have a faith that allows God to work; therefore, the works of righteousness will be manifest in the life, but it will not be us that do them. "True faith, which relies *wholly* upon Christ, will be manifested by obedience to all the requirements of God."[72]

"Yea, a man may say, Thou hast faith, and I have works: shew me thy faith without thy works, and I will shew thee my faith by my works" (James 2:18). When the works of God are manifested in the life, it testifies to the fact that saving faith is in the life. If any man claims to have faith but the works of God are not manifested through him, it is because he does not accept Christ into his heart by faith so that God can work through him. This is why "faith without works is dead" (verse 20). If there are no good works, it is because there is no faith exercised to claim them. The faith is dead because it does not

Chapter 4 — "Ye shall be free indeed"

bear fruit in revealing Christ's works, "for as the body without the spirit is dead, so faith without works is dead also" (verse 26).

Just as a dead man can accomplish nothing, even so, a faith that does not allow God to work in and through us accomplishes nothing. For instance, "Thou believest that there is one God; thou doest well: the devils also believe, and tremble" (verse 19). Believing that there is one God will save no one. Such a faith is, therefore, dead. But believing that God submits you unto Himself, forgives your sins, cleanses your heart and dwells in it, and, therefore, makes it impossible for sin to be manifested in your life as long as you continue to believe the promise, such a faith as this allows God to save you. This faith is a living faith, a saving faith.

There are three different things we can exercise faith in.

1. Facts that God declares as truth. Example: "Through faith we understand that the worlds were framed by the word of God, so that things which are seen were not made of things which do appear" (Heb. 11:3).
2. Facts that God declares will be truth. Example: "Behold, I come quickly" (Rev. 3:11).
3. Promises that become true the instant we believe them. Example: "Believe on the Lord Jesus Christ, and thou shalt be saved" (Acts 16:31).

When it comes to exercising faith, it helps to understand what kind of faith you are exercising. The third example of exercising faith is the most important because it results in calling forth the creative power of God's word on your behalf. This is that type of saving faith that depends upon the Word to do what it says. The reason why James says that faith without works is dead is because he is referring to the first example of exercising faith. Merely exercising the first two types of faith will not produce even a single good work. Therefore, the type

Saved by Works... Christ's Works!

of faith that brings forth no good works "is dead."

"If we say that *we* have no sin, we deceive ourselves, and the truth is not in us" (1 John 1:8). It is not here proposed that through living this life of faith we should say concerning ourselves, "*I* am sinless." "God does not look with favor upon those self-confident ones who loudly exclaim, '*I* am sanctified, *I* am holy, *I* am sinless.' These are Pharisees who have no foundation for their assertion. Those who, because of their sense of utter unworthiness, dare scarcely lift up their eyes to heaven, are nearer to God than those who claim so much piety. They are represented by the publican, who, with his head on his breast, prayed, 'God be merciful to me a sinner,' and went to his house justified, rather than the self-righteous Pharisee."[73]

But while we cannot, without being presumptuous, declare ourselves as sinless, we can safely declare that Christ is sinless, and Paul says, "*Put ye on the Lord Jesus Christ*, and make not provision for the flesh, to fulfil the lusts thereof" (Rom. 13:14). If we put on *Christ*, accepting *Him* into the heart, and consent for *Him* to do the works, how can we say, "*I* am sanctified, *I* am holy, *I* am sinless"? We cannot! But the man who truly believes can say, "I live; yet not I, but *Christ* liveth in me" (Gal. 2:20). All our righteousnesses are as filthy rags; therefore, the good I do, I do not, but *Christ* who dwelleth in me. *He* doeth the works. *He* is my sanctification; *He* is my righteousness; and *He* only is holy. If any evil work come from me, it cometh not from Christ, but from me, because He is not in me (Gal. 2:20; Isa. 64:6; John 14:10; 1 Cor. 1:30; Jer. 23:6; Rev. 15:4.)

We are never to say, "*I* cannot sin," because it is impossible for *us* to do anything but sin. *God* is the One who cannot sin, and the reason that the man born of God cannot sin is because God who cannot sin is living His life through him. Self is dead and, therefore, does no works. But God is alive and, therefore, does all the works. "Let the record-

Chapter 4 — "Ye shall be free indeed"

ing angels write the history of the holy struggles and conflicts of the people of God; let them record their prayers and tears; but let not God be dishonored by the declaration from human lips, '*I* am sinless; *I* am holy.' Sanctified lips will never give utterance to such presumptuous words."[74]

"'My little children, these things write I unto you, that ye sin not. And if any man sin, we have an Advocate with the Father, Jesus Christ the righteous.' Even those who are striving in sincerity to keep the law of God, are not always free from sin. Through some deceptive temptation, they are deceived, and fall into error. But when their sin comes home to their conscience, they see themselves condemned in the light of the holy precepts of God's law; but they do not war against the law which condemns them; they repent of their sin, and seek pardon through the merit of Christ, who died for their sins in order that they might be justified by faith in his blood. They do not avoid confession and repentance when the neglected law of God is brought to their attention, by exclaiming, as do the self-righteous pretenders to holiness, 'I am sanctified, I am holy, and I can not sin.' This is the class whom the apostle rebukes; for he says, 'If we say that we have no sin, we deceive ourselves, and the truth is not in us.' It is evident that where a claim to sinlessness is made, there the law of God has not been written in the heart; for the commandments of God are exceeding broad, and are discerners of the thoughts and intents of the heart. The apostle speaks words of encouragement to those who realize that they are sinners, and says, 'If we confess our sins, he is faithful and just to forgive us our sins, and to cleanse us from all unrighteousness.' 'If we say we have no sin,' when our thoughts, words, and actions, reflected from the law of God, the great moral mirror, reveal us as transgressors, we make God a liar, and prove that his word is not in us."[75]

"Many see much to admire in the life of Christ. But true love for

Saved by Works... Christ's Works!

Him can never dwell in the heart of the self-righteous. Not to see our own deformity is not to see the beauty of Christ's character. When we are fully awake to our own sinfulness, we shall appreciate Christ. The more humble are our views of ourselves, the more clearly we shall see the spotless character of Jesus. He who says, 'I am holy, I am sinless,' is self-deceived. Some have said this, and some even dare to say, 'I am Christ.' To entertain such a thought is blasphemy. Not to see the marked contrast between Christ and ourselves is not to know ourselves. He who does not abhor himself can not understand the meaning of redemption. To be redeemed means to cease from sin. No heart that is stirred to rebellion against the law of God has any union with Christ, who died to vindicate the law and exalt it before all nations, tongues, and peoples. Pharisaic self-complacency and bold assumptions of holiness are abundant. There are many who do not see themselves in the light of the law of God. They do not loathe selfishness; therefore they are selfish. Their souls are spotted and defiled. Yet with sin-stained lips they say, 'I am holy. Jesus teaches me that the law of God is a yoke of bondage. Those who say that we must keep the law have fallen from grace.'"[76] "That so-called faith in Christ which professes to release men from the obligation of obedience to God, is not faith, but presumption."[77]

In the history of the children of Israel, we find that after they had just come up out of Egypt God sought to make a covenant (an agreement or contract) with them that they might be to Him a peculiar treasure. "Now therefore, if ye will obey my voice indeed, and keep my covenant, then ye shall be a peculiar treasure unto me above all people: for all the earth is mine" (Ex. 19:5). In response to God's offer, all the children of Israel answered, "All that the LORD hath spoken we will do" (Ex. 19:8). It is interesting to notice that the terms of the agreement, "if ye will obey my voice indeed, and keep my covenant,"

Chapter 4 — "Ye shall be free indeed"

were not yet fully known to the Israelites at the moment of their compliance. The part of the covenant that they were to "keep" was not yet given to them. Moses, in reminding the Israelites of the time when God gave them His law, said, "And he declared unto you his covenant, which he commanded you to perform, even ten commandments; and he wrote them upon two tables of stone" (Deut. 4:13). The part of the covenant that God enjoined Israel to keep was His law—the Ten Commandments (Ex. 20:3-17)—and after hearing it and the judgments that He gave, the Israelites again declared, "All the words which the LORD hath said will we do" (Ex. 24:3). And again, "All that the LORD hath said will we do, and be obedient" (verse 7). God's part to perform in the covenant was to make them His special treasure, on the condition that they kept His law.

In agreeing to keep God's law, the children of Israel had failed to understand that "the heart is deceitful above all things, and desperately wicked" (Jer. 17:9). They failed to realize that great truth which was so many centuries later spoken by Christ, "without me ye can do nothing" (John 15:5). The Israelites felt that they could keep the law of God. But in doing so they were attempting to gather grapes off of a bramble bush, and they were to miserably fail. "Who can bring a clean thing out of an unclean? not one" (Job 14:4). So confidently did they declare that they would keep God's law, but not even six weeks passed before they were already engaged in apostasy. The terms of God's covenant, the law of the Ten Commandments, declared, "Thou shalt have no other gods before me. Thou shalt not make unto thee any graven image, or any likeness of any thing that is in heaven above, or that is in the earth beneath, or that is in the water under the earth: Thou shalt not bow down thyself to them, nor serve them" (Ex. 20:3-5). But they broke this law when they made a molten calf and worshiped it (Ex. 32:7, 8.)

Saved by Works... Christ's Works!

The apostle Paul speaks of the covenant that God then made with Israel as having a fault. "But now hath he," Jesus Christ (see Heb. 3:1; 4:14; 6:20; 8:1), "obtained a more excellent ministry, by how much also he is the mediator of a better covenant, which was established upon better promises. For if that first covenant had been faultless, then should no place have been sought for the second. For finding fault with them, he saith, Behold, the days come, saith the Lord, when I will make a new covenant with the house of Israel and with the house of Judah: Not according to the covenant that I made with their fathers in the day when I took them by the hand to lead them out of the land of Egypt; because they continued not in my covenant, and I regarded them not, saith the Lord. For this is the covenant that I will make with the house of Israel after those days, saith the Lord; I will put my laws into their mind, and write them in their hearts: and I will be to them a God, and they shall be to me a people: And they shall not teach every man his neighbour, and every man his brother, saying, Know the Lord: for all shall know me, from the least to the greatest. For I will be merciful to their unrighteousness, and their sins and their iniquities will I remember no more" (Heb. 8:6-12).

It is important to note that it was not God's law that had a fault needing correction and change, for "the law of the LORD is perfect, converting the soul" (Ps. 19:7), and "the law is holy, and the commandment holy, and just, and good" (Rom. 7:12); rather, the fault was in the agreement of the Israelites that they would in their own power keep the law. The fact that God's law is perfect, or without fault, serves as evidence that the old covenant is not the Ten Commandments, for Paul says that this covenant had a fault. The law of God never changes. "All his commandments are sure. They stand fast for ever and ever, and are done in truth and uprightness" (Ps. 111:7, 8). God may have done away with the first agreement/contract (covenant) that He made

Chapter 4 — "Ye shall be free indeed"

with the Israelites, but God's law wasn't done away with, nor did it change. In fact, in the new covenant agreement, God perpetuates His law saying, "I will put my law in their inward parts, and write it in their hearts" (Jer. 31:33). "Not in tables of stone" is God's law again written, "but in fleshy tables of the heart" (2 Cor. 3:3). The new covenant says absolutely nothing concerning an abrogation or change in God's moral law, but rather that it will now be found in the hearts of those whom the covenant embraces—those who believe. To further confirm that God's law does not change, we read the words of Jesus: "Till heaven and earth pass, one jot or one tittle shall in no wise pass from the law, till all be fulfilled" (Matt. 5:18). Are heaven and earth still in existence? Upon what planet do you rest your feet? Even so, God's law remains unchanged in even the smallest jot and tittle.

When God spoke to the children of Israel saying "thou shalt not . . .," it was not His intention that they should sigh in sadness because another restriction was placed upon them. He wanted them to understand that He was setting them free from sin through His promises that were made possible through the gift of the coming Messiah.

Just because God says "thou shalt not," it does not mean that He is setting another restriction upon man. For example, God made a promise to His faithful children saying, "When thou passest through the waters, I will be with thee; and through the rivers, they shall not overflow thee: when thou walkest through the fire, *thou shalt not* be burned; neither shall the flame kindle upon thee" (Isa. 43:2). This is a Bible promise and not a command at all. The Ten Commandments are to be literally understood as "The Ten Promises." "Every command is a promise."[78] When we read, "Thou shalt not commit adultery," we are not to read it with the connotation of, "You are not allowed to commit adultery anymore," but we are to read it as a blessed promise that sets us free from sin with the connotation, "You will no longer commit adultery! Isn't that wonderful!?" This is how our loving Savior intended we should look upon His "law of liberty" (James 1:25). If you accept it as true for yourself and apply these promises to your own soul, then "thou shalt not commit adultery," "thou shalt not steal," "thou shalt not bear false witness," etc.

When we read the two great commandments—"Thou shalt love the Lord thy God with all thy heart, and with all thy soul, and with all thy strength, and with all thy mind; and thy neighbour as thyself" (Luke 10:27)—the Lord intends that we read them with the same connotation of joy and happiness, knowing that by only believing these precious promises, they become true to us. The new heart upon which God's law, The Ten Commandments, is to be written is to be received by believing God's law, The Ten Promises, that were written in the tables of stone. This is why the psalmist wrote, "The law of the LORD is perfect, *converting the soul*" (Ps. 19:7). "Every one who *by faith* obeys God's commandments, will reach the condition of sinlessness in which Adam lived before his transgression."[79]

The promise of a change of heart is spoken of in Jeremiah 31:31-34 and Ezekiel 36:25-28. It is essential to notice that in all of these passages of Scripture we read the same two words spoken by God: "I" and "will." This is the key. The children of Israel declared, "All that the LORD hath spoken *we will* do," but they didn't realize that this was an impossibility for them. God, therefore, out of love for them, sought to teach them the lesson that without a change of heart there can be no true keeping of the law, for "the carnal mind is enmity against God: for it is not subject to the law of God, neither indeed can be" (Rom. 8:7). God knows this, and this is why He gives us the blessed assurance, "*I will* put my laws into their mind, and write them in their hearts" (Heb. 8:10). "A new heart also *will I* give you, and a new spirit *will I* put within you: and *I will* take away the stony heart out of your flesh, and

Chapter 4 — "Ye shall be free indeed"

I will give you an heart of flesh. And *I will* put my spirit within you, and cause you to walk in my statutes, and ye shall keep my judgments, and do them" (Eze. 36:26, 27).

God sought to teach Israel of old that their salvation consisted not in the sincerity of their saying, "All the words which the LORD hath said will *we* do," but that it consisted only in their believing, "All the words which the LORD hath said will *he* do." "Now all these things happened unto them for examples: and they are written for our admonition, upon whom the ends of the world are come. Wherefore let him that thinketh *he* standeth take heed lest *he* fall" (1 Cor. 10:11, 12).

Understanding this vital point, we see the whole gospel in one Old Testament Bible verse. "And *the LORD thy God will* circumcise thine heart, and the heart of thy seed, to love the LORD thy God with all thine heart, and with all thy soul, *that thou mayest live*" (Deut. 30:6). "It is God that circumcises the heart. *The whole work is the Lord's* from the beginning to the end."[80]

Many have said over and over again, "You'll never possess a perfect character. Stop wasting your time seeking after something you will never have." But Jesus has made it very plain that such people do not know what they are talking about. He says in unmistakable language, "Blessed are they which do hunger and thirst after righteousness: *for they shall be filled*" (Matt. 5:6). "If any man thirst, let him come unto me, and drink" (John 7:37). "*I will* give unto him that is athirst of the fountain of the water of life freely" (Rev. 21:6).

It has been said, "The warfare against self is the greatest battle that was ever fought."[81] And it is true that, "the Christian life is a battle and a march. But the victory to be gained is not won by human power. The field of conflict is the domain of the heart."[82]

While it is true that the warfare against self is the greatest battle ever fought, it can also be said that it is one of the easiest battles to win

119

Saved by Works... Christ's Works!

because you do not do the fighting. God says, "Ye shall not need to fight in this battle: set yourselves, stand ye still, and see the salvation of the LORD with you" (2 Chron. 20:17). The moment you attempt to fight, you lose, because it is impossible for you to obtain an atom of victory. Why? Because your nature is fallen. "You are not able, of yourself, to bring your purposes and desires and inclinations into submission to the will of God."[83] "No man can empty himself of self. We can only consent for Christ to accomplish the work."[84] "*You* cannot change your heart, *you* cannot of yourself give to God its affections; but you can choose to serve Him. You can give Him your will; *He will* then work in you to will and to do according to His good pleasure."[85] "*You* cannot atone for your past sins; *you* cannot change your heart and make yourself holy. But God promises to do all this for you through Christ. You believe that promise. You confess your sins and give yourself to God. You will to serve Him. Just as surely as you do this, *God will* fulfill His word to you. If you believe the promise,—believe that you are forgiven and cleansed,—*God supplies the fact*; you are made whole ... It is so if you believe it."[86]

God promises to fight the battle against self for us if we will but believe. He says, "*I will* take away the stony heart out of your flesh" (Eze. 36:26). *I will* destroy the power of selfishness in your heart; *I will* give you a new and good heart with My Son in it. Receive then this promise, *by faith*! Receive it by depending upon these very words alone, that *they* will create the thing that they promised. And understand that these words of promise cannot help but do the thing that they said, because they cannot lie even if they tried to, for their creative power would call forth into existence the thing that wasn't.

"Why is it so hard to lead a self-denying, humble life? Because professed Christians are not dead to the world. It is easy living after we are dead."[87]

Chapter 4 — "Ye shall be free indeed"

As soon as, *by faith*, you let God fight for you, the battle is instantly won. The type or strength of the temptation, the strongholds of self, the amount of power the devil summons to destroy you, should not even be considered. If God is fighting, *He will* win by the power of His immutable word. All that you must do is choose to believe that God will fight and win every battle for you. And when not only the battles but the war itself is finally over and you enter paradise, you will have no reason to boast of yourself because you made the choice to let God do everything for you, but you will only be able to say, "'It was God who worked in me both to will [choose] and to do of his good pleasure' (Phil. 2:13). I did not choose Him, but He chose me; and those who are lost, He chose them also, but they did not want to be chosen, and, grieved to the heart, He left them to their choice." (See also John 16:15 and Matthew 22:14.)

Right after the fall of the human race, God said to "that old serpent, called the Devil, and Satan" (Rev. 12:9), "*I will* put enmity between thee and the woman, and between thy seed and her seed" (Gen. 3:15). After sin, man naturally had a carnal mind, which is "enmity against God: for it is not subject to the law of God, neither indeed can be" (Rom. 8:7). Naturally, fallen man hates God, hates God's principles, and hates good, but God said that He would put in man a hatred against Satan's principles and a hatred against evil. So even though man cannot *do* good, because his heart is naturally evil and can therefore do only evil, God puts within him a *desire* for good and to do good.

We have an example of such a man in the Bible. Paul, speaking of himself in the past tense, said, "*I am carnal*, sold under sin. For that which I do I allow not: for what I would, that do I not; but what I hate, that do I. If then I do that which I would not, I consent unto the law that it is good. . . . For I know that in me (that is, in my flesh,) dwelleth

Saved by Works... Christ's Works!

no good thing: for to will is present with me; but how to perform that which is good I find not. For the good that I would I do not: but the evil which I would not, that I do. . . . I find then a law, that, when I would do good, evil is present with me. For I delight in the law of God after the inward man: But I see another law in my members, warring against the law of my mind, and bringing me into captivity to the law of sin which is in my members" (Rom. 7:14-23).

Paul is here saying that he wants to do good, that he desires to do good and not do evil, but that he cannot do it. This is the experience of those who are unconverted. They are not born again. They still have an evil heart. They are corrupt. But thanks be to God that He puts within them something that will reach out after good. When this desire reaches out after good, which it must of itself do naturally, God will fulfill the desire that He Himself implanted, and He does it at no cost.

So we do *nothing* to be saved then. God gives us a desire for something good even though we are evil, but since we can't fulfill this desire and obtain good by submitting to Him, He submits us to Himself. "*I will* take away the stony heart out of your flesh," He says (Eze. 36:26). When the heart is emptied of self, Jesus fills the heart. "*I will* dwell in them," He says (2 Cor. 6:16). And when Christ is in the heart, then it is that *He* that "worketh in you both to will [choose] and to do of his good pleasure" (Phil. 2:13). You do not choose the right; Jesus chooses it through you because you allow Him to by *your choice of faith.* You do not do His good pleasure; He does it for you; He does it through you. Remember, it is not we who have control of God's power, but *it is God's power that has control of us.* As long as you believe, you will find that good choices and works are manifest in your life.

We are bidden by the apostle Paul to "let this mind be in you, which was also in Christ Jesus" (Phil. 2:5). This mind is a converted

Chapter 4 — "Ye shall be free indeed"

mind, a good mind, from which good and only good can come forth. But we are not told to strive to make this mind be in us, but to *let* it be in us. Letting God give you a new mind and trying to make a new mind yourself are two distinctly different things. One requires a never-ending fruitless effort; the other requires only a simple, effortless faith in the creative power of God.

Jesus said, "*I . . . will* draw all men unto me" (John 12:32). "The sinner may resist this love, may refuse to be drawn to Christ; but if he does not resist *he will be drawn to Jesus*."[88] Resisting Christ's drawing love takes great effort. Why? Because He is determined to save you, and He will be on your track as long as an infinite God of measureless love possibly can. He loves you far too much to let you go. If you don't resist His love, you will be saved.

To resist Christ's drawing, in a practical sense, would be to ignore Him when He calls you to the secret place of prayer or to study His Word or to manifest kindness towards a burdened soul. Resisting His love is refusing to listen to His voice—to stifle conviction and seek to follow after selfishness.

These are the two dangers we have that can ruin us: 1) the danger of resisting Christ's drawing love, and 2) the danger of attempting to replace His good works with our own. Any effort we make to do good works is sin, plain, flat, and cold. Self-righteousness is just as much sin as is adultery or open rebellion against God. Man's polluted self-righteousness is in perfect antagonism with the spotless righteousness of Christ. "We are *all* as an unclean thing, and *all our righteousnesses are as filthy rags*" (Isa. 64:6). Attempting to do our own good works and resist temptation takes great effort. Why? Because the carnal heart hates doing these things—it is impossible for it to do them, and it is perfectly miserable to try. But God promises that He will do all this for you if you will but believe. Either of these two efforts will cost you

Saved by Works... Christ's Works!

your salvation.

If we were to draw a graph showing the amount of effort on both man's and God's part in the work of salvation, we should then put God's part as 100 percent and man's part as 0 percent. If we resist Christ's drawing love, then we put man's work in the negative, and therefore, when God gives His 100 percent to save us, some of it must be burnt up in reaching the zero mark and therefore the 100 percent that is necessary for man to be saved cannot be reached. If we attempt to do good works and resist evil, then we put man's part in the positive and block out some of God's part with our righteousnesses—perfect sin. And we know that "all that do wickedly, shall be stubble: and the day that cometh shall burn them up, saith the LORD of hosts" (Mal. 4:1).

Despite all of these things, throughout the Scriptures the lesson is continually repeated, "The secret of success is the union of divine power *with human effort*."[89] So what is our effort to be then? It is very simple. The effort that we are to make is to stop making efforts. Now, making effort to make no effort is the easiest thing you can do. Why? Because making effort to make no effort requires no effort. So then we have the two requirements to be saved: Believe and exist. You believe because God gave you the ability to acknowledge the power of His spoken word. This in itself requires no effort on your part. You exist because God spoke the word. This also requires no effort on your part. Therefore, you fill all the requirements necessary to be saved, and this most precious salvation is a perfectly *free* gift!

It does seem perfectly contradictory to say that when the Bible tells us we must make efforts if we expect to be saved it really means that we are to make no effort at all. To clarify this, it is to be made clear that we are to make no *physical* efforts. The efforts we are to make are the mental efforts to choose whom we will serve and to believe, to

Chapter 4 — "Ye shall be free indeed"

acknowledge the power of Christ's Word in relation to our own soul's salvation. In this part of the work of man's salvation, man must give 100 percent. But even this effort, *in a sense*, is not really ours. If we do not resist temptation and do not resist Christ's drawing love, we will be saved. The power of the love of Christ *will* draw out our souls to acknowledge that He is true, to acknowledge His power to save us. As long as you do not resist, you will, of sheer necessity, acknowledge Him as true in your behalf and you will therefore be saved. You can *only* choose.

To illustrate these things, imagine a conveyor belt that is pulling all the inhabitants of the earth toward heaven and through its gates—"I . . .will draw all men unto me" (John 12:32). If men will sit in place just where they are, they will be saved by the drawing of Christ's love. But if they insist upon keeping their sins and choosing this world over heaven, they will make efforts to affect this by walking away from the direction the conveyor belt is drawing them. Since God forces no man to be saved, He allows them to walk faster than the conveyor belt draws them in. If these continue in this path, God will leave them to their choice and they shall not enter into heaven, but they shall have this world with all its woes.

Now, if men decide they choose heaven over this world and in their zeal to obtain the heavenly treasure try to walk faster on the conveyor belt toward paradise by making their own efforts toward doing good works, they will come to the gates of paradise and run smack into them instead of going through them. Those gates will never allow such people to enter. In their shock and amazement, they will cry to Jesus saying, "Lord, Lord, have we not . . . done many wonderful works?" (Matt. 7:22). "Open unto us" (Luke 13:25). But Jesus will say unto them, "I never knew you: depart from me, ye that work iniquity" (Matt. 7:23).

Saved by Works... Christ's Works!

Their iniquity was found in their self-righteousness, in their efforts at righteousness, and in what *they* could do. The Scriptures declare, "All our righteousnesses are as filthy rags." That is to say that any effort man makes toward righteousness is polluted with sin, *except* for the effort of faith. If men choose heaven over this earth and let Christ do *all* of the saving, He will bring them safely through the gates of paradise.

"The work of the holy Spirit is *immeasurably great*."[90] "Man can accomplish nothing without God, and God has arranged His plans so far as to accomplish nothing in the restoration of the human race without the cooperation of the human with the divine. The part man is required to sustain is *immeasurably small*, yet in the plan of God it is just that part that is needed to make the work a success. We are laborers together with God. This is the Lord's own wise arrangement. The cooperation of *the human will* and endeavor with divine energy is the link that binds men up with one another and with God."[91] "Too much confidence is placed in man, too much reliance on human inventions. There is too little confidence in the power which God stands ready to give. 'We are laborers together with God.' 1 Corinthians 3:9. *Immeasurably inferior* is the part which the human agent sustains; but if he is linked with the divinity of Christ, he can do all things through the strength that Christ imparts."[92]

When you make the choice to believe, and believe only, that Christ does everything for you, you will, consciously or unconsciously, find Him choosing the right things for you and doing the right things for you without your having to choose or do anything, because *God's power is in control of you*. You must only choose to acknowledge God's power in behalf of your own soul. If you do this, then you have a new heart and you are under the control of that new heart. You do not control that new heart, that new heart controls you. You do not control

Chapter 4 — "Ye shall be free indeed"

that new heart with your choices and works, that new heart controls you with its own choices and works. And the choices and works it makes can be good and only good, because God said so. And since He said so, it is so.

Many Christians believe we need to exercise self-control, and it is true that self must be controlled, but self cannot control self for any purposes of good. So then, since self cannot control self and God requires that self be controlled, it then lies as inevitable that some power outside of ourselves must control us. That power is Christ! But we cannot exercise Christ-control, because if *we* are exercising Christ-control, then Christ is not in control because *we* are, in that we are exercising Him. When we consent to believe the promise that God will *cause* us to walk in His statutes (Eze. 36:27), we will walk in His statutes, not because we are in control but because He is. Now, it is possible for one to exercise self-control, but if one does exercise self-control, it is self-control and therefore whatever he controlled himself to do was evil because self did it—"All our righteousnesses are as filthy rags" (Isa. 64:6).

God says, "I will put my spirit within you, and *cause you* to walk in my statutes" (Eze. 36:27). The word "cause" in the original Hebrew means *to make*. God will make you keep His law if you will choose to keep it and believe His promise. But His making you keep His law does not mean you are forced to keep it. The law will be kept by His power if you are willing to let it be kept by Him, through you. God has not made us robots having no will of our own; He does not force us to do anything. But if we are willing, He will work in and through us to do His good pleasure. When we cry out to Him in faith saying, "Lord, I will; I want for You to control me," He controls us, not against our will, but according to our will. If man desires to no longer have God control Him, then God ceases to control him and another power takes

Saved by Works... Christ's Works!

the reins.

"All who love God and are loyal to his government, will be tempted to change leaders. But God has said, 'Thou shalt have no other gods before me.' 'Thou shalt love the Lord thy God with all thy heart, and with all thy soul, and with all thy mind, and with all thy strength.' The Lord accepts no half-hearted service. He demands the whole man. Religion is to be brought into every phase of life, carried into labor of every kind. The whole being is to be under *God's control*. We must not think that we can take supervision of our own thoughts. They must be brought into captivity to Christ. *Self cannot manage self; it is not sufficient for the work. Whoever tries to do this will be worsted. God alone can make and keep us loyal.*"[93]

To illustrate how God is to be *completely* in control of us while we merely go through the motions of God's will, as *if* we did it ourselves, imagine a storm at sea. In the midst of this storm is a ship which a child is seeking to steer safely to harbor through the ragged rocks and raging waves and wind. The weak and inexperienced child cannot possibly man the ship to safety and is doomed unless one comes to his aid. The child, seeing his perfect helplessness, tremblingly cries out for help. The captain of the ship, the child's father, instantly comes to his son's aid. But instead of shoving the helpless child aside, the father places his strong hands over his son's, and with one mighty jolt of his skilled arms, braces the ship to withstand the relentless storm and then guides it to safety.

The child's hands and arms lifelessly go through the motions of managing the ship, but it is the captain that successfully rescues the vessel. This was possible because of the child's perfect submission to his father's control and guidance. But suppose the child's will did not submit to his father's. Suppose the child decided to resist the captain's help and try to do things his own way. Suppose he steered the ship

Chapter 4 — "Ye shall be free indeed"

to the left while the captain sought to turn to the right. What then? Christ will not force anyone to be saved, but if they will be controlled, the Savior takes entire control of the matter and carries His children straight through heaven's pearly gates.

You have a new heart because God spoke His word to you, which created in you a new heart. You have been "born again . . . by the word of God" (1 Peter 1:23), and God says, "My word . . . that goeth forth out of my mouth . . . *it* shall accomplish that which I please" (Isa. 55:11). It is not *you*, because of *it,* that holiness is manifested in your life. You do not accomplish that which God pleases, *it* does—the Word does; Christ does. "In the beginning was the Word, and the Word was with God, and the Word was God. . . . All things were made by him; and without him was not any thing made that was made" (John 1:1, 3). The Word of God is the assurance that that which He has spoken will be and is so. Christ, whose "name is called The Word of God," is the One that makes it so (Rev. 19:13).

To prove that we don't need to make any physical efforts in the work of salvation, we will use an illustration. God says to man, "Go ye into all the world, and preach the gospel" (Mark 16:15). Upon hearing this command, for man to stay where he is and not preach the gospel would be a violation of the law and would therefore be sin. But if man's heart is good, it is perfectly impossible for him to sin by not preaching the gospel. So then, according to the Word of God, if man believes, and believes only, his heart is good and of necessity the gospel will be preached. But he need not make any physical effort to preach the gospel. God said that the gospel will be preached by them who believe they have a good heart with Christ in it. If a man then understands the command to preach the gospel, and through faith, and faith only, and not of works at all, has a good heart from God, there is no power in earth or hell that can hinder Christ, who is within that

Saved by Works... Christ's Works!

good heart, from causing the gospel to be preached. The *only* way the gospel cannot be preached by man is if his heart is evil through unbelief, through not acknowledging the authority and truthfulness of God's Word in behalf of his own soul. So we need then to believe *only* and let Christ preach the gospel through us. We need to stop preaching the gospel by putting forth our efforts of righteousness, for this is nothing but filthy rags, and in replacement of our sin, we need to let Christ preach His own gospel through us.

As long as you do not work out your own righteousness and do not resist Christ's drawing, everything that must happen in order for you to be saved *will happen*. Why? Because *God said it!* If you do these two things, and these two things only, you *will* be saved. True repentance and confession *will* be manifested in your life. You *will* live a life of prayer. You *will* forsake your sins, and you *will* believe God's promises unto your cleansing of sins from the past and unto works of God's righteousness at present. And the righteous, God says, go "into life eternal" (Matt. 25:46).

"In Jesus Christ neither circumcision availeth any thing, nor uncircumcision; but faith which worketh by love" Gal. 5:6. With those who were in mind when this scripture was originally written, circumcision was everything, and it was everything simply because of what it represented.

"And what circumcision represented to those people was works, and works only. It was the greatest of all works — greater than creation itself — because, as the rabbis put it, 'So great is circumcision, that but for it the Holy One, blessed be He, would not have created the world.' 'It is as great as all the other commandments;' 'equivalent to all the commandments of the law.' --Farrar's "Life of Paul," chapter 22, para. 5, note; chapter 35, para 4, note."[94]

"Yet this which to them was so great, the Lord sweeps away, as

Chapter 4 — "Ye shall be free indeed"

with a blast, in the words, 'Circumcision is nothing;' and in Christ Jesus, circumcision avails nothing. And, in view of what circumcision meant to them, this was simply to say that works are nothing, and in Christ Jesus works avail nothing.

"Then to all the others, who, in view of this, might be inclined to boast in their lack of works, and thus excuse sin, the Word is given with equal force: 'And uncircumcision is nothing;' 'In Jesus Christ neither . . . uncircumcision availeth anything:' which, in its connection, was simply to say that the absence of works is nothing; and in Christ Jesus the absence of works avails nothing. So, then, works are nothing, and the absence of works is nothing. In Christ Jesus neither works nor the lack of works avails anything.

"This Word of the Lord, therefore, utterly and forever excludes both classes from all merit, and from all ground of merit, in themselves, or in anything they ever did or did not do."[95]

The only thing that will ever avail anything is "*faith* which worketh by love" (Gal. 5:6). "Now to him *that worketh* is the reward not reckoned of grace, but of debt. But to him *that worketh not*, but believeth on him that justifieth the ungodly, his faith is counted for righteousness" (Rom. 4:4, 5).

Paul spoke to the Galatians saying, "O foolish Galatians, who hath bewitched you, that ye should not obey the truth, before whose eyes Jesus Christ hath been evidently set forth, crucified among you? This only would I learn of you, Received ye the Spirit by the works of the law, or by the hearing of faith? Are ye so foolish? having begun in the Spirit, are ye now made perfect by the flesh?" (Gal. 3:1-3).

There are many who, like the Galatians, begin their Christian life through a simple faith in Jesus Christ. They trust that He has forgiven their sins, cleansed their hearts, and given them a new life. Thus they have "begun in the Spirit" through the "hearing of faith." But

Saved by Works... Christ's Works!

upon taking their first steps in the Christian walk, they think that they, though begun in the Spirit, now have their characters made perfect by the flesh. That is to say, they think they are made perfect by what they (flesh and blood) can do, which is works. Paul says such people are bewitched. They have come under the power of witchcraft and sorcery. The works they do are works of self-righteousness, which is sin. God may wink at what they are doing during the time of their ignorance, but once they understand their fatal error, God commands them immediately to repent, for "every person who cherishes a known error, in faith or practice, is under the power of sorcery, and is practicing sorcery upon others. Satan employs him to mislead other souls."[96] (See also Act 17:30.)

God promises help to those struggling against the powers of evil. "Fear thou not," He says, "for I am with thee: be not dismayed; for I am thy God: I will strengthen thee; yea, I will help thee; yea, I will uphold thee with the right hand of my righteousness. . . . I the LORD thy God will hold thy right hand, saying unto thee, Fear not; I will help thee" (Isa. 41:10, 13).

Often people misunderstand what the Lord means when He promises to help them in the battle against sin and selfishness. When God says He will help us overcome evil, He means He will overcome evil for us. Let us imagine that a woman cries out to her husband for help because she is about to be attacked by a prowling lion. The husband, upon hearing his wife's cry, instantly appears with a high-powered rifle. His wife quickly darts behind him, and he kills the lion with one well-aimed blast. Now, did the wife receive help from her husband? Of course! But notice that the husband did not request of his wife to take part in the conflict. What would be the point of that? While she could possibly help her husband kill the lion, it just makes far more sense for him to do it himself. Is he not far more capable of dealing

Chapter 4 — "Ye shall be free indeed"

with wild beasts than is his wife? Would she not be far safer behind him? Would there be any point of endangering his wife's life by requiring that she help him execute the king of the jungle? And would God require us to take part in contending with the devil, when he, "as a roaring lion, walketh about, seeking whom he may devour" (1 Peter 5:8)? Oh how foolish it would be for a man to give his wife a rubber-band gun and tell her to help him fight off an approaching lion when he has a flamethrower on his back! And yet we so often look upon our Beloved as if He would do just that. Oh the crime of it all!

When we come to Jesus in faith crying, "Lord, help me!" (Matt. 15:25), it is our part to only let Him help us in the way that He desires. When we have learned to do this, then we can say with the psalmist, "The LORD is my strength and my shield; my heart trusted in him, and I am helped: therefore my heart greatly rejoiceth; and with my song will I praise him" (Ps. 28:7).

Do you see then how it is not as hard to be saved as many make it out to be? When there was a great multitude gathered together for battle against Israel of old, they were told, "Ye shall not need to fight in this battle" (2 Chron. 20:17), "for the battle is not yours, but God's" (verse 15). "Set yourselves, stand ye still, and see the salvation of the LORD with you . . . fear not, nor be dismayed . . . go out against them: for the LORD will be with you" (verse 17). Israel was told that the battle was not theirs, but God's, and therefore, He would be the One doing the fighting. If God took complete control and fought against Israel's enemies in literal battles, in which they might at least have put up a good resistance and fight of themselves, then why would God leave us to battle with the power of Satan's temptations against which we have no power to resist or fight whatsoever? "Thus saith the LORD . . . *I will* contend with him that contendeth with thee" (Isa. 49:25). "The LORD shall fight for you, and *ye shall hold your peace*" (Ex.

Saved by Works... Christ's Works!

14:14). If the battle is truly God's, then why in the world do we try to fight it ourselves? God does the work for us if we will only acknowledge His power in our behalf. Let this ever be settled in our minds.

Jesus says in most distinct terms, "There is none good but one, that is, God" (Matt. 19:17). So then God is the *only* One who is good, and He is the only One good *in and of Himself*. Now, we know that only someone who is good can do good (Matt. 7:18; 12:33; Luke 6:45). This being the case, it is inevitable that since God requires good works to be manifest in our lives, *He Himself must do the good works for us, through us*, for we have no goodness or righteousness of our own with which to do them. "As it is written, There is none righteous, no, not one," and as a natural result of this, "there is none that doeth good, no, not one" (Rom. 3:10, 12). Since these things are true, if we make any efforts of our own to do good, then by these efforts we are openly declaring Jesus a liar, for by our efforts at righteousness, we are declaring, in perfect opposition to the words of Jesus, that we have some goodness of our own with which we might do good. So then, if we make efforts to do good are we not declaring ourselves as God Himself? Oh the condemnation! Oh the blasphemy!

The reason that a man can be said to be a good man with a good heart (Matt. 12:35) when Jesus says that God is the only One who is good is because the fountain of that man's heart is good. And the reason the fountain of that heart is good is because Jesus is that fountain. The Lord is "the fountain of living waters" (Jer. 17:13). "If any man thirst," says Jesus, "let him come unto me, and drink" (John 7:37). "I will give unto him that is athirst of the fountain of the water of life freely" (Rev. 21:6).

If the heart is good because of the presence of Jesus, than the only way the heart can remain good is if Jesus remains there. The condition of the heart determines the type of works man will do, whether

Chapter 4 — "Ye shall be free indeed"

they are good works or whether they are evil. Satan, therefore, strives to get us to choose to remove Jesus from the throne of our hearts by urging us to put something else in His place. Satan's studied plan is to get man to fall for his temptations and to choose sin over the Savior, and we must remember that "the only safeguard against his power is found in the presence of Jesus."[97] Remove the presence of Jesus from the heart through the power of choice, and man is at the mercy of the evil one. But keep Jesus upon the throne of the heart, and the streams from the Fountain will be pure. They are not your streams, because you are not the fountain. They are the streams of life that come from the Lifegiver.

Upon observation, it seems that many will yet agree theoretically with this message of Christ our righteousness. But though they understand it, for some reason they don't *get* it. It doesn't sink down from their head to their heart. They understand and believe it as an abstract theory, but its concrete and practical application doesn't exist to them. These people need to realize what they must do to be saved. All that a man must do to be saved is to be saved. Choose to be saved—believe that God saves you, that you are born of God and are thus His child, and that Christ abides in your heart, making it impossible for sin to be manifested in your life. Then, when Satan tempts you to sin, you will realize that as God's child you do not want to do these evil things, for your heart is pure and its very nature recoils from all of the false pleasures of sin. You realize that the sinful feelings, desires, and cravings which seem like they are coming from your heart are really not coming from the heart and they need not be regarded as of *any* account. You are a child of God by faith in Christ Jesus (Gal. 3:26). As long as you hold to this position, perfect victory is yours and the devil cannot touch you. "While Satan can solicit, he cannot compel to sin."[98] And as for all evils, "Ye are of God, little children, and have overcome

Saved by Works... Christ's Works!

them: because greater is he that is *in* you, than he that is in the world" (1 John 4:4).

There are a number of people who get caught in the rut of thinking that the promises of God that are fulfilled to them are fulfilled to them only abstractly, not in a concrete and practical sense. This may be due to the fact that faith seems like an abstract thing, and so they conclude that the things they claim by faith must also be abstract. For whatever reason, some people's minds have the tendency to perceive that the things we receive from claiming God's promises by faith are abstract. This will be expressed in the following example.

A man is walking in the path that God has set before him and he comes to a dessert place where there is no water. He soon finds himself thirsty, so he kneels down and prays to God and asks for sustenance, claiming God's promise that He will provide water for him (Isa. 33:16). Then a man comes along, and seeing him, asks, "Sir, are you thirsty? Would you like some of my water?" But instead of replying, "Yes! I am thirsty and I would like some of your water," he says, "No. I am not thirsty. By faith my thirst is quenched, for God has provided for me."

Laugh if you will, but many people seem to express the same type of faith that this man did, a faith that claims God's promises in the abstract. This man was never satisfied. He never received the water that was so vital to sustain his life, but he insisted that he did and therefore tricked himself into believing that his thirst was satisfied when it really wasn't. Oh what foolishness! And what dangerous foolishness at that, for spiritually speaking, if our sins are only forgiven in the abstract, if Christ is in our hearts by faith, but only in some theoretical abstract sense, in some person outside of ourselves, we will be doomed in the judgment of God and will receive the punishment of eternal death. Why? Because our sins were never concretely forgiven and blotted

Chapter 4 — "Ye shall be free indeed"

out of the books of heaven and Jesus was never really in our hearts as our sanctification.

Now when we say, "Christ liveth in me; Jesus is in my heart by faith; I am dead unto sin; I am crucified with Christ," in which sense do we say it? In the abstract or the concrete? Paul says, "*I am* crucified with Christ . . . Christ liveth in *me*" (Gal. 2:20). That means *in him*, in Paul *himself*. But what is Paul? Paul is a man. And what is a man? The book of Genesis reveals exactly what a man is. "The LORD God formed man of the dust of the ground, and breathed into his nostrils the breath of life; and man became a living soul" (Gen. 2:7). Man is a living soul, which in the original Hebrew means "a breathing creature," and this living soul exists when you have a body combined with the breath of life (Body + Breath of Life = Living Soul). Paul was a living soul, a breathing creature. He was both a body and the breath of life put together. Therefore, a body and the breath of life put together was what Paul was composed of, and Paul was a concrete object, not an abstract object. Therefore, when Paul said, "Christ liveth in *me*," he was not speaking in a theoretical abstract sense which did him absolutely no good, but he was speaking in a practical and concrete sense which makes all the difference in the world, because Christ, the infinite of God of the universe, really lived in him and was practically and concretely doing good for and through him. "*I am* crucified with Christ," he said. Not some theoretical and abstract Paul person that appeared in some figment of his imagination, but *he* was crucified with Christ. Christ lived in *his* heart. Paul was sure of this. "*I am*," he said. Not somebody else, but *I am* crucified with Christ. Christ lived in *him*.

Paul was flesh and blood, and it was within this flesh and blood, it was within this living soul, that he said Christ dwelt. And this is how we are supposed to live. Christ is to live in us, concrete living

Saved by Works... Christ's Works!

souls that are composed of a concrete body and concrete breath of life. Christ is to live in the real you, and not just you, but you, yourself, and you, and nothing outside of you at all. If you merely claim the promise of Christ in the heart by faith in the abstract sense, then you might as well just hang up the idea of victory over sin. But if you will claim Christ in your heart by faith and receive this promise in the concrete sense, then victory will be seen in the life.

When one claims Christ into their heart by faith in the abstract sense, it will be manifest by the same lack of satisfaction that the man who drank no water will have. They will say, "Yes, yes! I know already. Christ is in my heart by faith, but . . ." The word "but" proves their unbelief. There is no lack of satisfaction when Christ dwells in the heart, and the fact that the soul is not satisfied is the evidence that Christ is not in the heart, and that proves that true faith is lacking. Abstract faith is just a form of unbelief that seems more like faith than no faith at all, and so many people accept abstract faith to feel more accomplished. But abstract faith *is no faith at all*. True faith that accepts God's promises in the concrete sense is the victory that overcomes the world.

"Having therefore these promises, dearly beloved, let us cleanse ourselves from all filthiness of the flesh and spirit, *perfecting holiness in the fear of God*" (2 Cor. 7:1). Many will look at this message of Christ our Righteousness as leaving no room for character improvement and that it therefore must be incorrect, because Paul says that we are to "go on unto perfection" (Heb 6:1), and they reason that if we are already perfect we cannot go on unto perfection. But Paul does not bid us to go on to improve something that is unrighteous, but to perfect, to make more complete, that which has already been made holy by the Word of God. We are to "perfect holiness" in the fear of God even though holiness is already perfect. The seed is perfect, the seedling is

Chapter 4 — "Ye shall be free indeed"

perfect, but it will get bigger, stronger, and more mature. A light is a light, and in a light is no darkness at all. That light is perfect, but as a light, it can always shine brighter. Thus we are to go on *in* perfection and *unto* a deeper completeness.

The kingdom of God is "as if a man should cast seed into the ground; And should sleep, and rise night and day, and the seed should spring and grow up, he knoweth not how. For the earth bringeth forth fruit of herself; first the blade, then the ear, after that the full corn in the ear" (Mark 4:26-28).

"The germination of the seed represents the beginning of spiritual life, and the development of the plant is a beautiful figure of Christian growth. As in nature, so in grace; there can be no life without growth. The plant must either grow or die. As its growth is silent and imperceptible, but continuous, so is the development of the Christian life. At every stage of development our life may be *perfect*; yet if God's purpose for us is fulfilled, there will be continual advancement. Sanctification is the work of a lifetime."[99]

The reason sanctification is called "the work of a lifetime" is because this part of sanctification is that which is making more perfect that which is already perfect. However, Paul says, "but ye are washed, but ye *are sanctified*, but ye are justified in the name of the Lord Jesus, and by the Spirit of our God" (1 Cor. 6:11). If you are *already* sanctified because Christ is in your heart, why would you need to be sanctified throughout the rest of your life? The reason is because one part of sanctification is unto the expelling of sin from the life, while the other part of sanctification is unto the beautification of the life, the shining brighter of the love of Jesus, the growing "unto the measure of the stature of the fulness of Christ" (Eph. 4:13).

Many people believe that while it is possible for them to live a sinless life, it will not happen. They believe that since it has always been,

Saved by Works... Christ's Works!

it always will be. They will quote saying that "a just man falleth seven times, and riseth up again" (Prov. 24:16). They will use this verse in support of their own poor selves, showing that they are considered as just before God even though they make mistakes along the way, and that in this verse they find comfort, since even though they know they can live without sinning, it will not happen. Oh what a way to interpret the Scriptures! The question to be considered is this, is the man described in Proverbs rendered as just (righteous) because he fell and got up, or because *despite* the fact that he fell, God got him up and justified him? Let us not say in *any* degree that sin is inevitable and that a man who sins is considered as righteous before God. No! A man is considered as righteous before God because God forgives him, makes him holy, and works righteousness through him because he believes. This is why that man is counted as just.

"He who has not sufficient faith in Christ to believe that *he can* keep him from sinning, has not the faith that will give him an entrance into the kingdom of God."[100] "Behold," says the Creator, "I am the LORD, the God of all flesh: *is there any thing too hard for me?*" (Jer. 32:27). "Believe ye that I am able to do this?... According to your faith be it unto you" (Matt. 9:28, 29).

The class of people who quote Proverbs 24:16, as above mentioned, also believe that everything they can ever do is unrighteous. However, since they put forth their efforts toward righteousness, God covers their unrighteous works by accounting their unrighteous works as if they were righteous. Now they do not say this meaning that they believe the law is changed. They believe that the law is unchangeable. However, even though they cannot keep the unchangeable law, they still try to *do* righteously, and they believe that God then looks at their works as righteous because of their efforts to keep the law. So by faith in God's power and by their own efforts, they believe they are made

Chapter 4 — "Ye shall be free indeed"

righteous. This is faith *and* works, not faith *which* works. Shall God, being just, turn sin into righteousness? Shall He call evil good? Shall the holy One justify sin itself? Never!

All should have faith in Christ as their personal Savior. Many Christians, however, will say, "We are to work in accordance with that faith. We show our faith by working . . ."[101] This is perfectly true when understood properly, but it is meant by these Christians in a way that is erroneous. We have a perfect illustration that reveals their mistake in the story of Abraham.

To give the whole story in short, in Genesis 15 God says to Abram, "He that shall come forth out of thine own bowels shall be thine heir. . . . Look now toward heaven, and tell the stars, if thou be able to number them: and he said unto him, So shall thy seed be" (Gen. 15:4, 5). In chapter 16, Abram's wife Sarai bares him no children, and so Sarai says to him, "Behold now, the LORD hath restrained me from bearing: I pray thee, go in unto my maid; it may be that I may obtain children by her" (Gen. 16:2). Abram consents to his wife's plea and marries Hagar, his wife's servant. Hagar then becomes pregnant and the sad story of a broken family begins.

In chapter 17, Abram is 99 years old and his wife Sarai is 90. God changes their names to Abraham and Sarah and then says to Abraham concerning his wife, "I will bless her, and give thee a son also of her: yea, I will bless her, and she shall be a mother of nations; kings of people shall be of her" (Gen. 17:16). "Then Abraham fell upon his face, and laughed, and said in his heart, Shall a child be born unto him that is an hundred years old? and shall Sarah, that is ninety years old, bear? . . . And God said, Sarah thy wife shall bear thee a son indeed" (Gen. 17:17, 19).

In chapter 18, God reconfirms His promise saying, "Sarah thy wife shall have a son" (Gen. 18:10). Sarah then laughs within herself at God's promise. "And the LORD said unto Abraham, Wherefore did Sarah laugh, saying, Shall I of a surety bear a child, which am old? Is any thing too hard for the LORD? At the time appointed I will return unto thee, according to the time of life, and Sarah shall have a son" (Gen. 18:13, 14). Finally, in chapter 21, we read of the fulfillment of God's promise. "And the LORD visited Sarah as he had said, and the LORD did unto Sarah as he had spoken. For Sarah conceived, and bare Abraham a son in his old age, at the set time of which God had spoken to him" (Gen. 21:1, 2).

There is nothing too hard for God, and when God says He will do something, *He will do it.* God had promised Abraham that he would have a son who would come forth from his own bowels. Abraham, in trying to help God fulfill His promise, showed his unbelief in the promise, and thus made way for much heartbreak in his own life and in the lives of others. "Whatsoever is not of faith is *sin*" (Rom. 14:23). When Abraham was 99 years old, he still manifested his unbelief in the promise of God by laughing at the idea that God would cause Sarah to get pregnant by him and have a son. "Whatsoever is not of faith *is sin*." Sarah herself later laughs at the promise of God, showing her own unbelief in His promise to her. *"Whatsoever is not of faith is sin."* What a terrible thing it is to laugh at the promise of God! To mock Christ and act as if we think Him an idiot is a wicked crime!

Christians today will admit that Christ is the One who is able to keep them from falling and that He will perform this for them until the day of His appearing (Jude 1:24; Phil. 1:6). They admit this because it is written in the Bible, and they believe it to be true. But they only believe it to be true in the light of their preconceived idea that they must live out their faith by helping God to fulfill His promise to them by doing works. Thus they manifest the unbelief of Abram and help to fill the world with woe. Their self-righteousness, they would not care

Chapter 4 — "Ye shall be free indeed"

to admit, is sin. This is why they fail again and again, and this is why they will not be admitted into heaven. By trying to help God fulfill His promises to them, they laugh at Him as did Abraham. They mock Jesus Christ Himself and declare Him a liar. They attribute to Christ the characteristics of Satan, the old forked-tongue serpent himself. If we want to be saved at last, we must believe the promise *only*, and then *stick to that choice*.

"Both Abraham and Sarah distrusted the power of God, and it was this error that led to the marriage with Hagar."[102] "Thinking it impossible that a child should be given her in her old age, Sarah suggested, as a plan by which the divine purpose might be fulfilled, that one of her handmaidens should be taken by Abraham as a secondary wife. Polygamy had become so widespread that it had ceased to be regarded as a sin, but it was no less a violation of the law of God, and was fatal to the sacredness and peace of the family relation."[103]

While it was a sin for Abraham to marry Hagar while he was still married to Sarah, in Abraham's mind it was not a sin. This is because the part of the law regarding the marriage relation was not fully understood by Abraham, and since "sin is not imputed when there is no law" (Rom. 5:13), God did not look at Abraham as having broken His law in marrying Hagar. Therefore Abraham still stood before God as just, as far as the marriage with Hagar was concerned. To Abraham, having a child with Hagar was a perfectly okay thing to do, but it was an act that revealed his hidden unbelief in the power of God. Abraham sinned, but in the eyes of God, his sin was his doubt in God's promise, not the marriage with Hagar. Abraham did not depend upon the word of God to do the thing that it said, but he trusted partly in what he could do.

So it is with many Christian's today. They will not believe that Christ will do good works for them if they merely believe His promises. Therefore they seek to help God fulfill His promises to them by putting forth their efforts toward doing good works. These works are self-righteous works, filthy rags, which will cost them their salvation. God is not so much on their case for their self-righteousness, for in their minds they truly believe that it is Christ's righteousness, but He is on their case for calling Him a liar by their unbelief. And in calling God a liar, they themselves are lying, for it is "impossible for God to lie" (Heb. 6:18).

"And he said unto me, It is done. I am Alpha and Omega, the beginning and the end. I will give unto him that is athirst of the fountain of the water of life *freely*. He that overcometh shall *inherit* all things; and I will be his God, and he shall be my son. But the fearful, and *unbelieving*, and the abominable, and murderers, and whoremongers, and sorcerers, and idolaters, and all *liars*, shall have their part in the lake which burneth with fire and brimstone: which is the second death" (Rev. 21:6-8). It is wicked unbelief in the promise of God that leads men to seek to aid Him in fulfilling to them His promises and to work for their salvation. This is clearly revealed in the experience of Abraham. But it is not to be left unnoticed that when Abraham believed God, when he depended upon the word of God to do the thing that it said, "it was accounted to him for righteousness" (Gal. 3:6). (See also James 2:23, Romans 4:3, and Genesis 15:6.)

Abraham most definitely needed to "work out his faith," but not in trying to produce a baby. God had promised to do that Himself. The way for Abraham to have worked out his faith would have been to prepare for the promised child soon to come. Supplying necessities such as baby clothes was the appointed way for him to work out his faith. Noah worked out his faith in the promise of a worldwide flood. He believed that promise, but he worked out his faith in preparing an ark, *not* in trying to produce water to cover the earth.

Chapter 4 — "Ye shall be free indeed"

When the soul is converted, a striking change is seen in the life. True repentance is manifested in confession and good works. But so many people mistake the *fruits of* conversion as the *steps to* conversion. They understand that repentance, confession, and good works are necessary if they expect to be saved, and so therefore they set out to repent, confess, and do good works. But this salvation is dependent upon what we can do. This is salvation by our own works. The fact that man focuses on repenting is evidence that he is not converted and that he is trying to perform some good deeds and penances that God might see his good works and finally convert him. Oh the poor souls that are stuck in this hopeless mire! May they see the love of God revealed in the message of the righteousness of Christ *by faith*, to the end that they might be saved!

"The principle that man can save himself by his own works lay at the foundation of every heathen religion . . . Wherever it is held, men have no barrier against sin."[104] Many will say that the teaching of salvation by grace through faith and faith only and not by works *at all*, if brought out in so striking a manner, will break down the last barriers against sin and a massive tide of evil will swell in as a result. But on the contrary! This life of faith and faith only and not of works *at all* will prove the greatest means of barring up the great tides of wickedness that are today manifest throughout the world.

Those who oppose this teaching with such an unfounded fear are of the conservative class. They say that we must not tell people that they do not have to do works to be saved, for then much evil will result and all the supposed good that has been accomplished will be wasted. But "we should not permit the spirit of conservatism to lead us to misrepresent our Lord."[105] These conservatives bar the way of salvation, and a solemn denunciation is pronounced against them by the Lord of all heaven, "Woe unto you, *lawyers*! for ye have taken away the key of

Saved by Works... Christ's Works!

knowledge: ye entered not in yourselves, and them that were entering in ye hindered" (Luke 11:52). "Woe unto you, scribes and Pharisees, hypocrites! for ye shut up the kingdom of heaven against men: for ye neither go in yourselves, neither suffer ye them that are entering to go in" (Matt. 23:13). "Woe unto them that call evil good, and good evil; that put darkness for light, and light for darkness; that put bitter for sweet, and sweet for bitter! . . . Which justify the wicked for reward, and take away the righteousness of the righteous from him!" (Isa. 5:20, 23).

"This is a faithful saying, and worthy of all acceptation, that Christ Jesus came into the world to save sinners" (1 Tim. 1:15). Though Jesus came to save sinners, Jesus will never save a single sinner. Sinners include those who take away the key of knowledge from others and allow them to remain in their sins. "To him that knoweth to do good, and doeth it not, to him it is sin" (James 4:17). "All unrighteousness is sin" (1 John 5:17). "Know ye not that the unrighteous shall not inherit the kingdom of God?" (1 Cor. 6:9). The sinners who will be saved by Christ's sacrifice will be saved because they have been made righteous through His blood and because He has worked righteousness in and through them. But for those who have not been made righteous by an indwelling Savior, "Behold, the day cometh, that shall burn as an oven; and all the proud, yea, and all that do wickedly, shall be stubble: and the day that cometh shall burn them up, saith the LORD of hosts, that it shall leave them neither root nor branch. . . . And ye shall tread down the wicked; for they shall be ashes under the soles of your feet in the day that I shall do this, saith the LORD of hosts" (Mal. 4:1, 3). Not those who have done wickedly and have since repented, not those who have once worked wickedness but have turned from their wicked ways by the power of an indwelling Savior, but those who still "*do wickedly*" shall be burnt to ashes.

Chapter 4 — "Ye shall be free indeed"

Jesus said, "Not every one that saith unto me, Lord, Lord, shall enter into the kingdom of heaven; but he that doeth the will of my Father which is in heaven. Many will say to Me in that day, Lord, Lord, have we not prophesied in thy name? and in thy name have cast out devils? and in thy name done many wonderful works? And then will I profess unto them, I never knew you: depart from me, ye that work iniquity" (Matt. 7:21-23).

But why will this class of people be lost? Was it not God's will for many wonderful works to be done in behalf of humanity? Did not Jesus Himself do these things when He was on earth? Of course! But these people did not do the will of God. "This is the will of God, even your sanctification" (1 Thess. 4:3). Their pleading question reveals their mistake, "Lord, Lord, have *we* not . . . done many wonderful works?" These workers of iniquity may have done deeds that may have resulted in good, but their deeds, in and of themselves, were evil, because they were done in self-righteousness: "*Have we not . . .* done many wonderful works?"

It is impossible for man to be a worker of iniquity when Christ is in the heart. If these people had a good heart with Christ in it, then they would have been both justified and sanctified. But these people could not retain their justification and be sanctified by Christ's works because their own works got in His way. Oh with what bitter remorse these people will cry, "The harvest is past, the summer is ended, and we are not saved" (Jer. 8:20). But shall we blame God for their loss? No! Perfect righteousness, perfect obedience was offered to them at an infinite cost in the free gift of Christ Jesus. But they have rejected Him who is life eternal and God leaves them with the choice they made.

This class of people had strongly preached to men saying, "Work out your own salvation with fear and trembling," and as a result, they themselves both feared and trembled, but the salvation part they never

Saved by Works... Christ's Works!

received, because they never understood the next verse, that *God was to work in them* both to choose and do His will (Phil. 2:12, 13). They were so caught up in their own works that there was no room for God's works to be manifested in their lives. Thus, they are finally left, having deprived themselves of the salvation that was so freely offered to them in Christ. They worked so hard to pay for a free gift that they never took it.

"There are persons who believe that they are right, when they are wrong. While claiming Christ as their Lord, and professedly doing great works in His name, they are workers of iniquity. 'With their mouth they show much love, but their heart goeth after their covetousness.' He who declares God's word is to them 'as a very lovely song of one that hath a pleasant voice, and can play well on an instrument: for they hear Thy words, but they do them not.' Ezekiel 33:31, 32."[106]

"Rather than give up some cherished idea, or discard some idol of opinion, many refuse the truth which comes down from the Father of light. They trust in *self,* and depend upon *their own* wisdom, and do not realize their spiritual poverty. They insist on being saved in some way by which *they* may perform some important work. When they see that there is no way of weaving self into the work, they reject the salvation provided."[107]

Legalists, those who harbor the spirit of conservatism, teach others saying, "*We* must keep the law, or we will be lost. We must have faith, yes! But we must have faith *and works.*" This is the cry of the self-righteous, "Have *we* not . . . done many wonderful works?" (Matt. 7:22). Liberalists, and those who teach that sinners will be saved, say, "The law need not be kept. Jesus will still save us as sinners as long as we believe that He does." This is the cry of sheer presumption, for God has plainly said, "The unrighteous shall not inherit the kingdom of God" (1 Cor. 6:9). But those who accept the message of Christ our

Chapter 4 — "Ye shall be free indeed"

Righteousness teach saying, "The law does in fact need to be kept, for no sinner will ever be saved. But since we cannot keep the law in any sense of the word, Jesus will keep it for us. He will keep it through us as He has promised if we will only believe."

"Faith, saving faith, is to be taught. The definition of this faith in Jesus Christ may be described in few words: It is the *act of the soul* by which the whole man is *given over to the guardianship and control of Jesus Christ.* He abides in Christ and Christ abides in the soul *by faith* as supreme. The believer commits his soul and body to God, and with assurance may say, *Christ is able* to keep that which I have committed unto Him against that day. All who will do this will be saved unto life eternal. There will be an assurance that the soul is washed in the blood of Christ and clothed with His righteousness and precious in the sight of Jesus."[108]

So then, is man saved by faith, by works, or by both faith and works? Neither. The Word of God says, *"By grace* are ye saved through faith" (Eph. 2:8). The Scripture does not say that man is saved by grace through faith *and works,* but through faith *only.* Nor do the Scriptures say that man is justified and sanctified by faith *and works,* but by faith *which works.* The apostle Peter unmistakably identifies those true Christians who will be saved and have their part in the "inheritance incorruptible, and undefiled, and that fadeth not away, reserved in heaven." He declares them as those, "who are *kept by the power of God through faith unto salvation"* (1 Peter 1:4, 5). "Kept by the power of God," meaning, *kept by the power of God;* "through faith," meaning, *through faith;* "unto salvation," meaning, *unto salvation; full and complete.*

The title of the gospel message is—Righteousness by Faith. "God is righteous" (Dan. 9:14), and "God is love" (1 John 4:8). Therefore, "righteousness is love,"[109] and love is a living, working, active principle. "Love is the *fulfilling* of the law" (Rom. 13:10). If love is not active in doing good, then it ceases to be love and becomes selfishness. Therefore, "righteousness is right doing,"[110] and we know that "faith, in itself, is an act of the mind."[111] "Faith is simply to take God at His word."[112] Faith is depending upon God's Word to do what it says and acknowledging in behalf of our own soul that it does do it because it cannot do anything else. The message is not right doing by right doing, but right doing by the acknowledgment of truth in behalf of our own soul. Oh how simple this is! How beautiful it is! Oh how great the love of Christ for us! He does *everything* for us! It is too good to be true, and yet *it is true!* This is our part in manifesting good works—faith! So beautiful, so simple, and oh so easy! "What shall we do, that we might work the works of God? . . . This is the work of God, *that ye believe*" (John 6:28, 29).

"Through faith also Sara herself received strength to conceive seed, and was delivered of a child when she was past age, because she judged *him faithful* who had promised" (Heb. 11:11). This text does not say that Sara judged the promise faithful, but that she judged the Author of the promise faithful. The characteristics of a promise are found in its author. To deny the truthfulness of either the promise or the author is to deny the truthfulness of both. If God cannot lie, then what He says must be true. This is the great issue at stake in the great controversy between Christ and Satan—the truthfulness of God's Word. So this is the question now, dear soul. Now comes the moment to decide. Will you acknowledge God as true, or as a liar? Before you answer, go to Gethsemane.

In Gethsemane Christ was brought face to face with the sacrifice He had promised to make to rescue the human race. "And what was to be gained by this sacrifice? How hopeless appeared the guilt and ingratitude of men! In its hardest features Satan pressed the situation

Chapter 4 — "Ye shall be free indeed"

upon the Redeemer: The people who claim to be above all others in temporal and spiritual advantages have rejected You. They are seeking to destroy You, the foundation, the center and seal of the promises made to them as a peculiar people. One of Your own disciples, who has listened to Your instruction, and has been among the foremost in church activities, will betray You. One of Your most zealous followers will deny You. All will forsake You. Christ's whole being abhorred the thought. That those whom He had undertaken to save, those whom He loved so much, should unite in the plots of Satan, this pierced His soul. The conflict was terrible. Its measure was the guilt of His nation, of His accusers and betrayer, the guilt of a world lying in wickedness. The sins of men weighed heavily upon Christ, and the sense of God's wrath against sin was crushing out His life. Behold Him contemplating the price to be paid for the human soul."[113]

"Throughout His life on earth He had walked in the light of God's presence. When in conflict with men who were inspired by the very spirit of Satan, He could say, 'He that sent Me is with Me: the Father hath not left Me alone; for I do always those things that please Him.' John 8:29. But now He seemed to be shut out from the light of God's sustaining presence. Now He was numbered with the transgressors. The guilt of fallen humanity He must bear. Upon Him who knew no sin must be laid the iniquity of us all. So dreadful does sin appear to Him, so great is the weight of guilt which He must bear, that He is tempted to fear it will shut Him out forever from His Father's love. Feeling how terrible is the wrath of God against transgression, He exclaims, 'My soul is exceeding sorrowful, even unto death.'"[114]

"The humanity of the Son of God trembled in that trying hour. He prayed not now for His disciples that their faith might not fail, but for His own tempted, agonized soul. The awful moment had come—that moment which was to decide the destiny of the world. The fate of humanity trembled in the balance. Christ might even now refuse to drink the cup apportioned to guilty man. It was not yet too late. He might wipe the bloody sweat from His brow, and leave man to perish in his iniquity. He might say, Let the transgressor receive the penalty of his sin, and I will go back to My Father. Will the Son of God drink the bitter cup of humiliation and agony? Will the innocent suffer the consequences of the curse of sin, to save the guilty? The words fall tremblingly from the pale lips of Jesus, 'O My Father, if this cup may not pass away from Me, except I drink it, Thy will be done.'"[115]

The True Witness declares, "I know thy works . . . thou sayest, I am rich, and increased with goods, and have need of nothing; and knowest not that thou art wretched, and miserable, and poor, and blind, and naked" (Rev. 3:15, 17).

"What is it that constitutes the wretchedness, the nakedness of those who feel rich and increased with goods?—It is the want of the righteousness of Christ. In their own righteousness they are represented as clothed with filthy rags, and yet in this condition they flatter themselves that they are clothed upon with Christ's righteousness. Could deception be greater? As is represented by the prophet, they may be crying, 'The temple of the Lord, the temple of the Lord are we,' while their hearts are filled with unholy traffic and unrighteous barter. . . . Christ looks mournfully upon his professed people who feel rich and increased in the knowledge of the truth, and who are yet destitute of the truth in life and character and unconscious of their destitute condition. In sin and unbelief, they lightly regard the warnings and counsels of his servants, and treat his ambassadors with scorn and contempt, while their words of reproof are regarded as idle tales. Discernment seems to have departed, and they have no power to discriminate between the light which God sends them and the darkness that comes from the enemy of their souls."[116]

Chapter 4 — "Ye shall be free indeed"

"When the doctrine we accept *kills sin in the heart*, purifies the soul from defilement, bears fruit unto holiness, we may know that it is the truth of God. When benevolence, kindness, tenderheartedness, sympathy, are manifest in our lives; when the joy of right doing is in our hearts; when we exalt Christ, and not self, we may know that our faith is of the right order."[117]

The problem man has is that his mind is naturally "enmity against God: for it is not subject to the law of God, neither indeed can be" (Rom. 8:7). This being the case, he must perish, for the law that demands the death of the transgressor declares, "Thou shalt love the Lord thy God with *all* thy heart, and with *all* thy soul, and with *all* thy mind" (Matt. 22:37). "And now also the axe is laid unto the root of the trees: every tree therefore which bringeth not forth good fruit is hewn down, and cast into the fire" (Luke 3:9).

The solution to man's problem is that the creative, irreversible, spoken word of the living God promises that if man will but believe that Christ forgives his sins and lives through him by abiding in his heart by faith, he shall be both justified and sanctified unto eternal life. He shall love God with everything he has and is, and he shall have the assurance of salvation. Oh what a precious Savior!

"Jesus prayed for us, and He asked that we might be one with Him, even as He is one with the Father. What a union is this! The Saviour has said of Himself, 'The Son can do nothing of Himself;' 'the Father that dwelleth in Me, *He doeth the works.*' John 5:19; 14:10. Then if Christ is dwelling in our hearts, *He will work* in us 'both to will and to do of His good pleasure.' Philippians 2:13. We shall work as He worked; we shall manifest the same spirit. And thus, loving Him and abiding in Him, we shall 'grow up into Him in all things, which is the head, even Christ.' Ephesians 4:15."[118]

Saved by Works... Christ's Works!

The Result

When Christ is *in* the heart, He is *on* the heart. The only way that Christ can be *on the heart* is if He is first *in it*. And when we love Christ as our Husband, we will have no time for ourselves. Love for self will be swallowed up in love for Christ. We will not spend our moments thinking about ourselves, our selfish interests, our selfish desires. Our every thought will center in Christ. Just as a bride cannot get her mind off of her groom, so we will not be able to get our minds off of Christ. Our hearts will constantly be springing up with love and gratitude to Christ for doing what He did for us and for offering to us the wedding garment that makes us His bride. Then, "the countenance is changed. Christ abiding in the heart shines out in the faces of those who love Him and keep His commandments. Truth is written there. The sweet peace of heaven is revealed. There is expressed a habitual gentleness, a more than human love."[119] Then it is that *true* obedience will come from the heart. Then it is that we are not under the law, but under grace. Then it is that we are converted.

When you love Christ, service to Him will not be something that insists upon you, but that you insist upon. Then it will be that "the love of Christ constraineth" you (2 Cor. 5:14). Not against your own will are you constrained, but because your heart is changed, it would be a constraining for you not to serve Christ. Your love for Christ, resulting from His love for you, makes you so eager to serve Him that you are "constrained" by your own desire to serve Him.

"The grace of Christ received into the heart, subdues enmity; it allays strife and fills the soul with love. He who is at peace with God and his fellow men cannot be made miserable. Envy will not be in his heart; evil surmisings will find no room there; hatred cannot exist. The heart that is in harmony with God is a partaker of the peace of heaven and will diffuse its blessed influence on all around. The

Chapter 4 — "Ye shall be free indeed"

spirit of peace will rest like dew upon hearts weary and troubled with worldly strife."[120]

"When Christ abides in the heart, there will be purity and refinement of thought and manner."[121] "If the heart has been renewed by the Spirit of God, the life will bear witness to the fact. While we cannot do anything to change our hearts or to bring ourselves into harmony with God; while we must not trust at all to ourselves or our good works, our lives will reveal whether the grace of God is dwelling within us. A change will be seen in the character, the habits, the pursuits. The contrast will be clear and decided between what they have been and what they are."[122]

The psalmist says, *"I delight to do thy will*, O my God: yea, thy law is within my heart" (Ps. 40:8). When by faith we accept God's law into our hearts, *even our feelings are changed!* We *will* delight to do God's will. Why? Because God *said* it! Therefore, it must be true. When Christ is accepted into the heart, "the natural inclinations are softened and subdued. New thoughts, *new feelings*, new motives, are implanted. A new standard of character is set up—the life of Christ. The mind is changed; the faculties are roused to action in new lines. Man is not endowed with new faculties, but the faculties he has are sanctified. The conscience is awakened. We are endowed with traits of character that enable us to do service for God."[123]

"All whose hearts are in sympathy with the heart of Infinite Love will seek to reclaim and not to condemn. Christ dwelling in the soul is a spring that never runs dry. Where He abides, there will be an overflowing of beneficence."[124] "The love of Christ is diffusive and aggressive. If it is dwelling in us, it will flow out to others,"[125] "not because of favors received from them, but because love is the principle of action."[126] "We shall come close to them till their hearts are warmed by our unselfish interest and love."[127]

Saved by Works... Christ's Works!

"Love modifies the character, governs the impulses, subdues enmity, and ennobles the affections. This love is as broad as the universe, and is in harmony with that of the angel workers. Cherished in the heart, it sweetens the entire life and sheds its blessing upon all around."[128] "When the love of Christ is enshrined in the heart, like sweet fragrance it cannot be hidden. Its holy influence will be felt by all with whom we come in contact. The spirit of Christ in the heart is like a spring in the desert, flowing to refresh all and making those who are ready to perish, eager to drink of the water of life."[129]

"If you are in communion with Christ, you will place His estimate upon every human being. You will feel for others the same deep love that Christ has felt for you. Then you will be able to win, not drive, to attract, not repulse, those for whom He died. None would ever have been brought back to God if Christ had not made a personal effort for them; and it is by this personal work that we can rescue souls. When you see those who are going down to death, you will not rest in quiet indifference and ease. The greater their sin and the deeper their misery, the more earnest and tender will be your efforts for their recovery. You will discern the need of those who are suffering, who have been sinning against God, and who are oppressed with a burden of guilt. Your heart will go out in sympathy for them, and you will reach out to them a helping hand. In the arms of your faith and love you will bring them to Christ. You will watch over and encourage them, and your sympathy and confidence will make it hard for them to fall from their steadfastness."[130] Dear friends, "If we love one another, God dwelleth in us, and his love is perfected in us" (1 John 4:12).

Those whose hearts are melted by Christ's love, and who as a result choose Him as their Husband and accept Him into their hearts by faith, accepting His offer to make them His bride, will be most strongly pursued by the devil, for he knows that those who love Christ

Chapter 4 — "Ye shall be free indeed"

above all are a great danger to his kingdom. The preaching of God's law is vital, for only those who see themselves as sinners, condemned to die, will seek after the Savior. But Satan can use the preaching of God's law for his own purposes of evil.

There are many who, upon hearing God's law preached to them, see their condemnation, feel their guilt, and are thus led to Christ, knowing that if anyone can save them it is He. In this way the law "brings them to Christ." But once brought to Christ, they need no longer be crushed under the condemnation of the law as Satan would have it. "There is therefore now no condemnation to them which are in Christ Jesus, who walk not after the flesh, but after the Spirit" (Rom. 8:1). If you walk after the Spirit, if you follow the Spirit, "if ye be led of the Spirit, ye are not under the law" (Gal. 5:18).

While it is good for us to hear the law of God preached to us, to examine ourselves, to see our terrible condition as sinners, and to tremble before the high demands of the law, we must not let the devil bring us back to being under the law's condemnation so that it crushes us. Christ's yoke is easy and His burden is light, but the devil would misrepresent this. If you are the bride of Christ, don't let Satan bring you down from this exalted position. It is no virtue to leave the bosom of our Savior and to continually fear for our salvation.

When the law of God is presented to sinners, it should be presented to them as having no mercy, for God's law has no mercy. The law can only say, "The wages of sin is death" (Rom. 6:23). It is dangerous to present the law of God as if it had mercy, that after all, it's not that bad to commit such and such little sins—I mean, hey, after all, we have to be balanced, right? Nonsense! With such balancing you will fall right into the lake of fire! When the law is preached, Jesus must also be preached, or the sinner would see no hope. Jesus has mercy, and when we preach the law's condemnation, we must also preach

Saved by Works... Christ's Works!

Jesus' mercy. But a clear and distinct line must be drawn between God's mercy and God's law, or else sinners might excuse their sins. When the law (condemnation) and Jesus (mercy) are preached, it must be made perfectly clear that *there is no such thing as a merciful law*. It must not be blurred in the minds of any that what God calls sin is sin, and those who sin *will die*. Christ promises to keep the law through and for us if we will but believe, but no sinner shall ever enter the kingdom of heaven.

There are many Christians who believe that we are saved by grace, and that we can do anything evil that we want and still be saved. But this cannot be right, for the whole Bible repeatedly declares that "the unrighteous shall not inherit the kingdom of God" (1 Cor. 6:9). There are fewer Christians who believe that because we are saved by grace we will do only good works. These are correct in their belief. But among this class of people are found many who do not serve God because it is their delight. They acknowledge themselves as God's servants, but not as His *children* and *bride*. They serve Him because they acknowledge Him as their Master and Lord, but not as their loving *Father* and *Husband*.

If people do not love God as their Father by believing that Christ is in their heart and that they are His children by faith, how it is that they think they are going to obtain the *inheritance* of heaven and eternal life? If they do not believe that Christ is in their heart and reckon themselves as His children, that God has, through Christ, adopted them as His children, can they expect to receive an inheritance? No. The Scriptures say, "the son of the bondwoman shall not be heir with the son of the freewoman" (Gal. 4:30). "For if they which are of the law be heirs, faith is made void, and the promise made of none effect" (Rom. 4:14). They cannot receive an inheritance unless they are children, because children, and children only, can receive an inheri-

Chapter 4 — "Ye shall be free indeed"

tance. But because these people, through their servant service, reckon themselves as mere servants, they reckon themselves as under the law, and they must then believe they are saved by their works. Do not their lives testify to this? By their life of serving God, not out of a delighted love-service as children and bride, having a new heart in which Christ dwells, but as a matter of duty as mere servants, they are, though unconsciously perhaps, seeking to obtain salvation by works. They are entangled with a yoke of bondage instead of being free with the yoke of Christ.

Let us say that one did choose to serve God only as a Master and not as a Husband. What would happen to such a person upon entering the gates of paradise? Would he then take delight in doing God's will, when for years and years it has been to him only a drudgery? Will he all of a sudden then take pleasure in doing those things in heaven that made his heart sigh in desolation when he was upon the earth? No. Such will not enter heaven. They would not take delight in doing God's will. They would want to do their own will and follow their own plans and selfish interests, and if these were crossed, their hearts would sigh in sadness and mar the sweet melody of heaven's sinless dwellers. Their only hope of salvation is in becoming Christ's bride *by faith*.

"There are many who, though striving to obey God's commandments, have little peace or joy. This lack in their experience is the result of a failure to exercise faith. They walk as it were in a salt land, a parched wilderness. They claim little, when they might claim much; for there is no limit to the promises of God. Such ones do not correctly represent the sanctification that comes through obedience to the truth. The Lord would have all His sons and daughters happy, peaceful, and obedient. Through the exercise of faith the believer comes into possession of these blessings. *Through faith*, every deficiency of character

Saved by Works... Christ's Works!

may be supplied, every defilement cleansed, every fault corrected, every excellence developed."[131]

"In the courts above, Christ is pleading for His church—pleading for those for whom He has paid the redemption price of His blood. Centuries, ages, can never lessen the efficacy of His atoning sacrifice. Neither life nor death, height nor depth, can separate us from the love of God which is in Christ Jesus; not because we hold Him so firmly, but *because He holds us so fast*. If our salvation depended on our own efforts, we could not be saved; but it depends on the One who is behind all the promises. Our grasp on Him may seem feeble, but His love is that of an elder brother; so long as we maintain our union with Him, no one can pluck us out of His hand."[132]

Dear reader, salvation is a *free gift*, it is an *inheritance* given to the *children* of God. Do you not see then that everything is based upon the relationship that we have with God as children and bride, and not as servants? When the bridegroom marries the bride, does not everything that belongs to him become hers without her having to make the slightest strain on her part to obtain it? "If the inheritance be of the law, it is no more of promise" (Gal. 3:18).

"When the Son of man shall come in his glory, and all the holy angels with him, then shall he sit upon the throne of his glory: And before him shall be gathered all nations: and he shall separate them one from another, as a shepherd divideth his sheep from the goats: And he shall set the sheep on his right hand, but the goats on the left. Then shall the King say unto them on his right hand, Come, ye blessed of my Father, inherit the kingdom prepared for you from the foundation of the world" (Matt. 25:31-34). Notice that Jesus tells those blessed of His Father to *inherit* the kingdom prepared for them. Peter speaks of this inheritance as "an inheritance incorruptible, and undefiled, and that fadeth not away, reserved in heaven for you" (1 Peter 1:4). If you

Chapter 4 — "Ye shall be free indeed"

do not choose to be wholly led by the Spirit of God and thus be God's child, if you do not choose the choice of faith to be God's child, if you do not let His love melt you to where you love Him with a child's love, and better, with a bride's love, but continue to wound Him by merely serving Him as nothing more than a servant, as if working for wages, then you are trying to turn the inheritance of eternal life into a matter of works, and in so doing, you will rob yourself of heaven at last!

Salvation does not consist of Christ, *and* the giving of tithes and offerings, *and* the doing of good works, *and* the keeping of the law. Salvation consists of Christ, Christ, and *only* Christ. Those who place themselves under the law declare that Christ is not enough for their salvation and that they must add to Him if they expect to be saved. Oh what folly! Do these not realize that it is this very act that will cost them their eternal life?

"What shall we say then? That the Gentiles, which followed not after righteousness, have attained to righteousness, even the righteousness which is of faith. But Israel, which followed after the law of righteousness, *hath not attained to the law of righteousness*. Wherefore? *Because they sought it not by faith, but as it were by the works of the law.* For they stumbled at that stumblingstone; As it is written, Behold, I lay in Sion a stumblingstone and rock of offence: and whosoever believeth on him shall not be ashamed" (Rom. 9:30-33).

The word gospel means good news, and *only* good news. Good news has absolutely nothing to do with bad news, and yet it seems that many preach a gospel of "good news" that is so deeply identified with bad news that the good news can scarcely be called good anymore. Who would want to be told that they can obtain salvation as a perfectly free gift that won't cost them anything but that few people will ever receive because it requires a lifetime commitment of struggles, sacrifices, and pain? Is that good news? Who would want to be told that

Saved by Works... Christ's Works!

they can have the next and better life for free, no strings attached, no small print to overlook, but that they will have to risk missing out on all the pleasures that this world has to offer in order to obtain it, and in the end they just might end up losing the joys of both worlds? Is that good news? No! That is a gospel that the loving Jesus never preached. The Lord in heaven does not intend that anyone need gamble their life here in hopes of obtaining a better life there. To all who will take the free gift, God gives to them the best of both worlds (see Mark 10:29, 30).

    Imagine the loving Savior calling all the children to come to Him so that He can share with them some really good news. The children quickly scramble together and gather about Him in eagerness to hear Him speak. One little girl even hops up on His lap and looks deep into His eyes, intently watching and waiting to catch every precious word that falls from His lips. Jesus begins to tell the children about how He wants to take them to a special place where there will be no more separation from loved ones, no more sickness, pain, death, or anything else that would ever make them feel sad again. He tells them that they will never get hurt there, that they will be only happy, and that they will live together with Him forever and will never get old or die. He tells them that He wants to do all of this for them, without it costing them a thing, and that He doesn't want them to even feel like they need to pay Him back for it. Every child's face instantly lights up with unspeakable joy, and the child on His lap throws her arms around Him and with grateful tears cries out, "Thank you, Jesus! Oh thank you so much! That just means so much to me!" She kisses Him on the cheek and sits back down on His lap, just as happy as can be. But then Jesus tells the children something else. He looks around at all the happy faces of the children about Him, and then rests His eyes upon the beaming face of the little girl in His lap and says, "The only

Chapter 4 — "Ye shall be free indeed"

problem is that you will probably never get there, because you aren't good enough now, and most likely never will be."

What, I ask you, do you think would be the children's response? Would not their hopes be crushed and their countenances sorrowed? What would be the response of the precious little girl sitting on Jesus' lap? Would not her tender heart be just smashed all to pieces? What would be your response, if as the parent of that little child, you saw and heard everything Jesus had just did and said? Would you not be indignant at such a cold and heartless thing to do and say? Now, what do you think God's response is, when His professed followers imitate this false Christ mentioned above? "With what judgment ye judge, ye shall be judged: and with what measure ye mete, it shall be measured to you again" (Matt. 7:2).

Paul says, "I am not ashamed of the gospel of Christ: for it is the power of God unto salvation to every one that believeth" (Rom. 1:16). The gospel of Christ means the good news of Jesus. And what does Paul say that this good news is? It is the power of God unto salvation. The good news *itself* is God's power to save man, for the gospel is expressed in the words of God, and it is the words of the gospel that have creative power to transform the sinner. But the good news is God's power to save only "every one that *believeth*." By merely believing that the gospel is true in your behalf, the good news itself creates a new heart in you. By believing that you are set free from the guilt of past sins and from the power that sin has over you, the creative power of the good news makes you fit to enter into the kingdom of God.

Stop trying to work for your salvation, you who have chosen Christ! Believe that God takes away your evil heart, that Christ *is in your heart*, that Christ *has saved you*, that Christ *has set you free*, and that your Father *has* an inheritance for you in heaven. Once you believe this such a love will spring up in your heart that the works will come, not because of some unwillful strain on your part, but because it would be an unwillful strain on your part to not do the works, for your heart is made new. Then it will be that the master called sin "shall not have dominion over you: for ye are not under the law, but under grace" (Rom. 6:14). Because "the grace of Christ" (Gal. 1:16), which is "the gospel of Christ . . . the power of God unto salvation" (Rom. 1:16), has given you "power to become the sons of God" (John 1:12), sin no longer has dominion over you. This is why you are not under the law of duty as a servant, but under the grace of God which has enabled you to love Him as a child and therefore serve Him. This is how Christ abides in your heart by faith, enabling you to live a perfectly sinless life.

The Lord Jesus said, "Love your enemies, bless them that curse you, do good to them that hate you, and pray for them which despitefully use you, and persecute you; That ye may be the children of your Father which is in heaven: for he maketh his sun to rise on the evil and on the good, and sendeth rain on the just and on the unjust" (Matt. 5:44, 45). Loving our enemies does not make us the children of God. This is a misconception. Rather, God, by making us His children with new hearts, causes us to love our enemies. Jesus said also, "Whosoever shall do the will of my Father which is in heaven, the same is my brother, and sister, and mother" (Mat. 12:50). Doing God's will does not make Christ our Brother. Rather, Christ, by making Himself our Brother, causes us to do God's will. When you read from the Scriptures, be careful that you do not read from effect to cause, because if you do, your life will be molded accordingly; rather, read from cause to effect.

Paul said, "Whatsoever ye do, do it heartily, as to the Lord, and not unto men; Knowing that of the Lord ye shall receive the reward of the inheritance: for ye serve the Lord Christ" (Col. 3:23, 24). In every aspect of life, into whatever line of work we are placed, no mat-

Chapter 4 — "Ye shall be free indeed"

ter where we are or what the duty is before us, we are to do it as if we were doing it for our Father in heaven. We are to do it with a heart full of the service of love. We are to take the greatest pleasure in pleasing Him who loved us first. If we will only live this way, then we shall always have something to be happy about. No matter how hard, annoying, or wearisome the task, we will take great delight in bringing joy to our Husband's heart, in bringing joy to the heart of Christ. And if you will do this, then know that "ye shall receive the reward of the inheritance." "Fear not, little flock; for it is your Father's good pleasure to give you the kingdom" (Luke 12:32).

If you will not accept Christ into your heart by faith and as a result love God out of a grateful heart that delights to serve Him as a bride would serve her beloved husband, then don't serve Him at all. The law that requires righteousness demands, "Thou shalt love the Lord thy God with all thy heart, and with all thy soul, and with all thy strength, and with all thy mind" (Luke 10:27). Christ "wants the whole heart and interest, or He will have none."[133] "I the LORD thy God am a jealous God" (Ex. 20:5). He says, "Set me as a seal upon thine heart, as a seal upon thine arm: for love is strong as death; jealousy is cruel as the grave: the coals thereof are coals of fire, which hath a most vehement flame. Many waters cannot quench love, neither can the floods drown it: if a man would give all the substance of his house for love, it would utterly be contemned" (S. of Sol. 8:6, 7).

Christ has given all of Himself to you, and He requires that you give all of yourself to Him. You are to own each other as your most precious of all possessions. "I am my beloved's, and my beloved is mine" is to be the language of your soul (S. of Sol. 6:3). But before this is possible, the kingdom of Satan must be broken by the kingdom of God.

When Christ "was demanded of the Pharisees, when the kingdom

Saved by Works... Christ's Works!

of God should come, he answered them and said, The kingdom of God cometh not with observation: Neither shall they say, Lo here! or, lo there! for, behold, the kingdom of God is within you" (Luke 17:20, 21). The Jews of old looked forward to a kingdom that the Messiah would establish on this earth, and they looked for its speedy fulfillment in the time of Christ, even though they did not believe Him to be the Messiah. But the True Messiah said, "My kingdom is not of this world" (John 18:36).

"The kingdom of God begins in the heart."[134] But how is it that the kingdom of God begins within the heart? Very simply! When the King's throne is in the heart, then of necessity His kingdom must be there also. "Not by the decisions of courts or councils or legislative assemblies, not by the patronage of worldly great men, is the kingdom of Christ established, but by the implanting of Christ's nature in humanity through the work of the Holy Spirit. 'As many as received Him, to them gave He power to become the sons of God, even to them that believe on His name: which were born, not of blood, nor of the will of the flesh, nor of the will of man, but of God.' John 1:12, 13. Here is the *only* power that can work the uplifting of mankind."[135]

Now, "we know that whosoever is born of God sinneth not . . . And we know that we are of God . . . And we know that the Son of God is come, and hath given us an understanding, that we may know him that is true, and we are in him that is true, even in his Son Jesus Christ. This is the true God, *and eternal life*" (1 John 5:18-20).

Jesus Christ is eternal life, and when He is abiding in the heart, we have eternal life. Though we can still choose to turn away from God and lose our inheritance, as long as we accept Christ into our hearts by faith, we have life eternal. We need not wait till Jesus comes to receive this promise—we may have it now, here, today, at this present moment.

Chapter 4 — "Ye shall be free indeed"

"And this is the record, that God hath given to us eternal life, and this life is in his Son. He that hath the Son hath life; and he that hath not the Son of God hath not life. These things have I written unto you that believe on the name of the Son of God; *that ye may know that ye have eternal life*, and that ye may believe on the name of the Son of God" (1 John 5:11-13). Not think, not reason, not speculate, but that you may *know* that you have eternal life.

Dear soul, simply make the choice of faith to believe that God takes away your sinful heart and that Christ lives in the new one that He gives you. Then God will not only be in the heart, but on the heart. Once this is done, the high demands of the law will be met, for "the righteousness of God is embodied in Christ. We receive righteousness by receiving Him. Not by painful struggles or wearisome toil, not by gift or sacrifice, is righteousness obtained; but it is freely given to every soul who hungers and thirsts to receive it. 'Ho, every one that thirsteth, come ye to the waters, and he that hath no money; come ye, buy, and eat, . . . without money and without price.' 'Their righteousness is of Me, saith the Lord,' and, 'This is His name whereby He shall be called, The Lord Our Righteousness.' Isaiah 55:1; 54:17; Jeremiah 23:6."[136] "Him that cometh to me I will in no wise cast out" (John 6:37).

Many perplexed and earnest souls, looking wistfully to heaven, with burning tears and broken hearts, cry out in an utter longing that envelops their whole being, "Lord! What must I do to be saved? Which of these many paths lead to heaven and eternal life? Which of these many signs tell the truth and point out the way of salvation?" The lovely voice of Jesus is heard in clear and distinct tones of understanding love, "*I am* the way, the truth, and the life" (John 14:6). "These things I have spoken unto you, that in me ye might have peace. In the world ye shall have tribulation: but be of good cheer; *I have* overcome

Saved by Works... Christ's Works!

the world" (John 16:33).

In that great day of victory, those depicted in Revelation as victorious overcomers will sing "the song of Moses" (Rev. 15:3). But what does the song of Moses say about the overcomers? Is it a song that tells of how *they* won the victory? Do the lines of that sacred hymn speak about how hard it was for them to overcome but how despite its miserable difficulty *they* still submitted to God and resisted the devil? Hear the words of that holy song as they echo down through the millenniums to our day. "I will sing unto the LORD, for *he* hath triumphed gloriously: the horse and his rider hath *he* thrown into the sea. *The LORD is my strength* and song, and *he is become my salvation*: he is my God, and I will prepare him an habitation; my father's God, and *I will exalt him. The LORD is a man of war*: the LORD is his name" (Ex. 15:1-3).

Chapter 4 — "Ye shall be free indeed"

The Doctrine of Witches

Trying so hard to keep the law;
Working and praying so much;
The harder I try, the harder I fall;
I get myself into a crunch.

Jesus sweetly says unto me,
"Oh please let Me live through you.
True you don't know how this can be;
Everyone else wonders too."

"Through Me so hard you've tried to live,
And you will never succeed.
My life *through you* I freely give;
I will root out every weed!"

"Your righteousness is, just filthy rags;
Your efforts to do good *are sin;*
Just hold up that little, tiny white flag;
And then for you *I will* win."

"Saved by My grace, through faith *all alone*;
Believing I'll do what I said;
Trusting yourself, while on your heart's throne;
You'll end up eternally dead!"

Saved by Works... Christ's Works!

Oh but you cry, "I must keep the law!
That is what the Bible teaches!"
"My dear little one, here is your great flaw:
That is the doctrine of witches!"

I keep the law, through you, My child,
If you let Me into your heart;
If you do not, sin will run wild,
And I will say, "Sinner, depart!"

The law will be kept, oh yes indeed!
But not by your efforts at all.
I'll stay in your heart, as the good seed,
And *I will* not let you fall.

"*I'll live My life, through you,* I said;
Not you, through Me, by works!
Take off that burden, heavy as lead;
I'm the One who does good works!"

The Holy Spirit flatters no man;
He comes to rebuke and reprove;
He does things according to His own plan;
The self-righteous rags to remove.

Salvation is said to be a free gift;
Why are you working so hard?
Good news is good, it helps to uplift,
But you the Savior have scarred.

Chapter 4 — "Ye shall be free indeed"

Stop teaching that false doctrine right now!
You're wounding the children of God!
You're knees before Satan do so lowly bow,
And you look at me like I am odd?

The Savior does offer, His free righteousness;
Those guilty rags off you He'll take.
By faith let Him live, His own righteousness;
It's your salvation at stake!

Chapter 5

"A way of escape"
1 Corinthians 10:31

"The thought that the righteousness of Christ is imputed to us, not because of any merit on our part, but as a free gift from God, is a precious thought. The enemy of God and man is not willing that this truth should be clearly presented; for he knows that if the people receive it fully, *his power will be broken.* If he can control minds, so that doubt and unbelief and darkness shall compose the experience of those who claim to be the children of God, he can overcome them with temptation. The simple faith that takes God at his word should be encouraged. God's people must have that faith which will lay hold of divine power; 'for by grace are ye saved through faith; and that not of yourselves: it is the gift of God.' Those who believe that God for Christ's sake has forgiven their sins should not, through temptation, fail to press on to fight the good fight of faith. Their faith should grow stronger until their Christian life, as well as their words, shall declare, 'The blood of Jesus Christ his Son cleanseth us from all sin.'"[1]

Of Jesus we read, "As many as *received* him, to them gave he power to become *the sons of God,* even to them that *believe* on his name: *Which were born . . . of God*" (John 1:12, 13). "Whosoever is born of God doth not commit sin; for his seed remaineth in him: and he cannot sin, because he is born of God" (1 John 3:9). To those who

Chapter 5 — "A way of escape"

receive Christ, those who *believe* Christ, is given power to become the sons of God. These people John says, "were born . . . of God." And by what means were they born of God? They were "*born again*, not of corruptible seed, but of incorruptible, *by the word of God*" (1 Peter 1:23). This word performed in their behalf when they received Christ, when they believed in Him. This word of God created them anew when they depended upon that creative word to do the thing that it said. The people who are born of God are called "the sons of God." The only way that we can become the children of God, and remain the children of God, is by receiving the promise of a new birth *by faith*, for Paul says, "Ye are all the *children of God by faith* in Christ Jesus" (Gal. 3:26).

To be born of God is to be born of the Spirit of God. "Except a man be born again, he cannot see the kingdom of God. . . . Except a man be born of water and of the Spirit, he cannot enter into the kingdom of God" (John 3:3-5). "Except ye be converted, and become as little children, ye shall not enter into the kingdom of heaven" (Matt. 18:3).

"The Spirit was to be given as a regenerating agent, and without this the sacrifice of Christ would have been of no avail. The power of evil had been strengthening for centuries, and the submission of men to this satanic captivity was amazing. Sin could be resisted and overcome only through the mighty agency of the Third Person of the Godhead, who would come with no modified energy, but in the fullness of divine power. It is the Spirit that makes effectual what has been wrought out by the world's Redeemer. It is by the Spirit that the heart is made pure. Through the Spirit the believer becomes a partaker of the divine nature. Christ has given His Spirit as a divine power to overcome all hereditary and cultivated tendencies to evil, and to impress His own character upon His church." [2]

Saved by Works... Christ's Works!

"As many as received him, to them gave he power to become the sons of God, even to them that *believe* on His name: Which were born, *not of blood, nor of the will of the flesh, nor of the will of man, but of God*" (John 1:12, 13). "So then *it is* not of him that *willeth*, nor of him that *runneth, but of God that sheweth mercy*" (Rom. 9:16). Those who are born again are not born again because of any willing or working on their part, but because God wills and works on His part, because God is merciful. Man must allow God to work by believing His promises, but God alone is the one who actually recreates the soul in Jesus.

"Whosoever is born of God doth not commit sin; for his seed remaineth in him: and he cannot sin, because he is born of God. In this the children of God are manifest, and the children of the devil: whosoever doeth not righteousness is not of God" (1 John 3:9, 10). "Little children, let no man deceive you: he that doeth righteousness is righteous, even as he is righteous. He that committeth sin is of the devil; for the devil sinneth from the beginning. For this purpose the Son of God was manifested, that he might destroy the works of the devil" (verses 7, 8).

Now, "we know that whosoever is born of God sinneth not" (1 John 5:18). "For whatsoever is born of God overcometh the world: and this is the victory that overcometh the world, *even our faith*" (verse 4). Faith is the victory that overcomes the world, and the reason for this is because faith is that which allows God's Word to cause us to be born again so that we "cannot sin."

Satan knows that He has absolutely no power over those who are the children of God by faith, for God has said of them, You cannot sin (1 John 3:9). Satan knows that all of his evil designs must bow to that all-powerful word which, once spoken, makes that which was spoken a fact that he cannot possibly reverse. When the weakest soul lays hold on the promise that he is the child of God, the strongest hold that Satan

Chapter 5 — "A way of escape"

has over him will instantly be wrenched from his grasp by the "quick, and powerful" Word of God (Heb. 4:12). Satan knows this, and he exerts himself to the utmost to destroy all who would be God's children.

In the wilderness of temptation, Satan came to Christ, tempting Him to commit the sin of unbelief. "If thou be the Son of God, command that these stones be made bread" (Matt. 4:3). Here Satan's insidious character is revealed. "*If* thou be the Son of God." "Christ was tempted to answer the 'if;' but He refrained from the slightest acceptance of the doubt. He would not imperil His life in order to give evidence to Satan."[3] Satan did not merely say to Christ, "Command that these stones be made bread." Satan's desire was to get Christ to consider whether or not He really was God's Son, to get Him to question, to doubt, God's Word. Therefore he asked, "*If* thou be the Son of God." Four verses ago, God had just declared from heaven, "This is my beloved Son, in whom I am well pleased" (Matt. 3:17). Satan wanted Christ to doubt that word and therefore call His Father a liar. But, "unless Christ should consent to temptation, He could not be overcome. Not all the power of earth or hell could force Him in the slightest degree to depart from the will of His Father."[4]

Satan comes to us with just such temptations. Satan knows that if he can get us to question or consider, even in the least, whether or not we are God's children, faith must then let go its hold on the sure promise of God's Word, because faith doesn't ask, "Is it so?" but says, "It is so."

Satan came to Eve in Eden saying, "Yea, hath God said, Ye shall not eat of every tree of the garden?" (Gen. 3:1). Thus he insinuates doubt into Eve's mind. If God said it, then there is no reason to question the matter. But Satan came to her saying, "Is that really what God said? Was God really speaking the truth?" When Eve paused to consider whether or not God had spoken the truth, she accepted the doubt.

Saved by Works. . . Christ's Works!

So Satan comes to us saying, "Has God said that you are His child? Has God said that Christ is in you? Is Christ *really* in you? Are *you* really His child?" If we pause to consider these questions, then we aren't God's children and Christ is not in us because faith would say, "*It is so,*" not, "Is it so?" Therefore, if we accept the doubt, then of necessity Christ must leave the heart because He abides in the heart *by faith.*

"Eve really believed the words of Satan, but her belief did not save her from the penalty of sin. She disbelieved the words of God, and this was what led to her fall. In the judgment men will not be condemned because they conscientiously believed a lie, but because they did not believe the truth, because they neglected the opportunity of learning what is truth. Notwithstanding the sophistry of Satan to the contrary, it is always disastrous to disobey God. We must set our hearts to know what is truth. All the lessons which God has caused to be placed on record in his word are for our warning and instruction. They are given to save us from deception. Their neglect will result in ruin to ourselves. Whatever contradicts God's word, we may be sure proceeds from Satan."[5]

As God's children, Satan tempts us by insinuating evil thoughts into our minds such as, "Oh how I wish I could just bust that guy's teeth out!" With astonishment we wonder how such a thought could come from us when by faith we have been claiming a new and good heart from God. Satan, a master at quoting Scripture, says to us, "'out of the heart of men, proceed evil thoughts' (Mark 7:21) and 'as he thinketh in his heart, so is he' (Prov. 23:7). If you are God's child, would you *really* be having such thoughts?"

Now is when the test comes. Should the startled soul doubt that he is God's child? Should he now put to question the promise that God gave him a new heart? Should he step back and just merely consider whether or not Christ is really abiding in his heart? *No! Never!* If he

Chapter 5 — "A way of escape"

gives the slightest consideration to such thoughts, he fails to believe God's promise and he has unconsciously declared within himself that God must not have fulfilled His word and that He is therefore a liar. And as a result of his *unbelief*, God's promise ceases to be fulfilled to him, for Christ abides in the heart *by faith*. He would now be left perfectly helpless in the hands of the devil.

"Temptation is no sin; the sin is in yielding to temptation."[6] "Temptation is enticement to sin, and this does not proceed from God, but from Satan and from the evil of our own hearts."[7] These are the only two sources of our temptations. Christ was "in the wilderness forty days, *tempted of Satan*" (Mark 1:13), and the apostle James said, "Every man is tempted, when he is drawn away *of his own lust*, and enticed" (James 1:14).

God's Word says that we will have a pure heart from Him the instant we believe the promise. So if we are claiming this promise and are tempted to do evil, and it *feels* like the temptation is coming from our heart, we must understand that this temptation is not coming from our heart, for God has cleansed our heart and it is pure and holy. The very nature of that heart recoils from evil because Christ is in it. Therefore, since the temptation is not from the heart, we need not pay it the least attention, for it is not a thing significant enough to consider. If the heart is pure and the Lord Jesus is there, why should we be concerned about the feelings of the body?

All the powers of hell cannot force a good heart to bring forth an evil work, for the Word of God has declared this to be impossible. Satan knows this, and therefore, when tempting us to do evil for the purpose of destroying us, his goal is not to increase the strength of his temptations and somehow force us to commit a sinful action, *but to change the condition of the heart from good to evil*. Satan knows that the heart is made good by the Word of God *through faith* and faith

Saved by Works. . . Christ's Works!

only, and since he cannot reverse the Word of God, his temptations are solely focused to get us to question, consciously or unconsciously, whether or not our heart is really good. If Satan can get us to question, to doubt, the promise that God has given us a new heart, then the heart must of necessity become evil, for the heart is good *only through faith*.

Satan's *only* hope in overcoming man is in getting him to believe his insinuated lies. Satan has lost *the* battle, and he has lost *the* war. But if he can get the Christian to believe that this is not the case, then he can at least win *a* battle. That is his studied effort. In every temptation ever recorded in the history of the Scriptures, Satan was only trying to get the tempted one to believe a lie. That is the *only* power that Satan has—the power of deception. Truth declares him as defeated, powerless, and nothing more than a conquered and fallen enemy, and so Satan weaves his insidious lies about to gain power over those who will accept them.

To accomplish his designs, Satan often plays with our feelings so that we will *feel* like our heart is not really good, that Jesus is not really in our heart, that we really do not believe, and that our hearts really desire to do evil. "Satan will, if he is unsuspected, give feelings and impressions."[8] *"There are thoughts and feelings suggested and aroused by Satan* that annoy even the best of men; but if they are not cherished, if they are repulsed as hateful, the soul is not contaminated with guilt, and no other is defiled by their influence."[9] If the devil can get us to trust in his insinuated thoughts and feelings and believe in them above the Word of God, then he wins the battle, for if we believe his insinuated thoughts and feelings, which are perfectly contrary to faith and to what the Word of God has declared, then we really don't believe the Word of God, and since we don't believe, then of necessity Christ must leave the heart, for He is there *only* through the channel of faith.

Chapter 5 — "A way of escape"

Practically speaking, let's say that Satan causes something to happen for the purpose of getting us to manifest an irritated temper toward someone. Immediately after the thing happens, instead of tempting us by saying, "Tell so-and-so to go jump off a cliff," Satan inserts his temptation into our minds as if it were our own thought saying, "What's your problem? Go jump off a cliff!" At the same time he does this, he inserts in us a feeling of irritation and anger. Without Christ in the heart *by faith,* we will instantly bark out in irritation, "Man what's your problem? Go jump off a cliff!"

When brought into such a situation as this, or the countless others that Satan will bring to us, we must not acknowledge within ourselves that we really *want* to do evil. If we do, then we will. If God has given us a new heart from which proceeds good desires, good impulses, good feelings, and good thoughts, then if we acknowledge the insinuated evil thoughts and feelings as true, that we really do *want* to do evil, then we are, consciously or unconsciously, telling God that He didn't really give us a good heart. When we do this, the heart instantly changes from good to evil, for the heart is only good when, *as by faith* (acknowledging God's Word as true), we claim the promise of a good heart. The instant we accept the insinuated evil thoughts and feelings as true they become true, for the heart has become evil through unbelief, and we have no barrier against sin.

Satan would tempt us to sin in such as way as to make us think that we have already committed the sin at heart, and since we have already committed the sin in our heart, he reasons, it is not anymore of a sin to commit the action. When he insinuates the evil thoughts and feelings in us, he would assume upon us that we have already been overcome by temptation in that we are thinking and feeling evil. But this evil is *from Satan.* If he can get us to *believe* that we have fallen to temptation and that we are therefore corrupt in heart, then we become corrupt in heart, for faith must then let go its hold upon the promise of God that we have a new and uncorrupt heart. *"Temptation is no sin*; the sin is in yielding to temptation."[10]

This is where we need to continually watch and pray. If we can only discern and acknowledge Satan's insinuations as false, by the power of God's keeping, then we are secure from *all* evil. And how are we kept from all evil? Well, what says the promise of the Word? "Now unto *him that is able to keep you from falling*" (Jude 1:24). So, since it is Him who will keep you from accepting Satan's insinuations, according to the promise, only believe that promise and *it is done*. The promise is, "*He will* keep the feet of his saints" (1 Sam. 2:9). "Now *the God of peace . . . Make you perfect* in every good work to do his will, working in you that which is wellpleasing in his sight" (Heb. 13, 20, 21), which includes rejecting Satan's insinuations. (Heb 13:20, 21.) Speak the words of simple faith, "I know whom I have believed, and am persuaded that *he is able* to keep that which I have committed unto him against that day" (2 Tim. 1:12). And do not only believe that He is able to keep you from accepting Satan's insinuations, but that *He will* keep you from accepting them. "Being confident of this very thing, that he which hath begun a good work in you *will perform it* until the day of Jesus Christ" (Phil. 1:6). Then it will be as it has always been, "According to your faith *be it unto you*" (Matt. 9:29). "We are secure, perfectly secure from the enemy's subtlety while we have unwavering trust in God."[11]

"There are thoughts and feelings suggested and aroused by Satan that annoy even the best of men; *but if they are not cherished, if they are repulsed as hateful, the soul is not contaminated with guilt,* and no other is defiled by their influence."[12] "Temptation is no sin; the sin is in yielding to temptation."[13]

Child of God, Satan will come to you and insinuate that you do not delight in prayer and the searching of the Scriptures. He will come to you insinuating that you do not delight to do God's will, that you do not take delight in doing the gospel work. But the Word of God says that when the law is in your heart by faith, *you do* delight to do God's will (Ps. 40:8). Satan will insinuate to you that you are in love with sin and all of the worlds engrossing pleasures and that you really have no heartfelt love for Christ. But these insinuations are all lies! Do not believe them! God has *said* that since you believe in His promise, you love Him and delight in doing His will. If you will only resist Satan's insinuated thoughts and feelings, it is only a matter of time before Satan is forced to leave you alone, for the all-powerful creative word of God says, "Resist the devil, *and he will flee from you*" (James 4:7). "Temptation is resisted when man is powerfully influenced to do a wrong action; and, knowing that he can do it, *resists, by faith*, with a firm hold upon divine power."[14]

The book of Proverbs says that as a man "thinketh in his heart, so is he" (Prov. 23:7). If a man thinks in his heart that he *really* wants to do evil, then he does want to do evil because his heart is evil as the result of his thinking/believing. If a man thinks in his heart that he *really* wants to do good, then he does want to do good because his heart has become good as the result of his thinking/believing. So it is that the words of Jesus hold true in both cases, "According to man's faith, it is unto him."

"'The prince of this world cometh,' said Jesus, 'and hath nothing in Me.' John 14:30. There was in Him nothing that responded to Satan's sophistry. He did not consent to sin. Not even by a thought did He yield to temptation. So it may be with us. Christ's humanity was united with divinity; He was fitted for the conflict by the indwelling of the Holy Spirit. And He came to make us partakers of the divine nature. So long as we are united to Him *by faith*, sin has no more do-

Saved by Works. . . Christ's Works!

minion over us. God reaches for the hand of faith in us to direct it to lay fast hold upon the divinity of Christ, that we may attain to perfection of character.

"And how this is accomplished, Christ has shown us. By what means did He overcome in the conflict with Satan? By the word of God. *Only by the word* could He resist temptation. 'It is written,' He said. And unto us are given 'exceeding great and precious promises: that by these ye might be partakers of the divine nature, having escaped the corruption that is in the world through lust.' 2 Peter 1:4. Every promise in God's word is ours. 'By every word that proceedeth out of the mouth of God' are we to live. When assailed by temptation, look not to circumstances or to the weakness of self, but to the power of the word. *All its strength is yours*. 'Thy word,' says the psalmist, 'have I hid in mine heart, that I might not sin against Thee.' '*By the word of Thy lips* I have kept me from the paths of the destroyer.' Psalm 119:11; 17:4."[15] Remember, "temptation is resisted when man is powerfully influenced to do a wrong action; and, knowing that he can do it, *resists, by faith*, with a firm hold upon divine power."[16]

Question: Does the prince of this world have something in you? If you say that he does, then he does because you believe it to be so. If you say that you only hope that he does not, then you are questioning whether or not he does, and therefore, you doubt the Word of God and have no barrier against sin. Now, if you say that he does not, then he does not, because Jesus says, "According to your faith *be it unto you*" (Matt. 9:29).

There are two ways Satan seeks to destroy us. He either tries to get us to doubt the Word of God, or tries to get us to believe that the Word of God will do something that it never said it would do. The first one is not having faith. The second one is presumption, a faith that is false.

"Faith is in no sense allied to presumption. Only he who has true

Chapter 5 — "A way of escape"

faith is secure against presumption. For presumption is Satan's counterfeit of faith. Faith claims God's promises, and brings forth fruit in obedience. Presumption also claims the promises, but uses them as Satan did, to excuse transgression. Faith would have led our first parents to trust the love of God, and to obey His commands. Presumption led them to transgress His law, believing that His great love would save them from the consequence of their sin. It is not faith that claims the favor of Heaven without complying with the conditions on which mercy is to be granted. Genuine faith has its foundation in the promises and provisions of the Scriptures.

"Often when Satan has failed of exciting distrust, he succeeds in leading us to presumption. If he can cause us to place ourselves unnecessarily in the way of temptation, he knows that the victory is his. God will preserve all who walk in the path of obedience; but to depart from it is to venture on Satan's ground. There we are sure to fall. The Saviour has bidden us, 'Watch ye and pray, lest ye enter into temptation.' Mark 14:38. Meditation and prayer would keep us from rushing unbidden into the way of danger, and thus we should be saved from many a defeat."[17]

Satan, having failed to get Christ to doubt the Word of God which said, "This is my beloved Son" (Matt. 3:17), now sought to get Jesus to believe a promise that God had never made. But again his aim was to get Christ to doubt God's Word if he could. "*If* thou be the Son of God, *cast thyself down*." And being a master of quoting the Scriptures, he cunningly reminded Christ, "For it is written, He shall give his angels charge concerning thee: and in their hands they shall bear thee up, lest at any time thou dash thy foot against a stone" (Matt. 4:6).

Christ defeated Satan in his first temptation with an "it is written," and Satan now sought to use the Word of God for his own purposes. But he did not quote all of God's promise. The promise of God said,

Saved by Works... Christ's Works!

"He shall give his angels charge over thee, *to keep thee in all thy ways*. They shall bear thee up in their hands, lest thou dash thy foot against a stone" (Ps. 91:11, 12).

"When Satan quoted the promise, 'He shall give His angels charge over Thee,' he omitted the words, 'to keep Thee in all Thy ways;' that is, in all the ways of God's choosing. Jesus refused to go outside the path of obedience. While manifesting perfect trust in His Father, He would not place Himself, unbidden, in a position that would necessitate the interposition of His Father to save Him from death. He would not force Providence to come to His rescue, and thus fail of giving man an example of trust and submission."[18] Should Christ be in the path of God's choosing and danger come upon Him He could be sure that God would keep Him. But to put Himself in a position where God had not promised Him protection would be presumption.

"Jesus declared to Satan, 'It is written again, Thou shalt not tempt the Lord thy God.' These words were spoken by Moses to the children of Israel when they thirsted in the desert, and demanded that Moses should give them water, exclaiming, 'Is the Lord among us, or not?' Exodus 17:7. God had wrought marvelously for them; yet in trouble they doubted Him, and demanded evidence that He was with them. In their unbelief they sought to put Him to the test. And Satan was urging Christ to do the same thing. God had already testified that Jesus was His Son; and now to ask for proof that He was the Son of God would be putting God's word to the test,—tempting Him. And the same would be true of asking for that which God had not promised. It would manifest distrust, and be really proving, or tempting, Him."[19]

"The tempter thought to take advantage of Christ's humanity, and urge Him to presumption. But while Satan can solicit, he cannot compel to sin. He said to Jesus, 'Cast Thyself down,' knowing that he could not cast Him down; for God would interpose to deliver

Chapter 5 — "A way of escape"

Him. Nor could Satan force Jesus to cast Himself down. Unless Christ should consent to temptation, He could not be overcome. Not all the power of earth or hell could force Him in the slightest degree to depart from the will of His Father."[20]

"Ye shall not tempt the LORD your God" (Deut. 6:16). This was the command Jesus quoted when Satan thought to lead Christ into presumption. But this was not merely a commandment. Quoting merely a commandment in the time of temptation does nothing to overcome sin. "Every command is a *promise.*"[21] Christ, by exercising faith in the promise that He would not tempt God, had the promise fulfilled to Him. So it was in the final temptation. When Satan said to Christ, "Fall down and worship me," Jesus quoted the promise of God saying, "*Thou shalt* worship the Lord thy God, and him only shalt thou serve" (Matt. 4:10). That command, that promise, fulfilled itself to Christ because He depended upon that word of promise to do what it said and acknowledged that it couldn't do anything else because of its creative power. Christ well knew of the creative power of the word. He knew that man was to live "*by every word that proceedeth out of the mouth of God*" (Matt. 4:4). He knew that "*the just shall live by his faith*" (Hab. 2:4). And He knew that faith was to take God at His word. This simple faith in God's Word, that ignored the insinuated thoughts and feelings of the devil, is what kept Christ from entering into presumption.

Satan will also tempt us to deal presumptuously with God. He will come to us saying things like, "Ask God for power to overcome temptation, and you shall have it. Hasn't God said, 'Ask and it shall be given you' (Matt. 7:7), and that the reason 'ye have not' is 'because ye ask not' (James 4:2)? Hasn't God promised that 'he shall give thee the desires of thine heart' (Ps. 37:4)? Are you not asking for a good thing? Surely it is according to His will for you to overcome temptation. It is

Saved by Works... Christ's Works!

true that you haven't received power to overcome sin in the past because you didn't really believe His Word, but now that you do and you understand what faith is, here is your chance to receive a necessary blessing as long as God fulfils His promises."

The first part of such a temptation is very plausible, but the very last part is deceitful. "As long as God fulfils His promises"? Such a statement as this would lead us to test God, because since we really "believe," it's just a matter of whether or not God does His part. But it is written, "Ye shall not tempt the LORD your God" (Deut. 6:16). To put God to the test, to prove whether or not He will do what He said, is tempting Him. But "we should not present our petitions to God to prove whether He will fulfill His word, but because He will fulfill it; not to prove that He loves us, but because He loves us."[22]

Some people might call it presumption for someone to say that Christ is in his heart because that would be saying he cannot sin. But when asked if Christ is in your heart, it would be sin to not speak according to faith and give an answer of question or doubt. If Paul wasn't afraid to declare before many, "Christ liveth in me" (Gal. 2:20), then why should we be? Paul was not afraid to claim that Christ was in his heart. But he would have great reason to fear if he didn't, for he would then be at the mercy of the enemy who has no mercy. Paul never said, "*I* cannot sin." It was impossible for *Paul* to do anything but sin. But Christ who was in Paul could not sin.

If one is continually accepting Christ into his heart by faith, he will see no sin manifested in his life. But when he comes to a better understanding of God's law, he may find that he *has sinned*. But he need not listen to the temptations of Satan and doubt the promise that Christ was in his heart when he did these things. Paul says, "Where no law is, there is no transgression" (Rom. 4:15). At the times of ignorance, God winks. If you have not known the law, God doesn't look

Chapter 5 — "A way of escape"

at you as having broken it, even though in a technical sense you have. But if you continue to break His law of which you have now come to an understanding of, then God considers it sin in you. "The times of this ignorance God winked at; but now commandeth all men every where to repent" (Acts 17:30). "If I had not come and spoken unto them, they had not had sin: but now they have no cloak for their sin" (John 15:22).

It should be well understood by now that temptation, though it may come at us strong and hard, is not so hard to overcome because we don't overcome it, God does. As long as we believe that God submits our wills unto Himself and that Christ dwells in our hearts, God overcomes for us. Satan strives to get us to doubt these promises, for if he fails to do this, he loses the battle because he cannot overcome the almighty Word. We must depend upon the Word of God to do what it says, knowing that it cannot possibly do anything else. As long as you are a child of God by faith in Christ Jesus with Him abiding in your heart, the devil cannot touch you. If you will only hold to this position, you cannot fail of victory. "*Through faith* the soul is kept from sin."[23]

If man will never commit the sin of unbelief, he will never commit any other sin. *Unbelief is the sin*, and the results of the unbelief are the actions of sin.

"There are those who have known the pardoning love of Christ and who really desire to be children of God, yet they realize that their character is imperfect, their life faulty, and they are ready to doubt whether their hearts have been renewed by the Holy Spirit. To such I would say, *Do not draw back in despair.*"[24] "Submit yourselves therefore to God [by faith]. Resist the devil [by faith], and he will flee from you" (James 4:7). For "this is the victory that overcometh the world, even our faith" (1 John 5:4), "and that not of yourselves: it is the gift of God" (Eph. 2:8). Faith is the victory, and this faith is a gift from God.

Saved by Works. . . Christ's Works!

"Thanks be to God, which *giveth* us the victory through our Lord Jesus Christ" (1 Cor. 15:57).

"We should not lose courage when assailed by temptation. Often when placed in a trying situation we doubt that the Spirit of God has been leading us. But it was the Spirit's leading that brought Jesus into the wilderness to be tempted by Satan."[25] The Scripture says that Jesus was "led up of the Spirit into the wilderness to be tempted of the devil" (Matt. 4:1). "When God brings us into trial, He has a purpose to accomplish *for our good*. Jesus did not presume on God's promises by going unbidden into temptation, neither did He give up to despondency when temptation came upon Him. Nor should we. 'God is faithful, who will not suffer you to be tempted above that ye are able; but will with the temptation also make a way to escape, that ye may be able to bear it.' He says, 'Offer unto God thanksgiving; and pay thy vows unto the Most High: and call upon Me in the day of trouble: I will deliver thee, and thou shalt glorify Me.' 1 Corinthians 10:13; Psalm 50:14, 15."[26]

Since the exercise of our faith, the human will, means everything to us, "how to exercise faith should be made very plain. To every promise of God there are conditions. If we are willing to do His will, all His strength is ours. Whatever gift He promises, is in the promise itself. 'The seed is the word of God.' Luke 8:11. As surely as the oak is in the acorn, so surely is the gift of God in His promise. If we receive the promise, we have the gift."[27] "*Remember that the exercise of faith is the one means of preserving it.* Should you sit always in one position, without moving, your muscles would become strengthless and your limbs would lose the power of motion. The same is true in regard to your religious experience. You must have faith in the promises of God. . . . Faith will perfect itself in exercise and activity."[28]

Again, the understanding we most need is "understanding how to

Chapter 5 — "A way of escape"

exercise faith. This is the science of the gospel. The Scripture declares, 'Without faith it is impossible to please God.' The knowledge of what the Scripture means when urging upon us the necessity of cultivating faith, is more essential than any other knowledge that can be acquired. We suffer much trouble and grief because of our unbelief, and our ignorance of how to exercise faith. We must break through the clouds of unbelief. We can not have a healthy Christian experience, we can not obey the gospel unto salvation, until the science of faith is better understood, and until more faith is exercised."[29]

Chapter 6

"This is life eternal"
John 17:3

"In His prayer to the Father, Christ gave to the world a lesson which should be graven on mind and soul. 'This is life eternal,' He said, 'that they might know Thee the only true God, and Jesus Christ, whom thou hast sent.' John 17:3. This is true education. It imparts power."[1] "Why is it that we do not realize the value of this knowledge? Why are not these glorious truths glowing in our hearts, trembling upon our lips, and pervading our whole being?"[2] "Now, as never before, we need to understand the true science of education. If we fail to understand this, we shall never have a place in the kingdom of God. 'This is life eternal, that they might know thee, the only true God, and Jesus Christ whom thou hast sent.' If this is the price of heaven, shall not our education be conducted on these lines? Christ must be everything to us."[3] "The experimental knowledge of God and of Jesus Christ whom He has sent, transforms man into the image of God. It gives to man the mastery of himself, bringing every impulse and passion of the lower nature under the control of the higher powers of the mind. It makes its possessor a son of God and an heir of heaven. It brings him into communion with the mind of the Infinite, and opens to him the rich treasures of the universe."[4]

But what does it mean to know God? Jeremiah gives us the an-

Chapter 6 — "This is life eternal"

swer, "Thus saith the LORD, Let not the wise man glory in his wisdom, neither let the mighty man glory in his might, let not the rich man glory in his riches: But let him that glorieth glory in this, that he understandeth and *knoweth* me, that I am the LORD which exercise lovingkindness, judgment, and righteousness, in the earth: for in these things I delight, saith the LORD" (Jer. 9:23, 24). To know God is to know His character, and this we can only know by learning about Him from His Word, His creation, and personal communion with Him.

Paul said, "I count all things but loss for the excellency of the knowledge *of* Christ Jesus my Lord: for whom I have suffered the loss of all things, and do count them but dung, that I may win Christ, And be found in him, not having mine own righteousness, which is of the law, but that which is through the faith of Christ, the righteousness which is of God by faith: That I may *know* him, and the power of his resurrection, and the fellowship of his sufferings, being made conformable unto his death" (Phil. 3:8-10).

Here, Paul shows that it is a knowledge *of* Christ that enables us to *know* Him. But he also brings out that if we want to know God we first need to have "the righteousness which is of God by faith." Not our own righteousness, but His righteousness. Paul also brings to view the same sort of thought when he was speaking to the saints at Ephesus saying, "I bow my knees unto the Father of our Lord Jesus Christ . . . That Christ may dwell in your hearts by faith; *that ye*, being rooted and grounded in love, May be able to comprehend with all saints what is the breadth, and length, and depth, and height; And to know the love of Christ, which passeth knowledge, that ye might be filled with all the fulness of God" (Eph. 3:14-19). To have Christ in the heart is to have His righteousness, and Paul desired this for those at Ephesus to the intent that they might comprehend and know the love of Christ which passeth knowledge. The condition of eternal life is to know God, and

Saved by Works. . . Christ's Works!

this knowledge we obtain when by faith we allow Him to dwell in our hearts. The precious promise is, "I will give them an heart to know me" (Jer. 24:7).

The character of God was declared to Moses as "merciful and gracious, longsuffering, and abundant in goodness and truth, Keeping mercy for thousands, forgiving iniquity and transgression and sin, and that will by no means clear the guilty" (Ex. 34:6, 7). Knowing God is *the condition* of receiving eternal life, and "when we know God as it is our privilege to know Him, our life *will be* a life of continual obedience. Through an appreciation of the character of Christ, through communion with God, sin will become hateful to us."[5]

Why did God declare His character to Moses? Because Moses asked God saying, "I beseech Thee, shew me Thy glory. And he [God] said, I will make all my goodness pass before thee, and I will proclaim the name of the LORD before thee" (Ex. 33:18, 19). In fulfillment of His promise to Moses that He would show him His glory, God declared His character to him. So then, the glory of God is His character. And "we all, with open face beholding as in a glass the glory of the Lord, are changed into the same image" (2 Cor. 3:18).

"As we near the close of earth's history, Satan redoubles his efforts to cast his hellish shadow over us, in order that he may cause us to turn our eyes away from Christ. If he can prevent us from beholding Jesus, we shall be overcome; but we must not permit him to do this."[6] "Satan invents unnumbered schemes to occupy our minds, that they may not dwell upon the very work with which we ought to be best acquainted. The archdeceiver hates the great truths that bring to view an atoning sacrifice and an all-powerful mediator. He knows that with him everything depends on his diverting minds from Jesus and His truth."[7]

Then, "let the mind dwell upon His love, upon the beauty, the perfection, of His character. Christ in His self-denial, Christ in His humiliation, Christ in His purity and holiness, Christ in His matchless love—this is the subject for the soul's contemplation. It is by loving Him, copying Him, *depending wholly upon Him*, that you are to be transformed into His likeness."[8] "Look unto me, and be ye saved, all the ends of the earth: for I am God, and there is none else" (Isa. 45:22).

God says, "Arise, shine; for thy light is come, and the glory of the LORD is risen upon thee. For, behold, the darkness shall cover the earth, and gross darkness the people: but the LORD shall arise upon thee, and His glory shall be seen upon thee" (Isa. 60:1, 2). But what is this darkness that covers the earth and the people? To answer this we read the writings of Paul. He says, "God, who commanded the light to shine out of darkness, hath shined in our hearts, to give the light of the knowledge of the glory of God in the face of Jesus Christ" (2 Cor. 4:6). Paul says that the knowledge of the glory—the character—of God is a light; therefore, when men do not have a right knowledge of God's character, they are in darkness.

"It is the darkness of misapprehension of God that is enshrouding the world. Men are losing their knowledge of His character. It has been misunderstood and misinterpreted. At this time a message from God is to be proclaimed, a message illuminating in its influence and saving in its power. His character is to be made known. Into the darkness of the world is to be shed the light of His glory, the light of His goodness, mercy, and truth."[9] "Lucifer in heaven had sinned in the light of God's glory. To him as to no other created being was given a revelation of God's love. Understanding the character of God, knowing His goodness, Satan chose to follow his own selfish, independent will. This choice was final. There was no more that God could do to save him. But man was deceived; his mind was darkened by Satan's sophistry. The height and depth of the love of God he did not know.

Saved by Works... Christ's Works!

For him there was hope in a knowledge of God's love. By beholding His character he might be drawn back to God."[10]

But how is the knowledge of God's character going to be made known to dispel the darkness? The command is, "Arise, shine; for thy light is come, and the glory of the LORD is risen *upon thee*" (Isa. 60:1). You are to shine God's character to the world, and Paul says just how this is to be done. "God," he says, "who commanded the light to shine out of darkness, hath shined in our hearts, to give the light of the knowledge of the glory of God" (2 Cor. 4:6). Who has shined in our hearts? God has! Notice that Paul didn't say that God has shined *on* our hearts, but *in* our hearts. God is the One who is shining, and the only way that He can shine *in* our hearts is if He is *in* our hearts. And for what purpose is He there? To give the light of the knowledge of His character. But before we can shine God's character, we must have it.

There are two things we need to do to obtain God's character. First, we must have God in the heart by faith, because He is the One who shines in the heart to make known the knowledge of His character. Second, we must behold God's character, for "we all, with open face beholding as in a glass the glory of the Lord, are changed into the same image" (2 Cor. 3:18). It is by beholding the standard of righteousness as revealed in Christ that we see our defects of character so that we might choose to have them expelled from the soul.

Jesus says, "I am the light of the world" (John 8:12), but He also says, "Ye are the light of the world. . . . Let your light so shine before men, that they may see your good works, and glorify your Father which is in heaven" (Matt. 5:14, 16). Jesus first says that we are the light of the world, and then He says that we *have* a light that we need to shine to the world. The reason we are the light of the world is because He who is the Light of the world in is us. He is our light, and we are to allow Him to shine through us. We are to be nothing but a window into heaven that men may see, not us, but Jesus only. The good works that men are to see as a result of our shining this light are not our works but His. We are the tool, He is the workman. We are the candle, He is the flame.

"But Jesus did not bid the disciples, 'Strive to make your light shine;' He said, 'Let it shine.' If Christ is dwelling in the heart, it is *impossible* to conceal the light of His presence. If those who profess to be followers of Christ are not the light of the world, it is because the vital power has left them; if they have no light to give, it is because they have no connection with the Source of light."[11]

"Those who have been enlightened by the truth are to be light bearers to the world. To hide our light at this time is to make a terrible mistake. The message to God's people today is: 'Arise, shine; for thy light is come, and the glory of the Lord is risen upon thee.'"[12] "Those who wait for the Bridegroom's coming are to say to the people, 'Behold your God.' The last rays of merciful light, the last message of mercy to be given to the world, is a revelation of His character of love. The children of God are to manifest His glory. In their own life and character they are to reveal what the grace of God has done for them."[13] "The light of His glory—His character—is to shine forth in His followers."[14]

"Christ is coming with power and great glory. He is coming with His own glory and with the glory of the Father. He is coming with all the holy angels with Him. [Matt. 16:27; 25:31] While all the world is plunged in darkness, there will be light in every dwelling of the saints. They will catch the first light of His second appearing. The unsullied light will shine from His splendor, and Christ the Redeemer will be admired by all who have served Him. While the wicked flee from His presence, Christ's followers will rejoice. [Rev. 6:15-17; Isa. 25:9] The patriarch Job, looking down to the time of Christ's second advent, said, 'Whom I shall see for myself, and mine eyes shall behold, and not a stranger.' Job 19:27, margin. To His faithful followers Christ has been a daily companion and familiar friend. They have lived in close contact, in constant communion with God. Upon them the glory of the Lord has risen. In them the light of the knowledge of the glory of God in the face of Jesus Christ has been reflected. Now they rejoice in the undimmed rays of the brightness and glory of the King in His majesty. They are prepared for the communion of heaven; for they have heaven in their hearts."[15] They are able to say with Paul, "I know whom I have believed, and am persuaded that *he is able* to keep that which I have committed unto him against that day" (2 Tim. 1:12).

Chapter 7

"Ye shall receive power"
Acts 1:8

"This shall be the covenant that I will make with the house of Israel; After those days, saith the LORD, I will put my law in their inward parts, and write it in their hearts; and will be their God, and they shall be my people" (Jer. 31:33). *"I will dwell in them"* (2 Cor. 6:16). *"A new heart also will I give you,* and a new spirit will I put within you: and I will take away the stony heart out of your flesh, and I will give you an heart of flesh. And *I will put my spirit within you,* and cause you to walk in my statutes, and ye shall keep my judgments, and do them" (Eze. 36:25-27).

The promise of a new heart is the same promise through which God's Spirit dwells in us. Jesus says to His followers on earth, "I will pray the Father, and he shall give you another Comforter, that he may abide with you for ever; Even the Spirit of truth; whom the world cannot receive, because it seeth him not, neither knoweth him: but ye know him; for he dwelleth with you, and shall be *in you.* I will not leave you comfortless: *I will come to you"* (John 14:16-18). Christ left His disciples on earth when He ascended to heaven, but He promised them His Spirit and then said, "I will come to you." Through the Holy Spirit, Christ was to be with His followers to the end of the world. The promise of the Holy Spirit then is the promise of Christ abiding in the heart.

"Those who see Christ in His true character, and receive Him into the heart, have everlasting life. It is *through the Spirit* that Christ dwells in us; and the Spirit of God, received into the heart by faith, is the beginning of the life eternal."[1] "The Holy Spirit is Christ's representative, but divested of the personality of humanity, and independent thereof. Cumbered with humanity, Christ could not be in every place personally. Therefore it was for their interest that He should go to the Father, and send the Spirit to be His successor on earth. No one could then have any advantage because of his location or his personal contact with Christ. By the Spirit the Saviour would be accessible to all. In this sense He would be nearer to them than if He had not ascended on high."[2]

"And I will put my spirit within you, and cause you to walk in my statutes, and ye shall keep my judgments, and do them" (Eze. 36:27). "The Holy Spirit was the highest of all gifts that He could solicit from His Father for the exaltation of His people. The Spirit was to be given as a regenerating agent, and without this the sacrifice of Christ would have been of no avail. The power of evil had been strengthening for centuries, and the submission of men to this satanic captivity was amazing. Sin could be resisted and overcome *only* through the mighty agency of the Third Person of the Godhead, who would come with no modified energy, but in the fullness of divine power. It is the Spirit that makes effectual what has been wrought out by the world's Redeemer. It is by the Spirit that the heart is made pure. Through the Spirit the believer becomes a partaker of the divine nature. Christ has given His Spirit as a divine power to overcome all hereditary and cultivated tendencies to evil, and to impress His own character upon His church."[3]

The promise of the Holy Spirit is to be received in the same way that all of God's promises are received, *by faith alone*. But there is of

Chapter 7 — "Ye shall receive power"

course that poor class of souls who seek by God's grace *and their own works* to obtain the free gifts of God. The Bible gives us an example of one who did just this.

"Now when the apostles which were at Jerusalem heard that Samaria had received the word of God, they sent unto them Peter and John: Who, when they were come down, prayed for them, that they might receive the Holy Ghost: . . . Then laid they their hands on them, and they received the Holy Ghost. And when Simon saw that through laying on of the apostles' hands the Holy Ghost was given, *he offered them money,* Saying, Give me also this power, that on whomsoever I lay hands, he may receive the Holy Ghost. But Peter said unto him, *Thy money perish with thee, because thou hast thought that the gift of God may be purchased with money.* Thou hast neither part nor lot in this matter: for thy heart is not right in the sight of God. *Repent therefore of this thy wickedness, and pray God, if perhaps the thought of thine heart may be forgiven thee"* (Act 8:14-22).

Seeking to purchase any of God's gifts, whether with our money, our possessions, good works, etc., is all an offense to God. God's gifts *are gifts*, and therefore, they are *free*, with no form of payment whatsoever required. The Holy Spirit, no less than any other gift of God, is perfectly free to all who will have Him. Even the thought that you can somehow barter with God to receive the gift of the Holy Spirit is a sin that needs to be repented of. It is a sin that needs God's forgiveness. You can give God all of your heart, money, talents, etc., but if you even so much as think that you will receive something from God for doing this, you need to repent, for this thought is wickedness.

Right before His ascension, Christ said to His disciples, "Ye shall receive power, after that the Holy Ghost is come upon you: and ye shall be witnesses unto me both in Jerusalem, and in all Judaea, and in Samaria, and unto the uttermost part of the earth" (Acts 1:8). So,

Saved by Works. . . Christ's Works!

"what was the result of the outpouring of the Spirit on the Day of Pentecost? The glad tidings of a risen Saviour were carried to the uttermost parts of the inhabited world. . . . One interest prevailed; one subject of emulation swallowed up all others. The ambition of the believers was to reveal the likeness of Christ's character and to labor for the enlargement of His kingdom."[4] But the Holy Spirit wasn't given to the disciples until "they were all with one accord" (Acts 2:1). Therefore, the reason the Spirit's power is not manifest today among God's people as it was in the apostle's time is because they are not in unity.

Jesus prayed for His disciples: "That they all may be one; as thou, Father, art in me, and I in thee, that they also may be one in us: that the world may believe that thou hast sent me. And the glory which thou gavest me I have given them; that they may be one, even as we are one: I in them, and thou in me, that they may be made perfect in one; and that the world may know that thou hast sent me, and hast loved them, as thou hast loved me" (John 17:21-23).

This unity, a unity so close that Jesus calls many people "one," is promised to us in the same way that we as individuals are promised a new heart—*by the Word*. The promise of the Word of God is, "*I will* give *them one heart*, and I will put a new spirit within you; and I will take the stony heart out of their flesh, and will give *them* an heart of flesh: That they may walk in my statutes, and keep mine ordinances, and do them: and they shall be my people, and I will be their God" (Eze. 11:19, 20).

If God's people desire to have that unity which will allow the Holy Spirit to be poured out as in the days of the apostles upon not just one, but all of His followers, then let them come together and claim the promise of the Holy Spirit so that the Holy Spirit may claim them.

When the disciples of old "lifted up their voice to God with one accord, and said, Lord, thou art God, which hast made heaven, and earth, and the sea, and all that in them is . . . grant unto thy servants, that with all boldness they may speak thy word, By stretching forth thine hand to heal; and that signs and wonders may be done by the name of thy holy child Jesus," then it was that "they were all filled with the Holy Ghost, and they spake the word of God with boldness. And the multitude of them that believed were of one heart and of one soul: neither said any of them that ought of the things which he possessed was his own; but they had all things common. And with great power gave the apostles witness of the resurrection of the Lord Jesus: and great grace was upon them all" (Acts 4:24, 29-33). "Before one book of the New Testament was written, before one gospel sermon had been preached after Christ's ascension, the Holy Spirit came upon the praying apostles. Then the testimony of their enemies was, 'Ye have filled Jerusalem with your doctrine.' Acts 5:28."[5]

"So mightily can God work when men give themselves up to the control of His Spirit."[6] "He who loves Christ the most will do the greatest amount of good. There is no limit to the usefulness of one who, by putting self aside, makes room for the working of the Holy Spirit upon his heart, and lives a life wholly consecrated to God."[7]

"The Saviour's life on earth was not a life of ease and devotion to Himself, but He toiled with persistent, earnest, untiring effort for the salvation of lost mankind. From the manger to Calvary He followed the path of self-denial and sought not to be released from arduous tasks, painful travels and exhausting care and labor. He said, 'The Son of man came not to be ministered unto, but to minister, and to give His life a ransom for many.' Matthew 20:28. This was the one great object of His life. Everything else was secondary and subservient. It was His meat and drink to do the will of God and to finish His work. [John 4:34] Self and self-interest had no part in His labor."[8]

When this same Jesus is in the heart of His followers, the works

Saved by Works. . . Christ's Works!

He did, they will do. "Those who are the partakers of the grace of Christ will be ready to make any sacrifice, that others for whom He died may share the heavenly gift. They will do all they can to make the world better for their stay in it. This spirit is the sure outgrowth of a soul truly converted. No sooner does one come to Christ than there is born in his heart a desire to make known to others what a precious friend he has found in Jesus; the saving and sanctifying truth *cannot be shut up in his heart*. If we are clothed with the righteousness of Christ and are filled with the joy of His indwelling Spirit, *we shall not be able to hold our peace*. If we have tasted and seen that the Lord is good we shall have something to tell. Like Philip when he found the Saviour, we shall invite others into His presence. We shall seek to present to them the attractions of Christ and the unseen realities of the world to come. There will be an intensity of desire to follow in the path that Jesus trod. There will be an earnest longing that those around us may 'behold the Lamb of God, which taketh away the sin of the world.' John 1:29."[9]

"To Jesus, who emptied Himself for the salvation of lost humanity, the Holy Spirit was given without measure [John 3:34]. So it will be given to every follower of Christ when the whole heart is surrendered for His indwelling. Our Lord Himself has given the command, 'Be filled with the Spirit' (Ephesians 5:18), and this command is also a promise of its fulfillment. It was the good pleasure of the Father that in Christ should 'all the fullness dwell,' and 'in Him ye are made full.' Colossians 1:19, R.V.; 2:10, R.V."[10]

"Christ has promised the gift of the Holy Spirit to His church, and the promise belongs to us as much as to the first disciples. But like every other promise, it is given on conditions. There are many who believe and profess to claim the Lord's promise; they talk about Christ and about the Holy Spirit, yet receive no benefit. They do not surren-

Chapter 7 — "Ye shall receive power"

der the soul to be guided and *controlled* by the divine agencies. *We cannot use the Holy Spirit. The Spirit is to use us.* Through the Spirit God works in His people 'to will and to do of His good pleasure.' Philippians 2:13. But many will not submit to this. They want to manage themselves. This is why they do not receive the heavenly gift. Only to those who wait humbly upon God, who watch for His guidance and grace, is the Spirit given. The power of God awaits their demand and reception. This promised blessing, *claimed by faith*, brings all other blessings in its train. It is given according to the riches of the grace of Christ, and He is ready to supply every soul according to the capacity to receive."[11]

"The promise of the Holy Spirit is not limited to any age or to any race. Christ declared that the divine influence of His Spirit was to be with His followers unto the end."[12] "The lapse of time has wrought no change in Christ's parting promise to send the Holy Spirit as His representative. It is not because of any restriction on the part of God that the riches of His grace do not flow earthward to men. If the fulfillment of the promise is not seen as it might be, it is because the promise is not appreciated as it should be. *If all were willing, all would be filled with the Spirit.* Wherever the need of the Holy Spirit is a matter little thought of, there is seen spiritual drought, spiritual darkness, spiritual declension and death. Whenever minor matters occupy the attention, the divine power which is necessary for the growth and prosperity of the church, and which would bring all other blessings in its train, is lacking, though offered in infinite plenitude."[13]

"Through the merits of Christ we have access to the throne of Infinite Power. 'He that spared not His own Son, but delivered Him up for us all, how shall He not with Him also freely give us all things?' Romans 8:32. The Father gave His Spirit without measure to His Son, and we also may partake of its fullness. Jesus says, 'If ye then, being evil, know how to give good gifts unto your children: how much more shall your heavenly Father give the Holy Spirit to them that ask Him?' Luke 11:13. 'If ye shall ask anything in My name, I will do it.' 'Ask, and ye shall receive, that your joy may be full.' John 14:14; 16:24."[14]

If men will but believe the promise of God, "*I will* give them one heart" (Eze. 11:19), they *will* come into the unity which will fit them to be able to receive an outpouring of the Holy Spirit as was given in the days of the apostles. Why will they receive it? Because *God said* that the instant they believe it is so, *it is so*, and since they believe it, *so it is*. All that remains for an outpouring of the Holy Spirit as was once given is for them to ask for it that they may receive it, for they have not because they ask not. God's promise that He will give them the Holy Spirit is in effect—all that awaits is for man to submit through faith and then the blessing will fall upon their heads through the channel of faith and they *shall have* what they asked for. Why shall they have what they asked for? Because *God said* that they shall have it.

So speaking in the present tense, when men come together believing only His spoken promises, they *have* what they ask for. When men will but do this, and this *only*, the "gospel of the kingdom shall be preached in all the world for a witness unto all nations; and then shall the end come" (Matt. 24:14).

God gave the prophet Ezekiel a beautiful view of what He will do for those praying and believing ones. He writes, "The hand of the LORD was upon me, and carried me out in the spirit of the LORD, and set me down in the midst of the valley which was full of bones, And caused me to pass by them round about: and, behold, there were very many in the open valley; and, lo, they were very dry.

"And he said unto me, Son of man, can these bones live? And I answered, O Lord GOD, thou knowest. Again he said unto me, Prophesy upon these bones, and say unto them, O ye dry bones, hear the word of

Chapter 7 — "Ye shall receive power"

the LORD. Thus saith the Lord GOD unto these bones; Behold, I will cause breath to enter into you, and ye shall live: And I will lay sinews upon you, and will bring up flesh upon you, and cover you with skin, and put breath in you, and ye shall live; and ye shall know that I am the LORD.

"So I prophesied as I was commanded: and as I prophesied, there was a noise, and behold a shaking, and the bones came together, bone to his bone. And when I beheld, lo, the sinews and the flesh came up upon them, and the skin covered them above: but there was no breath in them.

"Then said he unto me, Prophesy unto the wind, prophesy, son of man, and say to the wind, Thus saith the Lord GOD; Come from the four winds, O breath, and breathe upon these slain, that they may live. So I prophesied as he commanded me, and the breath came into them, and they lived, and stood up upon their feet, an exceeding great army.

"Then he said unto me, Son of man, these bones are the whole house of Israel: behold, they say, Our bones are dried, and our hope is lost: we are cut off for our parts. Therefore prophesy and say unto them, Thus saith the Lord GOD; Behold, O my people, I will open your graves, and cause you to come up out of your graves, and bring you into the land of Israel. And ye shall know that I am the LORD, when I have opened your graves, O my people, and brought you up out of your graves, And shall put my spirit in you, and ye shall live, and I shall place you in your own land: then shall ye know that I the LORD have spoken it, and performed it, saith the LORD" (Eze. 37:1-14).

The dry bones in the vision "are the whole house of Israel." God's people are represented here as being "dead in trespasses and sins" (Eph. 2:1)—dry bones—but God has bidden them to "awake thou that sleepest, and arise from the dead" (Eph 5:14). The Lord has a message for these dry bones, and He bids them, "O ye dry bones, *hear the word*

Saved by Works. . . Christ's Works!

of the LORD. Thus saith the Lord GOD unto these bones; Behold, *I will* cause breath to enter into you, and ye shall live: And *I will* lay sinews upon you, and will bring up flesh upon you, and cover you with skin, and put breath in you, and *ye shall live"* (Eze. 37:4-6).

This creative word of God, spoken to the dry bones, brings them to life. At the word of God the dry bones come together, sinews are laid upon them, and they are covered with flesh. Then once more the word of God works on their behalf. The words are spoken, "Thus saith the Lord GOD; Come from the four winds, O breath, and breathe upon these slain, that they may live" (Eze. 37:9). This breath represents the Holy Spirit. When Jesus appeared to the disciples after His resurrection, "he breathed on them, and saith unto them, Receive ye the Holy Ghost" (John 20:22).

At the word of God alone, breath comes into the lifeless bodies, "and they lived, and stood up upon their feet, *an exceeding great army"* (Eze. 37:10). When those who are destitute of the Spirit of God receive by faith the promise of the Holy Spirit, the promise of a new heart, they become part of God's exceeding great army. But what is the army for?

Paul gives the answer. "Finally, my brethren, be strong in the Lord, and in the power of his might. Put on the whole armour of God, that ye may be able to stand against the wiles of the devil. For we wrestle not against flesh and blood, but against principalities, against powers, against the rulers of the darkness of this world, against spiritual wickedness in high places. Wherefore take unto you the whole armour of God, that ye may be able to withstand in the evil day, and having done all, to stand. Stand therefore, having your loins girt about with truth, and having on the breastplate of righteousness; And your *feet shod with the preparation of the gospel of peace*; Above all, taking the shield of faith, wherewith ye shall be able to quench all the fiery darts

Chapter 7 — "Ye shall receive power"

of the wicked. And take the helmet of salvation, and the sword of the Spirit, which is the word of God" (Eph. 6:10-17).

The exceeding great army of dry bones that come to life by the word of God have their "feet shod with the preparation of the gospel of peace." Their mission is to carry the good news to the world. Soon, *very soon*, this army *will be* raised to life. Yea, *it is already rising!* Join it quickly by believing the Word of God! "And this gospel of the kingdom *shall be preached* in all the world for a witness unto all nations; and then shall the end come" (Matt. 24:14).

Our mission is like that of Ezekiel's, to prophesy, to preach to the dry bones the words of God. Our message to them is to be, "Awake thou that sleepest, and arise from the dead" (Eph. 5:14). When they accept the words that you preach to them, the words of the good news, and they believe them to be true in their own behalf, they "*shall live.*" They shall be converted, and then Jesus will come, for the mouth of the Lord has *spoken* it.

"The souls of those whom we desire to save are like the representation which Ezekiel saw in vision,—a valley of dry bones. They are dead in trespasses and sins, but *God would have us deal with them as though they were living.* Were the question put to us. 'Son of man, can these bones live.' our answer would be only the confession of ignorance. 'O Lord, thou knowest.' To all appearance there is nothing to lead us to hope for their restoration. Yet nevertheless the word of the prophecy must be spoken even to those who are like the dry bones in the valley. We are in no wise to be deterred from fulfilling our commission by the listlessness, the dullness, the lack of spiritual perception, in those upon whom the word of God is brought to bear. We are to preach the word of life to those whom we may judge to be as hopeless subjects as though they were in their graves. Though they may seem unwilling to hear or to receive the light of truth, without questioning or

Saved by Works... Christ's Works!

wavering we are to do our part. We are to repeat to them the message. 'Awake, thou that sleepest, and arise from the dead, and Christ shall give thee light.'"[15]

"The natural man receiveth not the things of the Spirit of God: for they are foolishness unto him: neither can he know them, because they are spiritually discerned" (1 Cor. 2:14). Because those to whom we preach are dead, having no spiritual discernment, we must preach to them *insinuating faith* into their minds. We must preach to them as though they *already accept the message* we are preaching. Then, the instant they accept the insinuation that they believe, *they do believe*, and since they believe, Christ dwells in their hearts and Satan's stronghold is broken. Then they can discern spiritual things, and they will join you in spreading the good news to the world.

Leave no room for misunderstandings as to what you are preaching, for your hearer's lives will be molded by their faith, but do not depend upon your ability to clearly present the truth. It is God alone who can convict of truth and convert souls. Your job is merely to speak the words of life to the dead; God is the one who resurrects them. It is good news that we preach, and we are to preach it, expecting our hearers to accept the wonderful truths God has given us.

"It is not the human agent that is to inspire with life. The Lord God of Israel will do that part, quickening the lifeless spiritual nature into activity. The breath of the Lord of hosts must enter into the lifeless bodies. In the judgment, when all secrets are laid bare, it will be known that the voice of God spoke through the human agent, and aroused the torpid conscience, and stirred the lifeless faculties, and moved sinners to repentance and contrition, and forsaking of sins. It will then be clearly seen that through the human agent faith in Jesus Christ was imparted to the soul, and spiritual life from heaven was breathed upon one who was dead in trespasses and sins, and he was

Chapter 7 — "Ye shall receive power"

quickened with spiritual life."[16]

"The Spirit of God, with its vivifying power, must be in every human agent, that every spiritual muscle and sinew may be in exercise. Without the Holy Spirit, without the breath of God, there is torpidity of conscience, loss of spiritual life. Many who are without spiritual life have their names on the church records, but they are not written in the Lamb's book of life. They may be joined to the church, but they are not united to the Lord. They may be diligent in the performance of a certain set of duties, and may be regarded as living men; but many are among those who 'have a name that thou livest, and art dead.' Unless there is genuine conversion of the soul to God; unless the vital breath of God quickens the soul to spiritual life; unless the professors of truth are actuated by heaven-born principle, they are not born of the incorruptible seed which liveth and abideth forever. Unless they trust in the righteousness of Christ as their only security; unless they copy his character, labor in his spirit, they are naked, they have not on the robe of his righteousness. The dead are often made to pass for the living; for those who are working out what they term salvation after their own ideas, have not God working in them to will and to do of his good pleasure.

"This class is well represented by the valley of dry bones Ezekiel saw in vision. Those who have had committed to them the treasures of truth, and yet who are dead in trespasses and sin, need to be created anew in Christ Jesus. There is so little real vitality in the church at the present time, that it takes constant labor to give men the appearance of life to the professed people of God. When the converting power of God comes upon the people, it will be made manifest by activity. They will become workers, and will esteem the reproach of Christ greater riches than the treasures of the world. They will have respect unto the crown of life, the immortal inheritance. They will not be dependent

Saved by Works... Christ's Works!

upon their ministers for their life and experience, but will realize that Christ is the Chief Shepherd of the flock. They will not think that their ministers are appointed of God to do their work for them. They will understand that they must work out their own salvation with fear and trembling, knowing that it is God that worketh in them to will and to do of his good pleasure."[17]

When the Holy Spirit is received into the heart by faith, then the fruits of the Spirit *will be* manifest in the life. "'The fruit of the Spirit is love, joy, peace, longsuffering, gentleness, goodness, faith, meekness, temperance' (Gal. 5:22, 23). This fruit can never perish but will produce after its kind a harvest unto eternal life.

"'When the fruit is brought forth, immediately he putteth in the sickle, because the harvest is come.' [Mark 4:29] Christ is waiting with longing desire for the manifestation of Himself in His church. When the character of Christ shall be perfectly reproduced in His people, then He will come to claim them as His own."[18]

"In the last day, that great day of the feast, Jesus stood and cried, saying, If any man thirst, let him come unto me, and drink" (John 7:37). "Ho, every one that thirsteth, come ye to the waters, and he that hath no money; come ye, buy, and eat; yea, come, buy wine and milk without money and without price" (Isa. 55:1). "He that believeth on me shall never thirst" (John 6:35). "And the Spirit and the bride say, Come. And let him that heareth say, Come. And let him that is athirst come. And whosoever will, let him take the water of life" (Rev. 22:17), and "*I will* give unto him that is athirst of the fountain of the water of life freely" (Rev 21:6).

Chapter 8

"There is a friend . . ."
Proverbs 18:24

Jesus says, "Greater love hath no man than this, that a man lay down his life for his friends" (John 15:13). "I am the good shepherd . . . and I lay down my life for the sheep. . . . No man taketh it from me, but I lay it down of myself" (John 10:14-18). "Henceforth I call you not servants . . . but I have called you friends . . . Ye have not chosen me, but I have chosen you" (John 15:15, 16).

Jesus has called us His friends, and He has manifested His love for us in living, dying, and living again for us. "He ever liveth to make intercession for them" (Heb. 7:25). Just as "a friend loveth at all times" (Prov. 17:17), even so, Jesus loves us at all times. And "I am persuaded, that neither death, nor life, nor angels, nor principalities, nor powers, nor things present, nor things to come, nor height, nor depth, nor any other creature, shall be able to separate us from the love of God, which is in Christ Jesus our Lord" (Rom 8:38, 39).

Though given as an accusation against Christ, the words hold true that Jesus is "a friend of publicans and sinners" (Luke 7:34), and nothing can ever change that. Jesus may not always be for the things that we do, but He will always be *for us*, and that is what constitutes a true friend. The most beautiful accusation against Jesus was given when the Pharisees and scribes said concerning Him: "This man receiveth

Saved by Works... Christ's Works!

sinners, and eateth with them" (Luke 15:2).

"The world's Redeemer accepts men *as they are*, with all their wants, imperfections, and weaknesses; and He will not only cleanse from sin and grant redemption through His blood, but will satisfy the heart-longing of all who consent to wear His yoke, to bear His burden."[1] "Ye are my friends, if ye do whatsoever I command you" (John 15:14). Christ is not saying here that fulfilling His commands causes Him to love us as His friends. He has loved us with a love stronger than friendship, stronger than the love of husband and wife, stronger than even death itself, and that, "while we were yet sinners" (Rom. 5:8). But Christ cannot properly call us His friends when we cherish evil, sin, and selfishness, for these things are hated and abhorred by Him. Jesus may love us as His friends, but He cannot, in a sense, call us His friends when our sinful hearts are at war with His sinless heart. "Whosoever therefore will be a friend of the world is the enemy of God" (James 4:4), but "he that loveth pureness of heart, for the grace of his lips the king shall be his friend" (Prov. 22:11).

While it may be true that we do not consider or love Christ as our friend, as revealed by our evil works, it will always be true that Christ considers and loves us as His friends. He holds us up as His friends, but we do not hold Him as ours. It must be heartbreaking for Jesus to have this one-way friendship with us.

The most essential element in building and maintaining a growing friendship is that of communication. People who were once the best of friends, through loss of communication between them, have become only mere acquaintances. The alienation from each other has caused the friendship to fade away to the point as if it never was. Jesus said, "This is life eternal, that they might know thee the only true God, and Jesus Christ, whom thou hast sent" (John 17:3). If we ever expect to have a blessed relationship with Jesus, and as a result be given the gift

Chapter 8 — "There is a friend . . ."

of eternal life, communication with Him is a positive necessity.

Prayer is talking to God. "Prayer is the opening of the heart to God as to a friend. Not that it is necessary in order to make known to God what we are, but in order to enable us to receive Him. Prayer does not bring God down to us, but brings us up to Him."[2] So many honest Christians have erroneous views as to what constitutes prayer. Prayer does not consist of getting down on our knees and thanking God for what He has so graciously given us and asking for more gifts that we might better serve Him. Prayer is talking to God as you would talk to a friend, but in most if not all cases, with far more respect. Prayer is opening up our hearts to God and pouring out before Him all of our thoughts and cares. When we talk to our friends, we tell them of our joys in life, of our sorrows, and also of those things that are constantly on our mind. We tell them about our relationship problems; we come to them in tears when our heart is broken; we seek for their sympathy and love. We ask for their advice, and we thank them for being there for us. Spending time and talking with our friends is one of our highest delights in life. Even when we have nothing specific that we want to tell them, no burdens to bring, no heavy heart to unload, we take great pleasure in just being with them and talking to them about whatever randomly comes to mind. So it is to be with God.

If we should have a friend nearby, we would most likely ask him for his opinion on various and random things throughout the entire day, from what job offer we should take, to what color socks we should wear. If God is our best friend, we will treat Him as our best friend; if God is our Husband, then we will treat Him as our Husband. And would it hurt to ask God what color socks we should wear? Would the Lord be offended that we want Him so involved with our lives as to ask Him such a thing? Never! It would be His utter delight to be that involved with us. We would ask our spouse and friends for their opinions of what we wear and what they think we should do. Should we not ask our Beloved?

When we think of what constitutes prayer, we often picture someone kneeling down with his eyes closed, hands folded, and saying, "Father in heaven, thank you for such and such things. Please forgive me for such and such things. Help me to do such and such things. Cause such and such things to happen. In the name of Jesus, Amen." While this may be suitable for publically spoken prayer, it will never suffice for secret prayer or talking to God throughout the day. If "prayer is the opening of the heart to God as to a friend," then such a prayer can scarcely be called a true prayer if it is the silent prayer of the soul. The many words we speak in prayer, the many common phrases we utter, the amount of things we ask for, or the amount of time we spend on our knees will not bring us an inch closer to heaven if the heart is not opened up to God as it would open up to a friend. Jesus said, "When ye pray, use not vain repetitions, as the heathen do: for they think that they shall be heard for their much speaking. Be not ye therefore like unto them: for your Father knoweth what things ye have need of, before ye ask him" (Matt. 6:7, 8).

When we pray, it is not for the purpose of informing God what we are thankful for, what we have done, who we are, or what we want and need. These things He already knows far better than we do. But don't cast off prayer because it seems like you are just telling God what He already knows. Prayer is "to enable us to receive Him," to establish that close friendship with Him, and for that relationship to grow into a deeper and still deeper love for Him until we love Him as our Husband and we give Him our hearts without stint or measure. Remember, "prayer does not bring God down to us, but brings us up to Him."

Some will point out that we should at times spend hours in prayer because this is what Jesus did and He is our example. This may be

Chapter 8 — "There is a friend . . ."

true, but it needs to be made clear that Jesus prayed differently than many Christians. Many Christians pray because they do not believe God's promises, but Jesus prayed *because He believed* God's promises. Many Christians pray because they think it will help them, but Jesus prayed because He *knew it helped Him.*

Those who think they will grow closer to God in their relationship to Him while they are neglecting true prayer need to understand that they are under a fatal deception of the devil. "The darkness of the evil one encloses those who neglect to pray."[3] "We must not neglect secret prayer, for this is the life of the soul. It is impossible for the soul to flourish while prayer is neglected. Family or public prayer alone is not sufficient. In solitude let the soul be laid open to the inspecting eye of God. Secret prayer is to be heard only by the prayer-hearing God. No curious ear is to receive the burden of such petitions. In secret prayer the soul is free from surrounding influences, free from excitement. Calmly, yet fervently, will it reach out after God. Sweet and abiding will be the influence emanating from Him who seeth in secret, whose ear is open to hear the prayer arising from the heart. By calm, simple faith the soul holds communion with God and gathers to itself rays of divine light to strengthen and sustain it in the conflict with Satan. God is our tower of strength."[4] "In order for a man's faith to be strong, he must be much with God in secret prayer."[5]

"Consecrate yourself to God in the morning; make this your very first work. Let your prayer be, 'Take me, O Lord, as wholly Thine. I lay all my plans at Thy feet. Use me today in Thy service. Abide with me, and let all my work be wrought in Thee.' This is a daily matter. Each morning consecrate yourself to God for that day. Surrender all your plans to Him, to be carried out or given up as His providence shall indicate. Thus day by day you may be giving your life into the hands of God, and thus your life will be molded more and more after

Saved by Works... Christ's Works!

the life of Christ."[6]

"Pray in your closet, and as you go about your daily labor let your heart be often uplifted to God. It was thus that Enoch walked with God. These silent prayers rise like precious incense before the throne of grace. Satan cannot overcome him whose heart is thus stayed upon God.

"There is no time or place in which it is inappropriate to offer up a petition to God. There is nothing that can prevent us from lifting up our hearts in the spirit of earnest prayer. In the crowds of the street, in the midst of a business engagement, we may send up a petition to God and plead for divine guidance, as did Nehemiah when he made his request before King Artaxerxes. A closet of communion may be found wherever we are. We should have the door of the heart open continually and our invitation going up that Jesus may come and abide as a heavenly guest in the soul."[7]

Jesus loves us. He is utterly thrilled when we come to talk with Him, and He is just itching to give us anything and everything that would gladden and refresh our hearts. Therefore, "if we come to God, feeling helpless and dependent, as we really are, and in humble, trusting faith make known our wants to Him whose knowledge is infinite, who sees everything in creation, and who governs everything by His will and word, He can and will attend to our cry, and will let light shine into our hearts. Through sincere prayer we are brought into connection with the mind of the Infinite. We may have no remarkable evidence at the time that the face of our Redeemer is bending over us in compassion and love, but this is even so. We may not feel His visible touch, but His hand is upon us in love and pitying tenderness."[8]

We must have communion with God if we ever expect to be saved, "but your iniquities have separated between you and your God, and your sins have hid his face from you, that he will not hear" (Isa. 59:2).

Chapter 8 — "There is a friend . . ."

"Some seem to feel that they must be on probation, and must prove to the Lord that they are reformed, before they can claim His blessing. But they may claim the blessing of God even now. They must have His grace, the Spirit of Christ, to help their infirmities, or they cannot resist evil. Jesus loves to have us come to Him just as we are, sinful, helpless, dependent. We may come with all our weakness, our folly, our sinfulness, and fall at His feet in penitence. It is His glory to encircle us in the arms of His love and to bind up our wounds, to cleanse us from all impurity."[9] "If my people, which are called by my name, shall humble themselves, and pray, and seek my face, and turn from their wicked ways; then will I hear from heaven, and will forgive their sin, and will heal their land" (2 Chron. 7:14).

"There are certain conditions upon which we may expect that God will hear and answer our prayers. One of the first of these is that we feel our need of help from Him. He has promised, 'I will pour water upon him that is thirsty, and floods upon the dry ground.' Isaiah 44:3. Those who hunger and thirst after righteousness, who long after God, may be sure that they will be filled. The heart must be open to the Spirit's influence, or God's blessing cannot be received."[10] If we expect to receive anything from God, we must cry out as did David when he said, "I stretch forth my hands unto thee: my soul thirsteth after thee, as a thirsty land" (Ps. 143:6). "As the hart panteth after the water brooks, so panteth my soul after thee, O God" (Ps. 42:1).

"Prayer is both a duty and a privilege. We must have help which God alone can give, and that help will not come unasked. If we are too self-righteous to feel our need of help from God, we shall not have His help when we need it most. If we are too independent and self-sufficient to throw ourselves daily by earnest prayer upon the merits of a crucified and risen Saviour, we shall be left subject to Satan's temptations."[11]

Saved by Works... Christ's Works!

"And this is the confidence that we have in him, that, if we ask any thing according to his will, he heareth us: And if we know that he hear us, whatsoever we ask, we know that we have the petitions that we desired of him" (1 John 5:14, 15). When we ask of God in prayer, we must always pray according to His will. "The assurance is broad and unlimited, and He is faithful who has promised. [Hebrews 10:23] When we do not receive the very things we asked for, at the time we ask, we are still to believe that the Lord hears and that He will answer our prayers. We are so erring and short-sighted that we sometimes ask for things that would not be a blessing to us, and our heavenly Father in love answers our prayers by giving us that which will be for our highest good—that which we ourselves would desire if with vision divinely enlightened we could see all things as they really are. When our prayers seem not to be answered, we are to cling to the promise; for the time of answering will surely come, and we shall receive the blessing we need most. But to claim that prayer will always be answered in the very way and for the particular thing that we desire, is presumption. God is too wise to err, and too good to withhold any good thing from them that walk uprightly. Then do not fear to trust Him, even though you do not see the immediate answer to your prayers. Rely upon His sure promise, 'Ask, and it shall be given you.'"[12] "Ye ask, and receive not, because ye ask amiss" (James 4:3).

"When we come to ask mercy and blessing from God we should have a spirit of love and forgiveness in our own hearts. How can we pray, 'Forgive us our debts, as we forgive our debtors,' and yet indulge an unforgiving spirit? Matthew 6:12. If we expect our own prayers to be heard we must forgive others in the same manner and to the same extent as we hope to be forgiven."[13]

"He that turneth away his ear from hearing the law, even his prayer shall be abomination" (Prov. 28:9). "If light and truth is within our

Chapter 8 — "There is a friend . . ."

reach, and we neglect to improve the privilege of hearing and seeing it, we virtually reject it; we are choosing darkness rather than light."[14] "If we close our eyes to the light for fear we shall see our wrongs, which we are unwilling to forsake, our sins are not lessened but increased. If light is turned from in one case, it will be disregarded in another."[15] Of God the psalmist says, "Thy law is the truth," and the prayers of those who turn away from hearing the truth and pray their prayers, not to know God's will and to do it, but for selfishness' sake, are an abomination. Shall such prayers, that are a sin in and of themselves, be heard in heaven? The psalmist answers, "If I regard iniquity in my heart, the Lord will not hear me" (Ps. 66:18).

One of the biggest problems people have in receiving answers to prayer is that of faith. To those who have this problem, Jesus simply answers, "Have faith in God." He continues, "For verily I say unto you, That whosoever shall say unto this mountain, Be thou removed, and be thou cast into the sea; *and shall not doubt in his heart,* but shall believe that those things which he saith shall come to pass; he shall have whatsoever he saith. Therefore I say unto you, What things soever ye desire, when ye pray, *believe that ye receive them, and ye shall have them*" (Mark 11:22-24).

When one prays to his Creator, "that giveth to all men liberally, and upbraideth not . . . let him ask in faith, nothing wavering. For he that wavereth is like a wave of the sea driven with the wind and tossed. For let not that man think that he shall receive any thing of the Lord" (James 1:5-7). God cannot bless the prayer of unbelief, "for whatsoever is not of faith is sin" (Rom. 14:23). And if we regard iniquity in our hearts and cherish any known sin, the Lord will not hear us. The very prayer, however earnest and touching, if it is prayed in unbelief, is an offense to God. It is a dishonor to Him. Of the one that prays a faithless prayer, can we not say that even his prayer is a sin? Jesus said, "If ye shall ask any thing in my name, I will do it" (John 14:14). Do you take Him at His word? Or do you accuse the righteous God of lying? "Every soul has the privilege of stating to the Lord his own special necessities and to offer his individual thanksgiving for the blessings that he daily receives. But the many long and spiritless, faithless prayers that are offered to God, instead of being a joy to Him, are a burden."[16]

Faith is one of the simplest concepts but is made to appear very complicated by confused people. Faith is a choice. The devil cannot force you to sin, and therefore, he cannot force you to doubt. The only thing you can do is choose to believe, and *that choice is your faith!* That choice is exercising your faith. It is choosing to acknowledge the truthfulness and power of God's spoken word and depending upon that word to do what it says, expecting it to do it. And having made the choice to believe, move forward, acknowledging that your prayer *is* heard and *is* answered. There is no need to question the matter, and if you do question it, then you do not believe it.

When praying, we need to take heed that we do not put God to the test, to see *if* He will fulfill His word. "Ye shall not tempt the LORD your God" (Deut. 6:16). To put God to the test, to prove whether or not He will do what He said, is tempting Him. "We should not present our petitions to God to prove whether He will fulfill His word, but because He will fulfill it; not to prove that He loves us, but because He loves us. 'Without faith it is impossible to please Him: for he that cometh to God must believe that He is, and that He is a rewarder of them that diligently seek Him.' Hebrews 11:6."[17]

"Jesus says, 'What things soever ye desire, when ye pray, believe that ye receive them, and ye shall have them.' Mark 11:24. There is a condition to this promise—that we pray according to the will of God. But it is the will of God to cleanse us from sin, to make us His children, and to enable us to live a holy life. So we may ask for these blessings,

Chapter 8 — "There is a friend . . ."

and believe that we receive them, and thank God that *we have* received them."[18] "And all things, whatsoever ye shall ask in prayer, believing, ye shall receive" (Matt. 21:22). All of the promises of God's Word, in all of their entirety, cannot possibly be hindered from fulfillment if you will meet the one condition of believing that God's all powerful word does what it says. And if you find it difficult to believe the power of His word, only notice the earth beneath you, the creation around you, and realize all this tangible matter was *spoken* into existence by the same word that spoke saying, "All things, whatsoever ye shall ask in prayer, believing, ye shall receive."

Jesus taught that if anyone requests something of the Lord, he should not ask only once for it. "And he spake a parable unto them to this end, that men ought always to pray, and not to faint; Saying, There was in a city a judge, which feared not God, neither regarded man: And there was a widow in that city; and she came unto him, saying, Avenge me of mine adversary. And he would not for a while: but afterward he said within himself, Though I fear not God, nor regard man; Yet because this widow troubleth me, I will avenge her, lest by her continual coming she weary me" (Luke 18:1-5).

"Christ here draws a sharp contrast between the unjust judge and God. The judge yielded to the widow's request merely through selfishness, that he might be relieved of her importunity. He felt for her no pity or compassion; her misery was nothing to him. How different is the attitude of God toward those who seek Him. The appeals of the needy and distressed are considered by Him with infinite compassion. . . . The unjust judge had no special interest in the widow who importuned him for deliverance; yet in order to rid himself of her pitiful appeals, he heard her plea, and delivered her from her adversary. But God loves His children with infinite love. To Him the dearest object on earth is His church."[19]

Saved by Works... Christ's Works!

"And, behold, a woman of Canaan came out of the same coasts" (Matt. 15:22). "The woman was a Greek, a Syrophenician by nation; and she besought him that he would cast forth the devil out of her daughter" (Mark 7:26). "And [she] cried unto him, saying, Have mercy on me, O Lord, thou son of David; my daughter is grievously vexed with a devil. But he answered her not a word. And his disciples came and besought him, saying, Send her away; for she crieth after us. But he answered and said, I am not sent but unto the lost sheep of the house of Israel. Then came she and worshipped him, saying, Lord, help me. But he answered and said, It is not meet to take the children's bread, and to cast it to dogs. And she said, Truth, Lord: yet the dogs eat of the crumbs which fall from their masters' table. Then Jesus answered and said unto her, O woman, great is thy faith: be it unto thee even as thou wilt. And her daughter was made whole from that very hour" (Matt. 15:22-28).

"The Saviour manifested divine compassion toward the Syrophenician woman. His heart was touched as He saw her grief. He longed to give her an immediate assurance that her prayer was heard; but He desired to teach His disciples a lesson, and for a time He seemed to neglect the cry of her tortured heart. When her faith had been made manifest, He spoke to her words of commendation and sent her away with the precious boon she had asked. The disciples never forgot this lesson, and it is placed on record to show the result of persevering prayer.

"It was Christ Himself who put into that mother's heart the persistence which would not be repulsed. It was Christ who gave the pleading widow courage and determination before the judge. It was Christ who, centuries before, in the mysterious conflict by the Jabbok, had inspired Jacob with the same persevering faith. And the confidence which He Himself had implanted, He did not fail to reward."[20] "There

Chapter 8 — "There is a friend . . ."

is no danger that the Lord will neglect the prayers of His people. The danger is that in temptation and trial they will become discouraged, and fail to persevere in prayer."[21] "Perseverance in prayer has been made a condition of receiving."[22] Not that persistent prayer brings God down to us so He can hear, but because it "brings us up to Him" so we can be blessed. "Why should the sons and daughters of God be reluctant to pray, when prayer is the key in the hand of faith to unlock heaven's storehouse, where are treasured the boundless resources of Omnipotence?"[23]

"Pray without ceasing" (1 Thess. 5:17). "We must pray always if we would grow in faith and experience. . . . Unceasing prayer is the unbroken union of the soul with God, so that life from God flows into our life; and from our life, purity and holiness flow back to God."[24] Jesus warns us, "Watch ye and pray, lest ye enter into temptation" (Mark 14:38). "Take ye heed, watch and pray: for ye know not when the time is" (Mark 13:33). "The end of all things is at hand: be ye therefore sober, and watch unto prayer" (1 Peter 4:7). "Take heed to yourselves, lest at any time your hearts be overcharged with surfeiting, and drunkenness, and cares of this life, and so that day come upon you unawares. For as a snare shall it come on all them that dwell on the face of the whole earth. Watch ye therefore, and pray always, that ye may be accounted worthy to escape all these things that shall come to pass, and to stand before the Son of man" (Luke 21:34-36). "And what I say unto you I say unto all, Watch" (Mark 13:37).

"The prayer of faith is the great strength of the Christian and will assuredly prevail against Satan. This is why he *insinuates* that we have no need of prayer."[25] "Without unceasing prayer and diligent watching we are in danger of growing careless and of deviating from the right path. The adversary seeks continually to obstruct the way to the mercy seat, that we may not by earnest supplication and faith obtain grace and power to resist temptation."[26] "Satan leads many to believe that prayer to God is useless, and but a form. He well knows how needful is meditation and prayer, to keep Christ's followers aroused to resist his cunning and deceptions. Satan's devices will divert the mind from these important exercises, that the soul may not lean for help upon the mighty One, and obtain strength from him to resist his attacks."[27]

"While engaged in our daily work, we should lift the soul to heaven in prayer. These silent petitions rise like incense before the throne of grace; and the enemy is baffled. The Christian whose heart is thus stayed upon God cannot be overcome. No evil arts can destroy his peace. All the promises of God's word, all the power of divine grace, all the resources of Jehovah, are pledged to secure his deliverance. It was thus that Enoch walked with God. And God was with him, a present help in every time of need. . . .

"Prayer is the breath of the soul. It is the secret of spiritual power. No other means of grace can be substituted, and the health of the soul be preserved. Prayer brings the heart into immediate contact with the Well-spring of life, and strengthens the sinew and muscle of the religious experience. Neglect the exercise of prayer, or engage in prayer spasmodically, now and then, as seems convenient, and you lose your hold on God. The spiritual faculties lose their vitality, the religious experience lacks health and vigor."[28]

"There is necessity for diligence in prayer; let nothing hinder you. Make every effort to keep open the communion between Jesus and your own soul."[29] But remember, all of your persevering prayers will not cause God to hear or answer you. Persevering prayer "does not bring God down to us" but is for the purpose of bringing "us up to Him."

"Let the soul be drawn out and upward, that God may grant us a breath of the heavenly atmosphere. We may keep so near to God that

Chapter 8 — "There is a friend . . ."

in every unexpected trial our thoughts will turn to Him as naturally as the flower turns to the sun."[30] "If we would but think of God as often as we have evidence of His care for us we should keep Him ever in our thoughts and should delight to talk of Him and to praise Him. We talk of temporal things because we have an interest in them. We talk of our friends because we love them; our joys and our sorrows are bound up with them. Yet we have infinitely greater reason to love God than to love our earthly friends; it should be the most natural thing in the world to make Him first in all our thoughts, to talk of His goodness and tell of His power. The rich gifts He has bestowed upon us were not intended to absorb our thoughts and love so much that we should have nothing to give to God; they are constantly to remind us of Him and to bind us in bonds of love and gratitude to our heavenly Benefactor. We dwell too near the lowlands of earth. Let us raise our eyes to the open door of the sanctuary above, where the light of the glory of God shines in the face of Christ, who 'is able also to save them to the uttermost that come unto God by Him.' Hebrews 7:25."[31]

"Prayer is heaven's ordained means of success in the conflict with sin and the development of Christian character. The divine influences that come in answer to the prayer *of faith* will accomplish in the soul of the suppliant all for which he pleads. For the pardon of sin, for the Holy Spirit, for a Christlike temper, for wisdom and strength to do His work, for any gift He has promised, we may ask; and the promise is, 'Ye shall receive.'"[32]

When asking our Lord for something, it is important to keep in mind the power of His word. This word of His has creative power to accomplish that which He says. God "calleth those things which be not as though they were" (Rom. 4:17), for when He calls them, *they are*. When praying then, we need to entreat God as did the centurion saying, "Speak the word *only*" and these things shall be. The word is pledged, "Ask, and *it shall be given you*" (Matt. 7:7), and "If ye shall ask any thing in my name, *I will do it*" (John 14:14). On this matter Christ has given His word, and that almighty word will be fulfilled, because since He said it, *it is so*. Meet only the conditions of receiving that which you ask for, and it shall be yours. There is no power in earth or hell that can keep that word from being fulfilled if you will only meet the conditions. Knowing this, we should pray, "Lord, if it lies within the domain of Your good will, let such and such things be so. And I know that if it does lie within Your will, then it is done, for You have spoken the word."

"Be earnest; be resolute. Present the promise of God, and then believe without a doubt. Do not wait to feel special emotions before you think the Lord answers. Do not mark out some particular way that the Lord must work for you before you believe you receive the things you ask of him; but trust his word, and leave the whole matter in the hands of the Lord, with full faith that your prayer will be honored, and the answer will come at the very time and in the very way your heavenly Father sees is for your good; and then live out your prayers. Walk humbly and keep moving forward."[33]

It needs to be remembered that we do not receive God's blessings merely because by faith we claim God's promises. No. We claim God's promises by faith, and because we do this, God's promises claim us and we cannot help but be blessed. When we believe that God's all-powerful word will be fulfilled to us, it is not that we have control of God's promises and blessings but that God's promises and blessings have control of us. We merely believe, but it is His word that is in authority and that performs according to our faith. And if we will only believe, Christ's Word says, "According to your faith *be it unto you*" (Matt. 9:29).

When God prepared a place for man to live, He did not merely provide just the bare necessities of life. "Why has He given you the

Chapter 8 — "There is a friend . . ."

singing birds and the gentle blossoms, but from the overflowing love of a Father's heart, that would brighten and gladden your path of life? All that was needed for existence would have been yours without the flowers and birds, but God was not content to provide what would suffice for mere existence. He has filled earth and air and sky with glimpses of beauty to tell you of His loving thought for you. The beauty of all created things is but a gleam from the shining of His glory. If He has lavished such infinite skill upon the things of nature, for your happiness and joy, can you doubt that He will give you every needed blessing?"[34]

The same God who formed the delicate rose petals and painted them with such care and love that He might enjoy watching your heart thrill as He placed them in your hands, is desiring, even this day, to abundantly lavish upon you all the blessings that you would enjoy but do not necessarily need. But, "ye have not, because ye ask not" (James 4:2). "It is a part of God's plan to grant us, in answer to the prayer of faith, that which He would not bestow did we not thus ask."[35] While it is true that you are always to "be content with such things as ye have" (Heb. 13:5), there is no evil in asking God for things you want even though you do not need them. The problem is coveting things you don't have and not being satisfied with what you do have, for this is telling God that what He has given you isn't sufficient for your happiness and that He is therefore unjust. Jesus says, "Verily, verily, I say unto you, Whatsoever ye shall ask the Father in my name, he will give it you. Hitherto have ye asked nothing in my name: ask, and ye shall receive, that your joy may be full" (John 16:23, 24). "Delight thyself also in the LORD: and he shall give thee the desires of thine heart" (Ps. 37:4).

God is desiring to give us all the blessings that heaven can bestow; He is only waiting for us to believe the implied promise: "He that spared not his own Son, but delivered him up for us all, how shall he not with him also freely give us all things?" (Rom. 8:32). "What man is there of you, whom if his son ask bread, will he give him a stone? Or if he ask a fish, will he give him a serpent?" (Matt. 7:9, 10). "Or if he shall ask an egg, will he offer him a scorpion?" (Luke 11:12). "If ye then, being evil, know how to give good gifts unto your children, how much more shall your Father which is in heaven give good things to them that ask him?" (Matt. 7:11).

"Our heavenly Father waits to bestow upon us the fullness of His blessing. It is our privilege to drink largely at the fountain of boundless love. What a wonder it is that we pray so little! God is ready and willing to hear the sincere prayer of the humblest of His children, and yet there is much manifest reluctance on our part to make known our *wants* to God. What can the angels of heaven think of poor helpless human beings, who are subject to temptation, when God's heart of infinite love yearns toward them, ready to give them more than they can ask or think, and yet they pray so little and have so little faith? The angels love to bow before God; they love to be near Him. They regard communion with God as their highest joy; and yet the children of earth, who need so much the help that God only can give, seem satisfied to walk without the light of His Spirit, the companionship of His presence."[36]

All the riches of the eternal world are at your fingertips. Your Father is holding them out to you to receive them by faith. But if you don't believe that He gives them to you and take them from Him, then they will avail you nothing because you won't use them, though they are spread out before you as a rich feast. "The effectual fervent prayer of a righteous man availeth much. Elias was a man subject to like passions as we are, and he prayed earnestly that it might not rain: and it rained not on the earth by the space of three years and six months. And

Chapter 8 — "There is a friend . . ."

he prayed again, and the heaven gave rain, and the earth brought forth her fruit" (James 5:16-18). How can such a thing as this be possible? Jesus answers, "Verily I say unto you, If ye have faith, and doubt not" (Matt. 21:21).

Jesus has illustrated that your life is more important to Him than His own. It is your happiness that is His highest delight to fill. It is perfectly irrelevant what our trouble is at the time, whether it is a lack a faith, separation from loved ones, confusion as to what path to take next in life, or anything that might trouble us. If we will go to our Friend and Lover, we *will* find comfort in His love.

"Keep your *wants*, your *joys*, your *sorrows*, your *cares*, and your *fears* before God. You cannot burden Him; you cannot weary Him. He who numbers the hairs of your head is not indifferent to the wants of His children. 'The Lord is very pitiful, and of tender mercy.' James 5:11. His heart of love is touched by our sorrows and even by our utterances of them. Take to Him everything that perplexes the mind. Nothing is too great for Him to bear, for He holds up worlds, He rules over all the affairs of the universe. Nothing that in any way concerns our peace is too small for Him to notice. There is no chapter in our experience too dark for Him to read; there is no perplexity too difficult for Him to unravel. No calamity can befall the least of His children, no anxiety harass the soul, no joy cheer, no sincere prayer escape the lips, of which our heavenly Father is unobservant, or in which He takes no immediate interest. 'He healeth the broken in heart, and bindeth up their wounds.' Psalm 147:3. The relations between God and each soul are as distinct and full as though there were not another soul upon the earth to share His watchcare, not another soul for whom He gave His beloved Son."[37]

"And this is the confidence that we have in him, that, if we ask any thing according to his will, he heareth us: And if we know that he hear us, whatsoever we ask, we know that we have the petitions that we desired of him" (1 John 5:14, 15). Why is it that if we know that God hears us that we can also know that we have the petitions that we desire of Him? It is simple. It is because it requires faith to acknowledge that God hears us. And faith claims the promises of God and acknowledges the creative power of His word.

Chapter 9

"Take no thought . . ."
Luke 12:22

"The gospel is a wonderful simplifier of life's problems. Its instruction, heeded, would make plain many a perplexity and save us from many an error. It teaches us to estimate things at their true value and to give the most effort to the things of greatest worth—the things that will endure."[1]

In today's world, upon becoming of age, the youth are often taught lessons of stress, worry, anxiety, and fear, which they had previously not known or understood. They are taught these things because they are pointed to the uncertain future and are told that they must make plans for themselves or their lives will be ruined and they shall come to want. If these teachings are accepted by the youth, they stress over obtaining an education, they are anxious about how they are going to go off on their own and provide for themselves, and they worry about how they are going to pay for a car and a home, and eventually support a family. These things may run even the most stouthearted youth into the ground with perplexing care and overwhelming stress, and as a result, they will not be fitted to do the work of God in preaching the gospel, for their attention is diverted. But it will not be this way for the true Christian.

One of the most stress-relieving and peace-bringing commands that has ever been given to humanity was spoken by the Lord Jesus Himself when He said, "Take no thought for your life" (Matt. 6:25). Continuing this command, Jesus reveals what exactly we are not to take thought for, namely, the necessities of life: food, water, and clothing. Anything and everything that is essential to life in today's world will be given to us from God and we are forbidden by the Lord Jesus to take thought for.

Many will agree that this is true, but only to a point. They are sure that while God will provide for them, they must give much thought for their lives, planning and devising so that they may obtain the essentials needed to live successfully in this world. Jesus said, "Take no thought, saying, What shall we eat? or, What shall we drink? or, Wherewithal shall we be clothed?" (Matt. 6:31). Many Christians will insist that though God's provision for our necessities is sure, we must give thought to what we will obtain an education in, what our lifework will be, and how we are going to go about it all, that God may be able to provide for us. This is not so. These professed Christians ask, "What shall I study to obtain a good job? What shall I do for a living? By what means shall I support myself?" These questions bear great similarities to the ones Jesus told us to "take no thought" for, for in today's world, an education and job are necessities.

Why does Jesus command us to take no thought for the things that are required for life? The Lord's answer is, "For your heavenly Father knoweth that ye have need of all these things" (Matt. 6:32). Here Jesus brings out the fact that God is our Father. If God is our Father, then we are His sons and daughters. This father-child relationship we are to have with God is deeply significant and extremely important. Jesus said, "Except ye be converted, and become as little children, ye shall not enter into the kingdom of heaven" (Matt. 18:3).

So what exactly is it about the little children that Jesus values

Chapter 9 — "Take no thought . . ."

so much as to make being like them a requirement to enter into His kingdom? It's simple. The child lives by faith. He trusts that his father will give him everything he needs. He is perfectly thoughtless when it comes to what he is going to eat and drink tomorrow, and the last thing that could ever pop into his mind is how he is going to support himself in the future. His is but dimly even aware of the fact. Everything is provided for, both his wants and needs, and yet he provides nothing for himself. What he needs is *just there* for him when he needs it, and that is all he knows. He does not know of the time and effort it took to provide these things for him, they are just there. He does not think about future wants. He plans nothing for himself because he has no need to. His father plans his life out for him. His largest sphere of living is in the present moment. Outside of this, he only knows the past. He is blind to thoughts of future self-provision, because he is thoughtlessly dependent upon his father's care.

This is the way of trust and dependence that Jesus lived, and we have been privileged to live this way as well. "The Son of God was surrendered to the Father's will, and dependent upon His power. So utterly was Christ emptied of self that He made no plans for Himself. He accepted God's plans for Him, and day by day the Father unfolded His plans. So should we depend upon God, that our lives may be the simple outworking of His will."[2] "Let this mind be in you, which was also in Christ Jesus" (Phil. 2:5). Like Christ, you are to make no plans for yourself, but you are to merely accept God's plans for you, and wait, day by day, as He unfolds to you His plans. "God's purposes know no haste and no delay."[3] "He hath made every thing beautiful in his time" (Eccl. 3:11). "Wait, I say, on the LORD" (Ps. 27:14).

The notion of planning out our life and telling God that this is His plan for us and that He needs to now bless it is a notion that God rejects. Who are you to tell God what His plan is for you? Should it not

Saved by Works... Christ's Works!

be He that reveals to you His plan for your life? When it comes to what position in life we will fill, we are not to study and follow after our own wants and preferences, "We need to follow more closely God's plan of life. To do our best in the work that lies nearest, to commit our ways to God, and to watch for the indications of His providence—these are rules that ensure safe guidance in the choice of an occupation."[4] But if we will not do this, we cannot expect God's fullest blessing.

"If we surrender our lives to His service, we can *never* be placed in a position for which God has not made provision. Whatever may be our situation, we have a Guide to direct our way; whatever our perplexities, we have a sure Counselor; whatever our sorrow, bereavement, or loneliness, we have a sympathizing Friend. If in our ignorance we make missteps, Christ does not leave us. His voice, clear and distinct, is heard saying, 'I am the Way, the Truth, and the Life.' John 14:6. 'He shall deliver the needy when he crieth; the poor also, and him that hath no helper.' Psalm 72:12."[5]

Having given His command to take no thought for our lives and His reason for it (see Matt. 6:24, 25), Jesus continued, "Seek ye first the kingdom of God, and his righteousness; and all these things shall be added unto you" (Matt. 6:33). "There are many whose hearts are aching under a load of care because they seek to reach the world's standard. They have chosen its service, accepted its perplexities, adopted its customs. Thus their character is marred, and their life made a weariness. In order to gratify ambition and worldly desires, they wound the conscience, and bring upon themselves an additional burden of remorse. The continual worry is wearing out the life forces. Our Lord desires them to lay aside this yoke of bondage. He invites them to accept His yoke; He says, 'My yoke is easy, and My burden is light.' He bids them seek first the kingdom of God and His righteousness, and His promise is that all things needful to them for this life shall be

Chapter 9 — "Take no thought . . ."

added. Worry is blind, and cannot discern the future; but Jesus sees the end from the beginning. In every difficulty He has His way prepared to bring relief. Our heavenly Father has a thousand ways to provide for us, of which we know nothing. Those who accept the one principle of making the service and honor of God supreme will find perplexities vanish, and a plain path before their feet."[6]

Because the promise of the Lord is sure, that all things needed for this life will be abundantly given if we seek first God's kingdom and righteousness, Jesus continues, "Take therefore no thought for the morrow: for the morrow shall take thought for the things of itself. Sufficient unto the day is the evil thereof" (Matt. 6:34). For the third time the Lord here enjoins us to "take no thought."

"If you have given yourself to God, to do His work, you have no need to be anxious for tomorrow. He whose servant you are, knows the end from the beginning. The events of tomorrow, which are hidden from your view, are open to the eyes of Him who is omnipotent.

"When we take into our hands the management of things with which we have to do, and depend upon our own wisdom for success, we are taking a burden which God has not given us, and are trying to bear it without His aid. We are taking upon ourselves the responsibility that belongs to God, and thus are really putting ourselves in His place. We may well have anxiety and anticipate danger and loss, for it is certain to befall us. But when we *really* believe that God loves us and means to do us good we shall cease to worry about the future. We shall trust God as a child trusts a loving parent. Then our troubles and torments will disappear, for our will is swallowed up in the will of God.

"Christ has given us no promise of help in bearing today the burdens of tomorrow. He has said, 'My grace is sufficient for thee' (2 Corinthians 12:9); but, like the manna given in the wilderness, His grace

Saved by Works... Christ's Works!

is bestowed daily, for the day's need. Like the hosts of Israel in their pilgrim life, we may find morning by morning the bread of heaven for the day's supply.

"One day alone is ours, and during this day we are to live for God. For this one day we are to place in the hand of Christ, in solemn service, all our purposes and plans, casting all our care upon Him, for He careth for us. 'I know the thoughts that I think toward you, saith the Lord, thoughts of peace, and not of evil, to give you an expected end.'"[7]

God sought to teach Israel of old that they need not take thought for the necessities of their lives. With all Israel gathered as his audience, Moses repeated some of their history to them saying, "Thou shalt remember all the way which the LORD thy God led thee these forty years in the wilderness, to humble thee, and to prove thee, to know what was in thine heart, whether thou wouldest keep his commandments, or no. And he humbled thee, and suffered thee to hunger, and fed thee with manna, which thou knewest not, neither did thy fathers know; that he might make thee know that man doth not live by bread only, but by every word that proceedeth out of the mouth of the LORD doth man live. Thy raiment waxed not old upon thee, neither did thy foot swell, these forty years" (Deut. 8:2-4).

It was not because of Israel's anxious care or worrisome thought that for forty years manna was daily provided for them. Neither was it because they stressed themselves out with fear, that their raiment waxed not old nor their feet became swollen while wandering in the wilderness all that time. They literally lived by, and found their essentials in, the same creative word of God that spoke the universe into existence. This same word declares that if we will "take no thought" for our lives but seek first God's kingdom and righteousness, He will surely provide for our every need. And since this is what the word

Chapter 9 — "Take no thought . . ."

says, it has to be true, for it is the creative word that cannot lie.

Jesus was tempted severely upon the subject of the cares of this world, the necessities of life. After "being forty days tempted of the devil," days in which "he did eat nothing" (Luke 4:2), our Lord was severely in need of food, and the devil came to Him and said, "If thou be the Son of God, command that these stones be made bread" (Matt. 4:3). But how did our Lord reply? Did He doubt in God's promise of provision? After being without food for forty days, did He give the slightest thought that God's promise that every needful thing would be provided had failed or would fail? Oh no! "He answered and said, It is written, Man shall not live by bread alone, *but by every word that proceedeth out of the mouth of God*" (verse 4).

Jesus was here tempted to go out of God's order to provide food for Himself. Yet He refused to do this. He trusted God like a child trusts a faithful and loving parent—implicitly. Whatever the parent says must be so. The thought never even enters the child's mind that anything otherwise might be possible, much less is that thought entertained. Christ was to rely upon His Father's promise of provision just like He requires it of us today. He wants us to believe the promise and understand that "man shall not live by bread alone, but by every word of God" (Luke 4:4). The promise of God's word is more sure than our daily bread, and it is far more sure than the possibility that our own efforts will provide for our every need. Jesus said that we are to live by every word and promise of God, yet how many Christians are there who insist that they must live by a bread of their own feeble and worried efforts, and for this reason they suffer under such a load of care!

To these Christians, Satan also brings his temptations to go out of God's order and to provide for their own necessities. He tempts them to worry, to fear, to doubt the sure Word of God and to rely upon their own efforts, and with these followers of Jesus, he has far more

Saved by Works. . . Christ's Works!

success. But this need not be if they will live by and believe God's promise.

"In the wilderness, when all means of sustenance failed, God sent His people manna from heaven; and a sufficient and constant supply was given. This provision was to teach them that while they trusted in God and walked in His ways He would not forsake them. The Saviour now practiced the lesson He had taught to Israel. By the word of God succor had been given to the Hebrew host, and by the same word it would be given to Jesus. He awaited God's time to bring relief. He was in the wilderness in obedience to God, and He would not obtain food by following the suggestions of Satan. In the presence of the witnessing universe, He testified that it is a less calamity to suffer whatever may befall than to depart in any manner from the will of God.

"'Man shall not live by bread alone, but by every word of God.' Often the follower of Christ is brought where he cannot serve God and carry forward his worldly enterprises. Perhaps it appears that obedience to some plain requirement of God will cut off his means of support. Satan would make him believe that he must sacrifice his conscientious convictions. But the only thing in our world upon which we can rely is the word of God. 'Seek ye first the kingdom of God, and His righteousness; and all these things shall be added unto you.' Matthew 6:33. Even in this life it is not for our good to depart from the will of our Father in heaven. When we learn the power of His word, we shall not follow the suggestions of Satan in order to obtain food or to save our lives. Our only questions will be, What is God's command? and what His promise? Knowing these, we shall obey the one, and trust the other."[8]

Far too many professed followers of Christ trust in their efforts or their money for their provision, but God speaks plainly regarding those who trust in riches instead of trusting in Him. "Children, how

Chapter 9 — "Take no thought..."

hard is it for them that trust in riches to enter into the kingdom of God!" (Mark 10:24). The problem is not riches, in and of themselves. The problem is *trusting* in riches, whether they be of large amount or small. "Charge them that are rich in this world, that they be not highminded, nor trust in uncertain riches, but in the living God, who giveth us richly all things to enjoy; That they do good, that they be rich in good works, ready to distribute, willing to communicate" (1 Tim. 6:17, 18).

In the parable of the sower, "they which are sown among thorns [are] such as hear the word, And the cares of this world . . . choke the word, and it becometh unfruitful" (Mark 4:18, 19). The cares of this world can be very deadly, robbing those who become engrossed in them of eternal life. Jesus said, "Seek not ye what ye shall eat, or what ye shall drink, neither be ye of doubtful mind. For all these things do the nations of the world seek after: and your Father knoweth that ye have need of these things" (Luke 12:29, 30). Do not become engrossed in "the cares of this world." Seek not to provide for your own necessities. Worldlings choose these things as their all-important portion, but Christians choose Christ as their all in all, believing that He will provide for them. "Some dwell upon what they shall eat and drink, and wherewithal they shall be clothed. These thoughts flow out from the abundance of the heart, as though temporal things were the grand aim in life, the highest attainment. These persons forget the words of Christ: 'Seek ye first the kingdom of God, and His righteousness; and all these things shall be added unto you.'"[9]

"Though their present needs are supplied, many are unwilling to trust God for the future, and they are in constant anxiety lest poverty shall come upon them, and their children shall be left to suffer. Some are always anticipating evil or magnifying the difficulties that really exist, so that their eyes are blinded to the many blessings which de-

Saved by Works... Christ's Works!

mand their gratitude. The obstacles they encounter, instead of leading them to seek help from God, the only Source of strength, separate them from Him, because they awaken unrest and repining."[10] The apostle warns, "Take heed, brethren, lest there be in any of you an evil heart of unbelief, in departing from the living God" (Heb. 3:12).

Paul speaks of a people who suppose "that gain is godliness"; "from such," he says, "withdraw thyself" (1 Tim. 6:5). He continues, "Godliness with contentment is great gain. For we brought nothing into this world, and it is certain we can carry nothing out. And having food and raiment let us be therewith content" (verses 6-8). How many Christians are honestly content having only food and raiment? Not many. Rather, these Christians desire to have more, to be richer so that they may be free from care and want and live "the easy life." They may sincerely think within themselves that they desire to be rich so that they can give more back to God, and this may even be, but they need to be careful not to forget that Jesus talks about the "deceitfulness of riches" which "choke the word" (Mark 4:19). Beware of insisting upon being rich, assuring yourselves that God will keep you safe. Riches have a deceitfulness to them.

Paul said, "They that will be rich fall into temptation and a snare, and into many foolish and hurtful lusts, which drown men in destruction and perdition. For the love of money is the root of all evil: which while some coveted after, they have erred from the faith, and pierced themselves through with many sorrows. But thou, O man of God, flee these things; and follow after righteousness, godliness, faith, love, patience, meekness. Fight the good fight of faith, lay hold on eternal life, whereunto thou art also called, and hast professed a good profession before many witnesses" (1 Tim. 6:9-12). "Thou therefore endure hardness, as a good soldier of Jesus Christ. No man that warreth entangleth himself with the affairs of this life; that he may please him who hath

Chapter 9 — "Take no thought . . ."

chosen him to be a soldier" (2 Tim. 2:3, 4).

The professed Christian's worldly wisdom is in constant combat with "the wisdom that is from above" (James 3:17). It makes the plain words of Scripture to mean the opposite of what they say. The words "take no thought for your life . . . [for] your heavenly Father knoweth that ye have need" (Luke 12:22, 30) are made to mean, "take much thought for your life, for though God knows you have need of things, He will not necessarily always provide them for you, and you need to have a little reserve laid up for times like these." The words "casting all your care upon him; for he careth for you" (1 Peter 5:7) are made to mean, "cast most of your cares upon God, but not quite all of them, because He doesn't care for you enough to take care of them *all* for you." The words "be careful for nothing; but in every thing . . . let your requests be made known unto God" (Phil. 4:6) are made to mean, "be careful for almost everything, because though you can take your troubles to the Lord who is your Shepherd, you shall come to want." The words, "seek ye first the kingdom of God, and his righteousness; and all these things shall be added unto you" (Matt. 6:33) are made to mean, "if you seek first the kingdom of God and His righteousness, the necessities of life will not necessarily be added, so you may have to seek these things first at times."

Do you note the wicked ring of unbelief in these twisted views of truth? It is this class of people who Jesus calls "of doubtful mind" (Luke 12:29). Paul asks, "What if some did not believe? shall their unbelief make the faith of God without effect? God forbid: yea, let God be true, but every man a liar" (Rom. 3:3, 4). These people of doubtful minds make the righteous God a liar through their unbelief! They proclaim to worldlings that they might as well remain worldlings, for there really is no God which will love, care, and provide for them. Their own corroding care that corrupts them will corrupt the innocent, and they must give an account to God for their influence, which is calculated to destroy souls and send them to perdition. "The wisdom of this world is foolishness with God" (1 Cor. 3:19).

Those who possess and cherish this worldly wisdom may say, "Oh, but things have always worked this way! We have always taken thought and care for the necessities of our lives." The words of Jesus to them are, "Full well ye reject the commandment of God, that ye may keep your own tradition" (Mark 7:9). If these people insist upon taking thought for their lives, which causes them to be anxious, worrisome, and stressed, and they do this because they obviously believe in a different Jesus than the One brought to view in the Scriptures, then let them live in their misery. It is your privilege as a child of your Father in heaven to let Him take all the thought and care of your life for you and let Him manage it.

It needs to be made clear, however, that laziness and slothfulness are not upheld by Jesus as characteristics to be obtained. We are not to sit around doing nothing and expect the Lord to drop food into our mouths. It is clearly written, "Go to the ant, thou sluggard; consider her ways, and be wise: Which having no guide, overseer, or ruler, Provideth her meat in the summer, and gathereth her food in the harvest" (Prov. 6:6-8). "I went by the field of the slothful, and by the vineyard of the man void of understanding; And, lo, it was all grown over with thorns, and nettles had covered the face thereof, and the stone wall thereof was broken down. Then I saw, and considered it well: I looked upon it, and received instruction" (Prov. 24:30-32). "How long wilt thou sleep, O sluggard? when wilt thou arise out of thy sleep? Yet a little sleep, a little slumber, a little folding of the hands to sleep: So shall thy poverty come as one that travelleth, and thy want as an armed man" (Prov. 6:9-11). "Slothfulness casteth into a deep sleep; and an

Chapter 9 — "Take no thought . . ."

idle soul shall suffer hunger" (Prov. 19:15). "The desire of the slothful killeth him; for his hands refuse to labour" (Prov. 21:25). "The hand of the diligent shall bear rule: but the slothful shall be under tribute" (Prov. 12:24). "The way of the slothful man is as an hedge of thorns: but the way of the righteous is made plain" (Prov. 15:19). "Behold, this was the iniquity of thy sister Sodom . . . abundance of idleness was in her and in her daughters" (Eze. 16:49).

While it is true that we are to be "not slothful in business" but "fervent in spirit; serving the Lord" (Rom. 12:11), we need to understand that there is a difference between working and worrying, striving and stressing, advancing and apprehending, taking action and being anxious, and forwarding things versus fretting over them. The Lord requires us to take action, to work, and to strive. But the Lord strictly forbids us to be anxious, fretful, worried, or stressed. You are to put forth effort, but let the weight of unseen results rest completely on your Father in heaven. He knows you have needs.

Many Christians get this notion from the world that there is both good and bad stress and that we should keep the former and dispose of the latter. But this idea is erroneous. Stress, both "good and bad," by its very nature destroys the peace of the soul. "Thou wilt keep him in perfect peace, whose mind is stayed on thee: because he trusteth in thee" (Isa. 26:3). To live a life of perfect peace means to live a life without stress. Paul says that "every man shall bear his own burden" (Gal. 6:5). But burdens, of themselves, do not destroy the peace of the soul. They can, if they are allowed to, but stress, of itself, will always destroy the peace of the soul. A person can be burdened without being stressed, and one can also be stressed without being burdened. Therefore, we may conclude that burdens and stress are not one and the same thing.

Jesus says twice, "Let not your heart be troubled" (John 14:1).

Saved by Works... Christ's Works!

This is a loving command, not merely a suggestion. Do not let your heart be troubled. Jesus said, "Peace I leave with you, my peace I give unto you: not as the world giveth, give I unto you. Let not your heart be troubled, neither let it be afraid" (John 14:27). Why do we not believe this promise? "Do we well to be thus unbelieving? Why should we be ungrateful and distrustful? Jesus is our friend; all heaven is interested in our welfare; and our anxiety and fear grieve the Holy Spirit of God."[11] But we have been commanded, "*Grieve not* the holy Spirit of God, whereby ye are sealed unto the day of redemption" (Eph. 4:30). To be stressed is to sin against God, to break the blessed command of the Lord Jesus. To be stressed is to doubt that He loves you and that He will take care of absolutely everything, both great and small, in your life. Satan may insinuate to you through thoughts and feelings that you are stressed, but you do not have to accept his lie. "Resist the devil, and he *will flee* from you" (James 4:7).

"We should not indulge in a solicitude that only frets and wears us, but does not help us to bear trials. No place should be given to that distrust of God which leads us to make a preparation against future want the chief pursuit of life, as though our happiness consisted in these earthly things. It is not the will of God that His people should be weighed down with care. But our Lord does not tell us that there are no dangers in our path. He does not propose to take his people out of the world of sin and evil, but he points us to a never-failing refuge. He invites the weary and care-laden, 'Come unto Me, all ye that labor and are heavy-laden, and I will give you rest.' Lay off the yoke of anxiety and worldly care *that you have placed on your own neck*, and 'take My yoke upon you, and learn of Me; for I am meek and lowly in heart: and ye shall find rest unto your souls.' Matthew 11:28, 29. We may find rest and peace in God, casting all our care upon Him; for he careth for us."[12] The command of Jesus, which forbids us to be stressed, is truly

Chapter 9 — "Take no thought . . ."

a "law of liberty" (James 1:25).

The apostle writes saying, "*let* the peace of God rule in your hearts" (Col. 3:15). He does not say, "*Strive to make* the peace of God rule in your hearts," but *let* it rule in your hearts. One requires a never-ending fruitless effort to obtain peace; the other requires only a simple, calm submission to the peace that God gives.

In the beginning after the fall, God said to Adam, "Cursed is the ground *for thy sake*" (Gen. 3:17). "God appointed labor as a blessing to man, to occupy his mind, to strengthen his body, and to develop his faculties. In mental and physical activity Adam found one of the highest pleasures of his holy existence. And when, as a result of his disobedience, he was driven from his beautiful home, and forced to struggle with a stubborn soil to gain his daily bread, that very labor, although widely different from his pleasant occupation in the garden, was a safeguard against temptation and a source of happiness. Those who regard work as a curse, attended though it be with weariness and pain, are cherishing an error. . . . Our Creator, who understands what is for man's happiness, appointed Adam his work. The true joy of life is found only by the working men and women. The angels are diligent workers; they are the ministers of God to the children of men. The Creator has prepared no place for the stagnating practice of indolence."[13]

God gave work to man to prove a blessing to him. But man has made work a curse to himself by learning to trust to his work, his efforts, and his money for provision, and as a result, he stresses himself out instead of trusting in his Creator and living in perfect peace. Just as man seeks to provide for his eternal life by his own works, by depending upon what *he* can do, even so men try to provide for their mortal lives the provision that God freely gives to them in this life. But they are only wasting their time and insulting their Savior.

Human effort and God's provision are two entirely separate things.

Saved by Works... Christ's Works!

It is not because you work that God provides. God provides for you while, in the meantime, you are working. Should God cease to make the seed to germinate, the plants to grow, the sun to shine, and the rain to fall, all the efforts of man to obtain his daily bread would prove utterly useless. Man might as well flap his arms in effort to fly as to provide the necessities of life for himself. And sooner would man have success trying to fly by flapping his arms than to provide for himself a single morsel of food with which to nourish his body.

But even the efforts of daily labor are to be performed *by faith*. The fourth commandment and promise is, "Six days *shalt thou* labour, and do all thy work" (Ex. 20:9). By believing this promise, the creative words of this promise will perform in your behalf. Oh how relieving it is to depend upon the creative promise of God to perform our daily work for us! Through us! Then when we become weary, we need not make any physical efforts to continue working because the word will cause us to get the job done. Oh the love that God has toward us! He has left *nothing* undone for His beloved. It is all a free gift! What an awesome Lover!

Christ has spoken the word saying, "Seek ye first the kingdom of God, and his righteousness; and all these things shall be added unto you" (Matt. 6:33). This is the spoken word of God, and whatever God says becomes a fact because of the creative power of His word. Therefore, if you will only fulfill the condition of seeking first God's kingdom and His righteousness, everything necessary for life will be provided for you, because if provision for life is not already, it will become, because the word of God itself will create the thing it spoke. Even if the very stones of the ground must turn into manna from heaven, all your needs will be provided for by the word of God. Jesus makes it clear that "man shall not live by bread alone, *but by every word that proceedeth out of the mouth of God*" (Matt. 4:4).

Chapter 9 — "Take no thought . . ."

When Christ sent forth the seventy to do missionary work, He gave the instructions, "Carry neither purse, nor scrip, nor shoes" (Luke 10:4). He sent them forth with nothing with which to provide for themselves, and the Lord asked them later saying, "When I sent you without purse, and scrip, and shoes, lacked ye any thing?" And what was the disciples' answer? "Nothing" (Luke 22:35).

"Matthew 'left all, rose up, and followed Him.' There was no hesitation, no questioning, no thought of the lucrative business to be exchanged for poverty and hardship. It was enough for him that he was to be with Jesus, that he might listen to His words, and unite with Him in His work.

"So it was with the disciples previously called. When Jesus bade Peter and his companions follow Him, immediately they left their boats and nets. Some of these disciples had friends dependent on them for support; but when they received the Saviour's invitation, they did not hesitate, and inquire, How shall I live, and sustain my family? They were obedient to the call; and when afterward Jesus asked them, 'When I sent you without purse, and scrip, and shoes, lacked ye anything?' they could answer, 'Nothing.' Luke 22:35."[14]

But how is it that the disciples lacked nothing? It is because the word was pledged, "Seek ye first the kingdom of God, and His righteousness; and all these things shall be added unto you" (Matt. 6:33). That spoken word provided for them. They had met the conditions of receiving the promised provision of the word and their needs were supplied. And if we will only fulfill the same conditions today, those same creative words will provide for us.

All of us have infirmities and necessities that seem to make life full of uncertainties, but this need not be so. The Lord Jesus said to Paul, "My grace is sufficient for thee: for my strength is made perfect in weakness. Most gladly therefore," Paul replied, "will I rather glory

Saved by Works... Christ's Works!

in my infirmities, that the power of Christ may rest upon me. Therefore I take pleasure in infirmities" and "in necessities . . . for when I am weak, then am I strong" (2 Cor. 12:9, 10). Oh if we would but trust in Christ's all sufficient grace, what a joy and pleasure would be ours!

While it is true that Christ does not condemn prudence or foresight when dealing with the things of this life, if the faintest trace of worry, stress, anxiety, or doubt ever enter the mind, these things must be immediately repulsed, for it is not the Lord's will for your heart to be thus troubled over the things of this world. He said, "Let not your heart be troubled" (John 14:1).

"If we will but listen, God's created works will teach us precious lessons of obedience and trust. From the stars that in their trackless courses through space follow from age to age their appointed path, down to the minutest atom, the things of nature obey the Creator's will. And God cares for everything and sustains everything that He has created. He who upholds the unnumbered worlds throughout immensity, at the same time cares for the wants of the little brown sparrow that sings its humble song without fear. When men go forth to their daily toil, as when they engage in prayer; when they lie down at night, and when they rise in the morning; when the rich man feasts in his palace, or when the poor man gathers his children about the scanty board, each is tenderly watched by the heavenly Father. No tears are shed that God does not notice. There is no smile that He does not mark.

"If we would but fully believe this, all undue anxieties would be dismissed. Our lives would not be so filled with disappointment as now; for everything, whether great or small, would be left in the hands of God, who is not perplexed by the multiplicity of cares, or overwhelmed by their weight. We should then enjoy a rest of soul to which many have long been strangers."[15]

"In the heart of Christ, where reigned perfect harmony with God, there was perfect peace. He was never elated by applause, nor dejected by censure or disappointment. Amid the greatest opposition and the most cruel treatment, He was still of good courage. But many who profess to be His followers have an anxious, troubled heart, because they are afraid to trust themselves with God. They do not make a complete surrender to Him; for they shrink from the consequences that such a surrender may involve. Unless they do make this surrender, they cannot find peace."[16]

"Those who take Christ at His word, and surrender their souls to His keeping, their lives to His ordering, will find peace and quietude. Nothing of the world can make them sad when Jesus makes them glad by His presence. In perfect acquiescence there is perfect rest. The Lord says, 'Thou wilt keep him in perfect peace, whose mind is stayed on Thee: because he trusteth in Thee.' Isaiah 26:3. Our lives may seem a tangle; but as we commit ourselves to the wise Master Worker, He will bring out the pattern of life and character that will be to His own glory. And that character which expresses the glory—character—of Christ will be received into the Paradise of God. A renovated race shall walk with Him in white, for they are worthy."[17]

Whatever your burden may be, take it to Jesus and *leave it with Him*. Do not get up off your knees with your burden still on your back and continue to go throughout your day. How strange would it be to ask a friend to carry something for you and upon his most joyful acceptance of the burden you never give it to him, or if you did, to immediately take it back. How would the one who offered to help feel if you did this? He was utterly delighted to do something to comfort you and make your life easier, but you withheld this blessing from him. How cruel! When you bring your burdens to Jesus, take them off your back, place them in His almighty hands, and, leaving the burden with Him, continue burden-free throughout your day. It is His greatest delight to

Saved by Works... Christ's Works!

bring you peace of mind and rest of soul. Don't refuse Him such a joy and make yourself miserable in the process.

Jesus invites you saying, "Come unto Me, all ye that labour and are heavy laden, and I will give you rest" (Matt. 11:28). "All the earth is mine" (Ex. 19:5). And shall not your Beloved lavish upon you everything you could want, much less the things you need? If you will just submit to the offer, "Take my yoke upon you, and learn of me; for I am meek and lowly in heart" (Matt. 11:29), if you will just obey the beautiful promise, "Take no thought for your life" (Matt. 6:25), if you will just now choose to seek God's kingdom and righteousness before everything else and choose to believe the promise that all things necessary for this life will be abundantly given to you, "ye shall find rest unto your souls," for His "yoke is easy" and His "burden is light" (Matt. 11:29, 30). "My God shall supply *all your need* according to his riches in glory by Christ Jesus" (Phil. 4:19).

Chapter 10

"All things . . ."
Romans 8:28

So often we grow up with the understanding that "all things work together for good to them that love God" (Rom. 8:28), while in reality, we don't really understand or believe it as we should. If this one Bible verse, which is a favorite of many, was thoroughly understood, believed, and accepted then the life of the Christian would be one of a constant comfort and joy, never to be interrupted by *anything*.

Into our lives come many little things that seem to ruin the few enjoyments of life and destroy our present peace. As for specifics, here are a few examples: we get bitten by mosquitoes while berry picking; we stub our toe before breakfast; we are gossiped about by friends; we lose our wallets and purses while shopping; we get sick on our vacation; we get hot and thirsty at the beach; we spill water on our new book; we run out of toilet paper when company is over; we forget to bring our lunch to the picnic; our best friends let us down when we really need them; we get interrupted when busy; the gift we bought for someone is delivered broken; the phone rings when we are sleeping; we leave our car window open and it rains; we get stains our on new clothes; a slug crawls out of our salad; a fly lands in our soup; we burn our food; we can't find the keys; our glasses break; someone cuts us off on the road; we slam our fingers in the door; the light goes

Saved by Works... Christ's Works!

out when it's dark; we can't find our tools we were just using; the restroom is closed; we get a flat tire on the way to the airport; we get stuck talking to someone that never stops; we must work long when we are weary, etc. All of these little things and many others that harass, annoy, perplex, and distress us often ruin the soul's present peace, and we are told by some that it is all of these little things that come from God.

Is it really true that God gives attention to such very small matters as stubbing our toes? Oh yes. The Bible makes it very clear. God says that, "He shall give his angels charge over thee, to keep thee in all thy ways. They shall bear thee up in their hands, lest thou dash thy foot against a stone" (Ps. 91:11, 12). Yes! God even has His angels bear us up in their own hands so that we do not stub our toes. What a thoughtful Creator! What a care He must have for us! Oh how it must pain Him to see us hurt! Although God does, in fact, allow us to stub our toes at times, how many times we have not stubbed them because of His thoughtful care for us we will only know in heaven.

Now, there are far greater things in life that much more effectually destroy our joy, happiness, and very desire for life, other than things as small as stubbing our toes. In the straight and narrow path, we are often delayed by obstacles, attacked by perplexities, saddened by failures, appalled at the standards, weary of temptations, condemned by our sins, worn with unending toil, and afflicted by some unforeseen event. We travel over slippery rocks. We must go barefoot through the thorns. We stumble and fall. The clouds hide the Son's loving warmth and cut off His bright rays of guiding light, while casting a dark shadow over our path. The storm's wind chills us, the rain slows us down, and we get stuck in the mud. Standing fastened where we are, we see the traces of those who have gone before us and notice the blood and tears that mark them. The prostrate forms of loved ones are scattered

Chapter 10 — "All things . . ."

low along the path. They have fallen from weariness and exhaustion. Looking forward, we see in this path only sacrifice, self-denial, pain, torture, and misery, and yet we are told that real Christians are happy people. How can this be? How can everything great and small that ruins and blights the very joy of life be said to come from God? Is God really the author of these things? Is it really God's will for us to suffer abuse, mistreatment, privation, and pain?

To be very plain, no. God is not the originator of these things that wound and hurt us. Sin is the author of our pain, and this pain may come to us through man or mere circumstances. But the pain we receive from sin is, in fact, God's will for us; it comes from God. How so? you ask. Because God permits it. Jesus Christ commands us, saying, "Resist not evil" (Matt. 5:39). And why does He command such an awkward thing as this? The whole world is out of harmony with this principle, and everyone seeks to defend themselves. The reason that Christ commands us to "resist not evil" is because He has pledged Himself as our defense.

So often we as Christians insist upon defending ourselves from harm when Jesus has told us that He will defend us from harm and that we need not fear of being wounded. We insist upon resisting evil ourselves, and once we get hurt, we complain to God and ask why He allowed us to be injured. Imagine a soldier having a bodyguard who has sworn to protect him even at the cost of his own life. On the battlefield, an enemy charges toward the solder for an attack. At the last second, the bodyguard jumps in between the soldier and his oncoming enemy and quickly raises his sword to block the deadly blow. Immediately, the soldier shoves him out of the way, attempts to block the blow himself, and ends up wounded as a result. Then, the weirdest thing happens! The soldier instantly becomes angry at the bodyguard for allowing him to get hurt and starts complaining about him! What a soldier! And yet this is the very thing we do to Christ, our great Bodyguard. But, "When we realize His great love we should be willing to trust everything to the hand that was nailed to the cross for us."[1]

God's promise that He will protect us is clear enough. "Fear thou not; for I am with thee: be not dismayed; for I am thy God: I will strengthen thee; yea, I will help thee; yea, I will uphold thee with the right hand of my righteousness" (Isa. 41:10). "When thou passest through the waters, I will be with thee; and through the rivers, they shall not overflow thee: when thou walkest through the fire, thou shalt not be burned; neither shall the flame kindle upon thee" (Isa. 43:2). "A thousand shall fall at thy side, and ten thousand at thy right hand; but it shall not come nigh thee. . . . There shall no evil befall thee, neither shall any plague come nigh thy dwelling. . . . Thou shalt tread upon the lion and adder: the young lion and the dragon shalt thou trample under feet" (Ps. 91:7-13). "Behold, I give unto you power to tread on serpents and scorpions, and over all the power of the enemy: and nothing shall by any means hurt you" (Luke 10:19). "No weapon that is formed against thee shall prosper" (Isa. 54:17).

The reassuring words of the men of the past declare to us: "The LORD is our defence" (Ps. 89:18). "He is my defence; I shall not be moved" (Ps. 62:6). "The LORD . . . is our help and our shield" (Ps. 33:20). "The LORD is my rock, and my fortress, and my deliverer; The God of my rock; in him will I trust: he is my shield, and the horn of my salvation, my high tower, and my refuge, my saviour; thou savest me from violence" (2 Sam. 22:2, 3). "He shall deliver thee in six troubles: yea, in seven there shall no evil touch thee" (Job 5:19). "What shall we then say to these things? If God be for us, who can be against us?" (Rom. 8:31).

What we need to understand far more thoroughly than we do is that "except the LORD keep the city, the watchman waketh but in

Chapter 10 — "All things . . ."

vain" (Ps. 127:1). We are to say with the psalmist, "Some trust in chariots, and some in horses: but we will remember the name of the LORD our God" (Ps. 20:7).

"God cares for everything and sustains everything that He has created. He who upholds the unnumbered worlds throughout immensity, at the same time cares for the wants of the little brown sparrow that sings its humble song without fear. When men go forth to their daily toil, as when they engage in prayer; when they lie down at night, and when they rise in the morning; when the rich man feasts in his palace, or when the poor man gathers his children about the scanty board, each is tenderly watched by the heavenly Father. No tears are shed that God does not notice. There is no smile that He does not mark."[2] "Not a sigh is breathed, not a pain felt, not a grief pierces the soul, but the throb vibrates to the Father's heart."[3]

"His heart of love is touched by our sorrows and even by our utterances of them. . . . Nothing that in any way concerns our peace is too small for Him to notice. There is no chapter in our experience too dark for Him to read; there is no perplexity too difficult for Him to unravel. No calamity can befall the least of His children, no anxiety harass the soul, no joy cheer, no sincere prayer escape the lips, of which our heavenly Father is unobservant, or in which He takes no immediate interest. 'He healeth the broken in heart, and bindeth up their wounds.' Psalm 147:3. The relations between God and each soul are as distinct and full as though there were not another soul upon the earth to share His watchcare, not another soul for whom He gave His beloved Son."[4]

Our God, who sees "the end from the beginning" (Isa. 46:10), always knows what is best for us, and unless He moves out of the way and permits evil to come through to us, a single hair of our head, which He has indeed numbered (Matt. 10:30), cannot even be ruffled.

"The Father's presence encircled Christ, and nothing befell Him but that which infinite love permitted for the blessing of the world. Here was His source of comfort, and it is for us. He who is imbued with the Spirit of Christ abides in Christ. The blow that is aimed at him falls upon the Saviour, who surrounds him with His presence. Whatever comes to him comes *from* Christ. He has no need to resist evil, for Christ is his defense. Nothing can touch him except by our Lord's permission, and 'all things' that are permitted 'work together for good to them that love God.' Romans 8:28."[5] "All our sufferings and sorrows, all our temptations and trials, all our sadness and griefs, all our persecutions and privations, in short, all things work together for our good. All experiences and circumstances are God's workmen whereby good is brought to us."[6]

If the Lord Jesus is truly our Defense, our Shield, and our Deliverer, then whatever comes to us has to pass Him first. Christ gently assures His weary followers, "I know the thoughts that I think toward you . . . thoughts of peace, and not of evil" (Jer. 29:11). Then He gives the command of rest, "Be careful for nothing" (Phil. 4:6). The word "careful" in the original Greek means *anxious* or, if we take the literal breakdown of the word, *care-full*, meaning *full of care*. The word "nothing" in the original Greek really means *nothing*. You are not to care for yourself, but "casting all your care upon him," you are to believe that "he careth for you" (1 Peter 5:7). You are not to care for yourself because God cares *for* you; He cares in place of you; He cares instead of you. This is one reason why He said not to resist evil. Those who love Jesus and yet resist evil are resisting what He sees as best for them; they are resisting that very thing which will work together for their own good; they are resisting that which comes to them from Love Himself. "Faith is trusting God—believing that He loves us and knows best what is for our good. Thus, instead of our own, it leads us to choose His way."[7]

Chapter 10 — "All things . . ."

Jesus said, "Abide in me" (John 15:4). If we will abide in Christ and allow Him to abide in us, then we are protected by His presence, for we are within Him. "He that dwelleth in the secret place of the most High shall abide under the shadow of the Almighty" (Ps. 91:1). We read concerning the Lord, "He shall cover thee with his feathers, and under his wings shalt thou trust" (verse 4). These feathers with which God covers us are far more impenetrable than dragons' scales. Nothing, absolutely *nothing*, can penetrate these holy feathers of love. If we choose to abide under His wings, if we claim His promise of protection with the choice of faith, then *nothing* bad can happen to us unless infinite Love gently moves these wings aside to allow the evil in.

All the purposes of wicked men and angels to bring about your sorrow and demise through location or circumstances cannot defeat God's command to bless you. "Behold," says the prophet, "I have received commandment to bless: and he hath blessed; and I cannot reverse it" (Num. 23:20). "How shall I curse, whom God hath not cursed? or how shall I defy, whom the LORD hath not defied?" (verse 8).

"When trials arise that seem unexplainable, we should not allow our peace to be spoiled. However unjustly we may be treated, let not passion arise. By indulging a spirit of retaliation we injure ourselves. We destroy our own confidence in God, and grieve the Holy Spirit. There is by our side a witness, a heavenly messenger, who will lift up for us a standard against the enemy. He will shut us in with the bright beams of the Sun of Righteousness. Beyond this Satan cannot penetrate. He cannot pass this shield of holy light."[8]

We have the great blessing, joy, and privilege of abiding under Christ's almighty wings of protection, and we have also been given the command, "Let your conversation be without covetousness; and be content with such things as ye have: for he hath said, I will never leave thee, nor forsake thee" (Heb. 13:5). As long as we have Christ

Saved by Works... Christ's Works!

as our Shepherd, our Provider and Protector, we shall have no wants or needs. What could we ever covet while we are resting under His wings?

Do we have any examples when evil was allowed to pass this circle of protection and it was said to come *from* God? Oh yes! After those great and many evils befell the faithful Job, he inspirationally declared, "the LORD gave, and the LORD hath taken away," and to finish it, as we always should, he said, "blessed be the name of the LORD" (Job 1:21). Joseph was sold into slavery by his own brothers. To all appearances, this could not have come from God. It was a wicked sin of his brothers to treacherously sell him over to the Egyptians to bear the unenviable position of a slave. But God permitted this great evil to come upon Joseph, and Joseph later declared to his brothers, "Be not grieved, nor angry with yourselves, that ye sold me hither: for God did send me before you to preserve life" (Gen. 45:5). "Ye thought evil against me; but God meant it unto good, to bring to pass, as it is this day, to save much people alive" (Gen. 50:20). Do we need any more examples?

"Oh why," we ask ourselves, "does God allow such trials and afflictions to come to me? Can't He find a better way to work things out for my good?"

"Many who sincerely consecrate their lives to God's service are surprised and disappointed to find themselves, as never before, confronted by obstacles and beset by trials and perplexities. They pray for Christlikeness of character, for a fitness for the Lord's work, and they are placed in circumstances that seem to call forth all the evil of their nature. Faults are revealed of which they did not even suspect the existence. Like Israel of old they question, 'If God is leading us, why do all these things come upon us?'

"It is because God is leading them that these things come upon them. Trials and obstacles are the Lord's chosen methods of discipline and His appointed conditions of success. He who reads the hearts of men knows their characters better than they themselves know them. He sees that some have powers and susceptibilities which, rightly directed, might be used in the advancement of His work. In His providence He brings these persons into different positions and varied circumstances that they may discover in their character the defects which have been concealed from their own knowledge. He gives them opportunity to correct these defects and to fit themselves for His service. Often He permits the fires of affliction to assail them that they may be purified.

"The fact that we are called upon to endure trial shows that the Lord Jesus sees in us something precious which He desires to develop. If He saw in us nothing whereby He might glorify His name, He would not spend time in refining us. He does not cast worthless stones into His furnace. It is valuable ore that He refines. The blacksmith puts the iron and steel into the fire that he may know what manner of metal they are. The Lord allows His chosen ones to be placed in the furnace of affliction to prove what temper they are of and whether they can be fashioned for His work."[9]

"Our sorrows do not spring out of the ground. God 'doth not afflict willingly nor grieve the children of men.' Lamentations 3:33. When He permits trials and afflictions, it is 'for our profit, that we might be partakers of His holiness.' Hebrews 12:10. If received in faith, the trial that seems so bitter and hard to bear will prove a blessing. The cruel blow that blights the joys of earth will be the means of turning our eyes to heaven."[10]

"In every affliction God has a purpose to work out for our good. Every blow that destroys an idol, every providence that weakens our hold upon earth and fastens our affections more firmly upon God, is a bless-

Saved by Works... Christ's Works!

ing. The pruning may be painful for a time, but afterward it 'yieldeth the peaceable fruit of righteousness.' We should receive with gratitude whatever will quicken the conscience, elevate the thoughts, and ennoble the life. The fruitless branches are cut off and cast into the fire. Let us be thankful that through painful pruning, we may retain a connection with the living Vine; for if we suffer with Christ, we shall also reign with him. The very trial that taxes our faith the most severely and makes it seem as though God had forsaken us, is to lead us more clearly to him, that we may lay all our burdens at the feet of Christ, and experience the peace which he will give us in exchange. Let no Christian feel that he is forsaken when the hour of trial comes upon him. Not a sparrow falls to the ground without your heavenly Father's notice. God loves and cares for the feeblest of his creatures, and we cannot dishonor him more than by doubting his love to us. O let us cultivate that living faith that will trust him in the hour of darkness and trial! Living faith in the merits of a crucified Redeemer will carry men through the fiery furnace of affliction and trial, and the form of the Fourth will be with them in the furnace, however fierce its heat; and they will come forth from its flame with not even the smell of the fire on their garments."[11]

"The Lord permits trials in order that we may be cleansed from earthliness, from selfishness, from harsh, unchristlike traits of character. He suffers the deep waters of affliction to go over our souls in order that we may know Him and Jesus Christ whom He has sent, in order that we may have deep heart longings to be cleansed from defilement, and may come forth from the trial purer, holier, happier. Often we enter the furnace of trial with our souls darkened with selfishness; but if patient under the crucial test, we shall come forth reflecting the divine character."[12]

Here is the reason God allows us to suffer all types of trials and afflictions. God allows us to stub our toes to test us, to see if we will

Chapter 10 — "All things . . ."

praise Him still or if we will burst out with cursing and swearing. He allows us to come to utter want to see if we will trust in Him for provision. He allows our friends to abuse us to see if we will cherish a spirit of revenge and seek to abuse them back. He allows us to be put in positions where harassments attack us on all sides to see if we will remain cheerful and bear the test patiently. He allows all of these things for the purpose of fitting us for heaven. "All things," says Paul, "are for your sakes" (2 Cor. 4:15).

No wonder the apostle James could so earnestly say to his brethren, "Count it all joy when ye fall into divers temptations" (James 1:2). Everything that harasses, annoys, afflicts, saddens, or wounds us is a precious token of Christ's love for us and is evidence that He is working for our salvation. The next time someone annoys you, the next time your patience is tried, the next time you suffer loss, the next time you find yourself without means to purchase necessities, the next time you stub your toe or can't find your pencil, it is your wonderful privilege to rejoice and be exceedingly glad—to take joy in the blessing of abiding under His wings and to give praise to the name of Jesus. Some may think that this would be a ridiculously absurd way to handle your troubles, but let them suffer if they will. You have the privilege of being utterly ecstatic when misfortune comes your way, while they can only be unhappy and unpleasant. While they are crying in sorrow, you will be laughing in joy. If you will live in such a state as this, there will be far fewer instances where you will frown, and you will find that your facial muscles will quickly tire from smiling.

That is not to say that while you are in front of others you should roll around on the floor in hysterical laughter when your cell phone breaks—your audience might think you have a problem. Nor is it to say that you must jump around excitedly when your best friend dies, but you are never to question why God has allowed this to happen to

Saved by Works... Christ's Works!

you. The answer is clear enough. Say rather with Paul, "I have learned, in whatsoever state I am, therewith to be content" (Phil. 4:11).

"God's children are always being tested in the furnace of affliction. If they endure the first trial, it is not necessary for them to pass through a similar ordeal the second time; but if they fail, the trial is brought to them again and again, each time being still more trying and severe. Thus opportunity after opportunity is placed before them of gaining the victory and proving themselves true to God. But if they continue to manifest rebellion, God is compelled at last to remove His Spirit and light from them."[13]

"God's love for His children during the period of their severest trial is as strong and tender as in the days of their sunniest prosperity."[14] "If we do represent Christ, we shall make His service appear attractive, as it really is. Christians who gather up gloom and sadness to their souls, and murmur and complain, are giving to others a false representation of God and the Christian life. They give the impression that God is not pleased to have His children happy, and in this they bear false witness against our heavenly Father."[15]

"The bright and cheerful side of our religion will be represented by all who are daily consecrated to God. We should not dishonor God by the mournful relation of trials that appear grievous. All trials that are received as educators will produce joy. The whole religious life will be uplifting, elevating, ennobling, fragrant with good words and works. The enemy is well pleased to have souls depressed, downcast, mourning and groaning; he wants just such impressions made as to the effect of our faith. But God designs that the mind shall take no low level. He desires every soul to triumph in the keeping power of the Redeemer."[16]

Jesus said, "Come unto me, all ye that labour and are heavy laden, and I will give you rest. Take my yoke upon you, and learn of me; for

Chapter 10 — "All things . . ."

I am meek and lowly in heart: and ye shall find rest unto your souls. For my yoke is easy, and my burden is light" (Matt. 11:28-30). If you will go to Christ and rest under His wings at every moment, trusting that everything that comes to you, both the evil and the good, really comes from Christ Himself, and if you will choose to believe that it comes from Him because He loves you, you will far better understand this rest that He has promised. "If you will seek the Lord and be converted every day; *if you will of your own spiritual choice be free and joyous in God*; if with gladsome consent of heart to His gracious call you come wearing the yoke of Christ,—the yoke of obedience and service,—all your murmurings will be stilled, all your difficulties will be removed, all the perplexing problems that now confront you will be solved."[17]

Chapter 11

"The truth shall make you free"
John 8:2

You are a sinner; you have broken God's law and are condemned to eternal death.[1] But because God loves you, He gave His Son Jesus to die for you so that you can live forever.[2] Knowing what Jesus did for you brings you to repentance in which you are really sorry for your sins.[3] Jesus is the One who gave you this sorrow as a gift, and if you come to Him asking for His forgiveness, He gives you that as well.[4] As long as you believe that He does, God now considers you as if you had never sinned, and you are justified by faith.[5] This faith has been given to you as a free gift from God so that you can receive all of His other gifts.[6] Now that you have been made righteous as if you had never sinned, you must remain this way if you expect to inherit God's kingdom.[7]

Since it is impossible for *you* to live righteously,[8] the only possible way that righteousness can be lived out in your life is if you let *Christ* dwell in your heart by faith and live righteously for you, in place of you, instead of you.[9] It is His righteous works and efforts, and not a speck of yours.[10] Since your heart must be emptied of self before it can be filled with Christ, and since you cannot empty your heart of self, God says that He will do it for you and then abide in your heart by faith.[11] Because Christ is now in your heart and sin, which includes

Chapter 11 — "The truth shall make you free"

not doing good, is expelled from your present life, you are therefore sanctified by faith, and He is your sanctification and righteousness.[12] You do not now live a sinless life because you are in control of God's power but because God's power is in control of you because you believe.[13] As long as you use the gift of choice, or faith, which you already have, and by this gift continue to believe that God does all of these things for you through Christ and the power of His *spoken* word, you will be saved.[14] And if you do this, you may *know* that you have eternal life, here and now.[15] But it is not because *you* chose Jesus that you are saved; *He chose you* and worked in you to choose Him.[16] You merely consented.

Now you live a life of perfect peace.[17] Christ is your Beloved.[18] Your every need is provided for, and even though you may not see how it is so, it is so, because *God said it.*[19] Nothing can happen to you unless your Beloved allows it to happen because He loves you.[20] You have received the promise of the Holy Spirit because you have asked for it and believe that you have received it and God's promise is fulfilled to you.[21] You do not now have control of the Holy Spirit, but the Holy Spirit now has control of you.[22] This gospel of Jesus is going to all the world through you and others, and Jesus will come back just as soon as everyone knows the truth of this gospel.[23]

Saved by Works... Christ's Works!

If Men Only Knew...

If men only knew,
Just how good,
How good the good news is;
Could they help but be saved?
Would they not shout His praise?
And do the good works that He did?

If men only knew,
Just how good,
How good the good news is;
Could they help but find peace?
From their sins find release?
And rejoice in salvation that is?

If men only knew,
Just how good,
How good the good news is;
Knowing of His great love,
Could they help but sing like a dove?
And love Him just how He is?

If men only knew,
How good it is,
How the news is just so good;
Could they help but be blessed?
Would they not find sweet rest?
And do for Him all that they could?

Chapter 11 — "The truth shall make you free"

If men only knew,
Just how good,
How good the good news is;
Could they help but cry out,
To those all about,
Of the goodness and love that are His?

If men only knew,
Just how good,
How very good the news is;
But oh how sad,
That they are not glad,
Will you tell them how good the news is?

If only they knew!
If only they knew!
Quick let us tell them and fast!
With love in our heart,
Let us go and impart,
And wait not till the harvest is past.

And now that you know,
Just how good,
How very good the news is,
Your lips can't stay sealed,
His love will be revealed,
And they'll know of the good news that is.

Source References

All quoted references are authored by Ellen G. White unless otherwise indicated.

Chapter 1

1. *Christ's Object Lessons*, p. 112.
2. *The Review and Herald*, July 26, 1892, par. 3, 4.
3. *Testimonies to Ministers and Gospel Workers*, pp. 105-111.
4. *Testimonies on Sabbath-School Work*, pp. 64, 65.
5. *Testimonies for the Church*, vol. 5, p. 707.
6. *The Great Controversy*, pp. 595, 596.
7. *The Review and Herald*, September 11, 1894, par. 4.
8. *The Great Controversy*, p. 596.
9. Ibid., p. 388.
10. *The Review and Herald*, December 15, 1885, par. 16.
11. Ibid., August 13, 1959, par. 2.
12. *Faith and Works*, pp. 77, 78.
13. *The Great Controversy*, pp. 596-600, italics added.
14. *Thoughts from the Mount of Blessing*, p. 145.
15. *Testimonies for the Church*, vol. 3, pp. 252, 253.
16. *Thoughts from the Mount of Blessing*, pp. 146, 147.

Chapter 2

1. *Education*, p. 57.
2. *Christ's Object Lessons*, p. 333.
3. *Steps to Christ*, p. 47, italics added.
4. *Thoughts from the Mount of Blessing*, p. 61.
5. *The Ministry of Healing*, p. 176, italics added.
6. *Education*, p. 289.
7. *The Desire of Ages*, p. 679.
8. *Testimonies for the Church*, vol. 5, p. 515.
9. *General Conference Bulletin*, March 2, 1897, par. 24.
10. *Steps to Christ*, pp. 47, 48, italics added.
11. *Christ's Object Lessons*, p. 118.

Source References

12. *Thoughts from the Mount of Blessing,* pp. 93, 94.
13. *The Desire of Ages,* p. 324.
14. *Our High Calling,* p. 348.
15. *Thoughts from the Mount of Blessing,* p. 141.
16. *The Desire of Ages,* p. 207.
17. *Steps to Christ,* p. 72, italics added.
18. *The Desire of Ages,* p. 480.
19. *Christ's Object Lessons,* p. 331.
20. *The Upward Look,* p. 73.
21. *Testimonies for the Church,* vol. 1, pp. 240, 241.
22. *Steps to Christ,* p. 46.
23. *Christ's Object Lessons,* p. 187.
24. *The Desire of Ages,* p. 483.
25. Ibid., p. 417.
26. Ibid., p. 49.
27. *Christ's Object Lessons,* p. 196.
28. *The Desire of Ages,* p. 116.
29. Ibid., p. 131.
30. *The Review and Herald,* June 23, 1896, par. 1.
31. *The Desire of Ages,* p. 466.
32. Ibid., p. 58.
33. *Christ's Object Lessons,* p. 237.
34. *The Desire of Ages,* p. 655.
35. Ibid., p. 107.
36. *Patriarchs and Prophets,* p. 628.
37. *The Desire of Ages,* p. 749.
38. Ibid., pp. 755, 756.
39. Ibid., pp. 489, 490.
40. *Christ's Object Lessons,* p. 237.
41. *The Desire of Ages,* p. 587.
42. *The Youth's Instructor,* January 1, 1854, par. 5.
43. *The Great Controversy,* p. 642.
44. *The Desire of Ages,* p. 588.
45. *The Review and Herald,* December 15, 1896, par. 16.

Saved by Works... Christ's Works!

Chapter 3

1. *The Signs of the Times,* November 24, 1887, par. 6.
2. *Testimonies for the Church,* vol. 1, p. 620.
3. *Early Writings,* p. 72.
4. *Testimonies for the Church,* vol. 1, p. 167, italics added.
5. *Special Testimonies on Education,* p. 115, italics added.
6. *Steps to Christ,* p. 47, italics added.
7. *Testimonies for the Church,* vol. 5, pp. 513, 514, italics added.
8. Manuscript Releases, vol. 9, p. 300, italics added.
9. *The Desire of Ages,* p. 316.
10. *The Review and Herald,* November 3, 1904, par. 4.
11. *Education,* pp. 253, 254.
12. *The Desire of Ages,* pp. 428, 429, italics added.
13. *Testimonies for the Church,* vol. 1, p. 413.
14. *Testimonies for the Church,* vol. 1, p. 620.
15. Manuscript Release, vol. 9, p. 300.
16. *The Review and Herald,* October 18, 1898, par. 7.
17. *Christ's Object Lessons,* p. 330.
18. *The Desire of Ages,* p. 311.
19. *The Review and Herald,* March 10, 1904, par. 26.
20. *The Desire of Ages,* p. 490, italics added.
21. *The Youth's Instructor,* April 25, 1901, par. 11.
22. *The Great Controversy,* p. 597.
23. Manuscript Release, vol. 9, p. 301, italics added.
24. *The Desire of Ages,* p. 210.
25. *Selected Messages,* bk. 1, p. 394.
26. *Gospel Workers,* 1892, p. 441.
27. *The Ministry of Healing,* p. 159.

Chapter 4

1. *Thoughts from the Mount of Blessing,* p. 150.
2. *Steps to Christ,* p. 103.
3. *The Youth's Instructor,* February 1, 1856, par. 6.
4. *Testimonies for the Church,* vol. 1, p. 139.
5. *Thoughts from the Mount of Blessing,* p. 64.

Source References

6. *The Review and Herald*, August 11, 1891, par. 6.
7. *The Desire of Ages*, p. 422.
8. Ibid., p. 360.
9. *Christ's Object Lessons*, p. 97, italics added.
10. *Testimonies for the Church*, vol. 1, p. 160.
11. *Steps to Christ*, p. 59.
12. *Thoughts from the Mount of Blessing*, p. 142.
13. *Christ's Object Lessons*, p. 159.
14. Ibid., p. 96.
15. *Steps to Christ*, p. 47.
16. Ibid., p. 51, italics added.
17. *The Desire of Ages*, p. 173, italics added.
18. Ibid., p. 324.
19. *Steps to Christ*, p. 52, italics added.
20. *Thoughts from the Mount of Blessing*, p. 146.
21. *Testimonies for the Church*, vol. 1, p. 413.
22. *The Desire of Ages*, p. 172.
23. *Christ's Object Lessons*, p. 99.
24. *Steps to Christ*, p. 67.
25. *Thoughts from the Mount of Blessing*, p. 118, italics added.
26. *Steps to Christ*, p. 27, italics added.
27. *The Desire of Ages*, p. 176.
28. *Steps to Christ*, p. 51.
29. *The Review and Herald*, May 21, 1908, par. 2.
30. *Education*, p. 254, italics added.
31. Ibid., p. 253.
32. Ibid., p. 126, italics added.
33. *The Review and Herald*, July 25, 1899, par. 13, italics added.
34. *General Conference Bulletin*, April 23, 1901, par. 2, italics added.
35. Ibid., May 17, 1909, par. 20.
36. *Steps to Christ*, p. 58.
37. *Christ's Object Lessons*, p. 97.
38. *Special Testimonies for Ministers and Workers*, p. 54.
39. *The Desire of Ages*, p. 668, italics added.
40. *Christ's Object Lessons*, pp. 97, 98, italics added.
41. *Thoughts from the Mount of Blessing*, p. 18.

Saved by Works... Christ's Works!

42. *Christ's Object Lessons,* p. 312.
43. *Patriarchs and Prophets,* p. 509, italics added.
44. *The Desire of Ages,* p. 385.
45. Ibid., italics added.
46. *Thoughts from the Mount of Blessing,* p. 87, italics added.
47. *Christ's Object Lessons,* p. 117.
48. *Thoughts from the Mount of Blessing,* pp. 54, 55.
49. *Christ's Object Lessons,* p. 115.
50. *Thoughts from the Mount of Blessing,* p. 114, italics added.
51. *Special Testimonies for Ministers and Workers,* no. 9, p. 62, italics added.
52. *Education,* p. 253.
53. *Faith and Works,* pp. 38, 39, italics added.
54. Ibid., p. 66.
55. *The Desire of Ages,* p. 324.
56. *The Great Controversy,* p. 469, italics added.
57. *Steps to Christ,* p. 69.
58. *Christ's Object Lessons,* p. 381.
59. Ibid., p. 406
60. *Steps to Christ,* p. 18, italics added
61. Ibid., p. 61, italics added.
62. *The Desire of Ages,* p. 300.
63. *The Review and Herald,* June 4, 1895, par. 7, italics added.
64. *The Desire of Ages,* p. 249, italics added.
65. *The Ministry of Healing,* p. 455.
66. *Steps to Christ,* p. 62.
67. Ibid., pp. 62, 63, italics added.
68. *The Desire of Ages,* p. 82.
69. Ibid., p. 324.
70. *The Signs of the Times,* February 15, 1905, par. 5.
71. *Steps to Christ,* pp. 69, 70.
72. *Patriarchs and Prophets,* p. 73, italics added.
73. *The Review and Herald,* May 21, 1908, par. 3.
74. *The Acts of the Apostles,* p. 561, italics added.
75. *The Signs of the Times,* April 30, 1896, par. 5.
76. *The Review and Herald,* September 25, 1900, par. 10.
77. *Steps to Christ,* p. 61.

Source References

78. *Education*, p. 126.
79. *The Signs of the Times*, July 23, 1902, par. 14, italics added.
80. *Selected Messages*, bk. 1, p. 392, italics added.
81. *Steps to Christ*, p. 43.
82. *Thoughts from the Mount of Blessing*, p. 141.
83. Ibid., p. 142.
84. *Christ's Object Lessons*, p. 159.
85. *Steps to Christ*, p. 47, italics added.
86. Ibid., p. 51, italics added.
87. *Testimonies for the Church*, vol. 1, p. 131.
88. *Steps to Christ*, p. 27, italics added.
89. *Patriarchs and Prophets*, p. 509.
90. *The Review and Herald*, November 29, 1892, par. 3, italics added.
91. Manuscript Releases, vol. 4, pp. 113, 114, italics added.
92. *Christ's Object Lessons*, p. 82, italics added.
93. *The Review and Herald*, September 14, 1897, par. 14, italics added.
94. A.T. Jones and E. J. Waggoner, *Lessons on Faith*, p. 28.
95. Ibid., p. 28.
96. *The Signs of the Times*, May 18, 1882, par. 18.
97. *The Desire of Ages*, p. 341.
98. Ibid., p. 125.
99. *Christ's Object Lessons*, p. 65, italics added.
100. *The Review and Herald*, March 10, 1904, par. 26, italics added.
101. *Australasian Union Conference Record*, July 12, 1899, par. 5.
102. *Patriarchs and Prophets*, p. 147.
103. Ibid., p. 145.
104. *The Desire of Ages*, pp. 35, 36.
105. *The Youth's Instructor*, May 4, 1893, par. 5.
106. *Thoughts from the Mount of Blessing*, p. 146.
107. *The Desire of Ages*, p. 280.
108. *The Ellen G. White 1888 Materials*, p. 495, italics added.
109. *Thoughts from the Mount of Blessing*, p. 18.
110. *Christ's Object Lessons*, p. 312.
111. Manuscript Releases, vol. 9, p. 300.

112. *Testimonies for the Church,* vol. 1, p. 620.
113. *The Desire of Ages,* p. 687.
114. Ibid., p. 685.
115. Ibid., p. 690.
116. *The Review and Herald,* August 7, 1894, par. 3.
117. *Thoughts from the Mount of Blessing,* p. 146, italics added.
118. *Steps to Christ,* p. 75, italics added.
119. *Christ's Object Lessons,* p. 102.
120. *Thoughts from the Mount of Blessing,* p. 27.
121. Ibid., p. 24.
122. *Steps to Christ,* p. 57.
123. *Christ's Object Lessons,* pp. 98, 99, italics added.
124. *Thoughts from the Mount of Blessing,* p. 22.
125. Ibid., p. 36.
126. Ibid., p. 38.
127. Ibid., p. 36.
128. Ibid., p. 38.
129. *Steps to Christ,* p. 77.
130. *Christ's Object Lessons,* p. 197.
131. *The Acts of the Apostles,* pp. 563, 564, italics added.
132. Ibid., pp. 552, 553, italics added.
133. *Testimonies for the Church,* vol. 1, p. 139.
134. *The Desire of Ages,* p. 506.
135. Ibid., p. 509, italics added.
136. *Thoughts from the Mount of Blessing,* p. 18.

Chapter 5

1. *The Review and Herald,* December 24, 1908, par. 2, italics added.
2. *The Desire of Ages,* p. 671.
3. Ibid., p. 124.
4. Ibid., p. 125.
5. *Patriarchs and Prophets,* p. 55.
6. *The Review and Herald,* May 20, 1884, par. 8.
7. *Thoughts from the Mount of Blessing,* p. 116.
8. *Testimonies for the Church,* vol. 1, p. 413.

9. *The Review and Herald*, March 27, 1888, par. 15, italics added.
10. Ibid., May 20, 1884, par. 8, italics added.
11. *Our High Calling*, p. 22.
12. *The Review and Herald*, March 27, 1888, par. 15, italics added.
13. Ibid., May 20, 1884, par. 8.
14. *The Youth's Instructor*, July 20, 1899, par. 10.
15. *The Desire of Ages*, p. 123, italics added.
16. *The Youth's Instructor*, July 20, 1899, par. 10, italics added.
17. *The Desire of Ages*, p. 126.
18. Ibid., p. 125.
19. Ibid., pp. 125, 126.
20. Ibid., p. 125.
21. *Education*, p. 126.
22. *The Desire of Ages*, p. 125.
23. Ibid., p. 210, italics added.
24. *Steps to Christ*, p. 64, italics added.
25. *The Desire of Ages*, p. 126.
26. Ibid., pp. 126, 129, italics added.
27. *Education*, p. 253.
28. *In Heavenly Places*, p. 104 italics added.
29. *The Review and Herald*, October 18, 1898, par. 7.

Chapter 6

1. *Christ's Object Lessons*, p. 114.
2. Ibid., p. 133.
3. *The Christian Educator*, August 1, 1897, par. 4.
4. *Christ's Object Lessons*, p. 114.
5. *The Desire of Ages*, p. 668, italics added.
6. *Sabbath-School Worker*, July 1, 1894, par. 5.
7. *The Great Controversy*, p. 488.
8. *Steps to Christ*, p. 70.
9. *Christ's Object Lessons*, p. 415.
10. *The Desire of Ages*, pp. 761, 762.
11. *Thoughts from the Mount of Blessing*, p. 41, italics added.

12. *Testimonies for the Church,* vol. 7, p. 62.
13. *Christ's Object Lessons,* pp. 415, 416.
14. Ibid., p. 414.
15. Ibid., pp. 420, 421.

Chapter 7

1. *The Desire of Ages,* p. 388, italics added.
2. Ibid., p. 669.
3. Ibid., p. 671, italics added.
4. *The Acts of the Apostles,* p. 48.
5. *The Desire of Ages,* p. 671.
6. *The Acts of the Apostles,* p. 49.
7. *The Desire of Ages,* p. 250.
8. *Steps to Christ,* p. 78.
9. Ibid., pp. 78, 79, italics added.
10. *Thoughts from the Mount of Blessing,* p. 20.
11. *The Desire of Ages,* p. 672, italics added.
12. *The Acts of the Apostles,* p. 49.
13. Ibid., p. 50, italics added.
14. *The Great Controversy,* p. 477.
15. *The Review and Herald,* January 17, 1893, par. 6, italics added.
16. Ibid., par. 7.
17. Ibid., par. 9, 10.
18. *Christ's Object Lessons,* pp. 68, 69.

Chapter 8

1. *Steps to Christ,* pp. 46, 47, italics added.
2. Ibid., p. 93.
3. Ibid., p. 94.
4. Ibid., p. 98.
5. *Testimonies for the Church,* vol. 4, p. 235.
6. *Steps to Christ,* p. 70.
7. Ibid., pp. 98, 99.
8. Ibid., p. 97.

9. Ibid., p. 52.
10. Ibid., p. 95.
11. *The Review and Herald*, July 24, 1883, par. 19.
12. *Steps to Christ*, p. 96.
13. Ibid., p. 97.
14. *The Great Controversy*, p. 597.
15. *Testimonies for the Church*, vol. 2, p. 70.
16. *Testimonies for the Church*, vol. 9, p. 278.
17. *The Desire of Ages*, p. 125.
18. *Steps to Christ*, p. 51, italics added.
19. *Christ's Object Lessons*, pp. 165, 166.
20. Ibid., p. 175.
21. Ibid.
22. *Steps to Christ*, p. 97.
23. Ibid., p. 94.
24. Ibid., p. 97.
25. *Testimonies for the Church*, vol. 1, p. 296, italics added.
26. *Steps to Christ*, p. 94.
27. *Spiritual Gifts*, vol. 4b, p. 84.
28. *Gospel Workers*, pp. 254, 255.
29. *Steps to Christ*, p. 98.
30. Ibid., p. 99.
31. Ibid., p. 102.
32. *The Acts of the Apostles*, p. 564.
33. *The Youth's Instructor*, September 1, 1886, par. 4.
34. *Thoughts from the Mount of Blessing*, p. 96.
35. *The Great Controversy*, p. 525.
36. *Steps to Christ*, p. 94, italics added.
37. Ibid., p. 100.

Chapter 9

1. *The Ministry of Healing*, p. 363.
2. *The Desire of Ages*, p. 208.
3. Ibid., p. 32.
4. *Education*, p. 267.
5. *Christ's Object Lessons*, p. 173.

6. *The Desire of Ages*, p. 330.
7. *Thoughts from the Mount of Blessing*, pp. 100, 101, italics added.
8. *The Desire of Ages*, p. 121.
9. *Testimonies for the Church*, vol. 1, p. 500.
10. *Patriarchs and Prophets*, p. 293.
11. Ibid., p. 294.
12. Ibid., italics added.
13. Ibid., p. 50.
14. *The Desire of Ages*, p. 273.
15. *Steps to Christ*, pp. 85, 86.
16. *The Desire of Ages*, p. 330.
17. Ibid., p. 331.

Chapter 10

1. *Steps to Christ*, p. 103.
2. Ibid., p. 85.
3. *The Desire of Ages*, p. 356.
4. *Steps to Christ*, p. 100.
5. *Thoughts from the Mount of Blessing*, p. 71.
6. *The Ministry of Healing*, p. 489.
7. *Education*, p. 253.
8. *Christ's Object Lessons*, pp. 171, 172.
9. *The Ministry of Healing*, pp. 470, 471.
10. *Thoughts from the Mount of Blessing*, p. 10.
11. *The Review and Herald*, April 10, 1894, par. 9.
12. *Christ's Object Lessons*, p. 175.
13. *SDA Bible Commentary*, vol. 4, p. 1146.
14. *The Great Controversy*, p. 621.
15. *Steps to Christ*, p. 116.
16. *Testimonies for the Church*, vol. 6, p. 365.
17. *Thoughts from the Mount of Blessing*, p. 101.

Source References

Chapter 11

1. Isaiah 33:22; Romans 3:23; 6:23; James 4:12; 1 John 3:4
2. John 3:16; Romans 5:8
3. Romans 2:4
4. Acts 5:31; 1 John 1:9
5. Romans 5:1
6. Romans 12:3; Ephesians 2:8
7. Malachi 4:1-31; John 5:17; 1 Corinthians 6:9
8. Job 14:4; Isaiah 64:6; Jeremiah 13:23; 17:9; Matthew 7:18; 12:33, 34; Luke 6:45; Romans 8:7; James 3:11, 12
9. Genesis 4:25; Mark 1:1; Luke 1:35; Ephesians 3:17; Philippians 2:13; 1 John 3:9
10. Isaiah 64:6; Jeremiah 23:6; Philippians 2:13
11. Jeremiah 31:33; Ezekiel 36:26; 2 Corinthians 6:16; Ephesians 3:17; 1 John 5:20
12. Act 26:18; 1 Corinthians 1:30; James 4:17
13. Psalms 33:6, 8, 9; Ephesians 3:17; 1 John 3:9
14. Psalms 33:6, 8, 9; Romans 5:9; 2 Corinthians 13:5; Ephesians 2:8; Colossians 2:6; James 1:21
15. 1 Timothy 6:15, 16; 1 John 5:11-13, 20
16. John 15:16; Philippians 2:13
17. John 14:1, 27
18. Song of Solomon 2:16
19. Matthew 6:31-34
20. Romans 8:28
21. Matthew 21:22; John 14:16-18
22. Luke 4:1; Acts 1:2; 8:19, 20
23. Matthew 24:14; Acts 1:8

We invite you to view the complete
selection of titles we publish at:

www.TEACHServices.com

or write or email us your praises,
reactions, or thoughts about this
or any other book we publish at:

TEACH Services, Inc.
P.O. Box 954
Ringgold, GA 30736

info@TEACHServices.com

www.ingramcontent.com/pod-product-compliance
Lightning Source LLC
Chambersburg PA
CBHW070537160426
43199CB00014B/2285